BANKS OF THE WORLD

BANKS OF THE WORLD

Roger Orsingher

TRANSLATED BY D. S. AULT

Walker and Company • New York

CONTENTS

3. THE SEVEN INTERNATIONAL BANKING AND FINANCIAL INSTITUTIONS OF WASHINGTON

4. THE BANKS AND EUROPEAN INTEGRATION

5. THE 110 MOST IMPORTANT COMMERCIAL BANKS IN THE WORLD

6. THE 475 CENTURY-OLD BANKS OF THE WORLD

PREFACE

Bank: derived from the Italian word *banco*, bench or counter: public or private credit institution, whose function is to receive money on deposit, to employ it profitably and to facilitate its circulation in the form of notes, bonds or bills of exchange.

Banking — one of the specialised forms of commerce — appeared, as did the latter, in conjunction with the civilisations of the past and was nearly always at the basis of their prosperity.

It is impossible with the documents so far discovered, whatever their kind, to determine when banking operations first took place or to give a continuous uninterrupted account of their evolution.

Inscriptions reveal the existence, a thousand years before our era, of organisations carrying out what would nowadays be called banking operations. Recent excavations have uncovered the temple of Uruk in Chaldea (Mesopotamia), a relic of the Babylonian Empire, and have shown that the foundation of the oldest banking building in the world took place more than 3,300 years before our era.

A history of banking would therefore have to cover at least thirty-three centuries.

But in the case of the ancient world, and indeed of more recent epochs, texts do not exist in sufficient quantities, nor do they give sufficiently precise information, for us to be able to give an account of successive techniques in banking operations, in exact chronological sequence. Nevertheless they enable one to plot sufficient landmarks, even if they are at times very widely spaced, to determine the principal stages in the development of an industry which occupies an important place in modern economic systems.

On examining the data inherited from the past and collated by the historian, one becomes convinced that banks, in their first primitive beginnings and later in more highly developed forms, did not enjoy a steady and harmonious development. Like other human institutions, banking enterprises experienced throughout the civilised world all the political and economic vicissitudes inherent in human history; they emerged and evolved, then disappeared to be rediscovered and reinvented as fresh civilisations arose, adapting themselves constantly in order to meet more efficiently the needs of commerce, whatever obstacles they encountered.

In the world of antiquity, two events are important landmarks in the history of banking.

The first of these was the drawing up of the Code of Hammurabi, by King Hammurabi, the true founder of the Babylonian Empire (1728–1686 B.C.). This is one of the most important documents from this period. Bank operations by temples and great landowners had become so numerous and so important that the king thought it necessary to lay down standard rules of procedure, which he caused to be inscribed on a block of diorite, 2·25 metres tall, which was discovered during the excavation of the Acropolis of Susa and is preserved in the Museum of the Louvre in Paris.

The Code contains about 150 paragraphs which deal with nearly all cases arising from loans, interest, pledges, guarantees, the presence or absence of evidence, natural accidents, loss, theft, etc. The Code has been translated by the French archaeologist, Père Scheil.

The second event was the invention of money.

In antiquity the Sumerian, Babylonian, Hittite and Assyrian banks functioned without the aid of a currency. The standard of value of the period was either barley, silver, copper, bronze or electrum (an alloy of gold and silver).

Who invented money? Perhaps the Chinese, but no certainty exists on this point.

However, one name remains in the history books: Gyges. In 687 B.C. Gyges, king of Lydia, freed his country from the domination of a Hittite dynasty and transformed his capital — Sardis — into an important commercial centre.

In Lydia, electrum was to be found in great abundance in the quartz lodes of Tholus and in the sands of the Pactolus. King Gyges caused it to be cast in ingots of identical shape and of a uniform weight, and a triple emblem to be engraved on the ingots; one of the emblems was the effigy of a fox, the great Lydian god; this emblem was an official guarantee of value.

In this way money came into use.

In the pre-Christian era there naturally existed more than one type of bank: indeed, four rather different types can be distinguished; eastern banks, banks of the Greek city-states, hellenistic banks with a modified type in Egypt, and the Roman bank. In Chapter 1 the chief stages in the historical development of banking will be shown, by a brief description in each phase of the nature of banking practices and the activities of the establishments that perform them.

In the long development of the human race, bankers have at times profoundly influenced the course of history. The banks, whose very existence depends on a settled culture, fertilised the civilisation of Antiquity, of the Middle Ages, and of Modern Times. They will surely remain an essential element in future civilisations.

In part at least, the history of the world has been made and will continue to be made by the banking profession even when the banker is reduced to the role of a mere distributor.

Today in all the countries of the world, whether they are capitalist or communist, banks are more than ever essential to the economy, finance, currency, commerce, industry and agriculture. Whether it be in Paris, London, Frankfurt, Tokyo, Washington, Moscow or Peking, public and private banks are helped and supported by the respective governments and they co-operate in implementing the great productive schemes projected by the various social systems, greedy for wealth and power.

In the whole world credit is such a pressing and vital necessity that banks, even though depersonalised and dehumanised, retain all their prestige and all their power.

Banks symbolise money, the established order, as immutable as their heavy freestone buildings. Their monumental doors, their facades, are like some temple of a universal religion, which has its priests, its devotees, its initiates, its mysteries. They reassure some, they anger others. Banks, symbols of thrift and enterprise, are a part of our world. They form the life-giving circulatory system of the nations as veins and arteries form that of living creatures.

The evolution of the modern economy implied a correlative evolution in the banking system and compelled an adaptation to the multiple and changing imperatives of political economy. Banks are at the centre of all activities. The capitalist in the administration of his wealth, the trader or the industrialist in the financing of his business, are necessarily and constantly brought to the counter of a bank, which thus becomes more and more closely integrated into the intense life of modern society.

Banks and industries support one another, become inter-dependent. Industrial methods are adopted by banks; the factory owner asks the advice of the bank. Banks are not merely money-lenders but also influential advisers and efficient associates and collaborate with industrialists in the elaboration and adoption of programmes of rationalisation which permit the conquest of national markets and invasion of foreign markets.

Banks are not merely one element among others in the formid-able expansion of economic activity; they are also to a large extent the authors and creators of this expansion. By steadily extending their deposit system, forming reservoirs of capital, fed by every sector of the economy, to be lent out again to commerce and industry, they provide commercial and industrial undertakings with the stimulus and the means to embark on vast enterprises.

In this way a new concept of the bank takes form — that of director of the national economy. This role, which banks are assuming more and more every day under the imperious pressure of economic circumstances, is of transcendental importance: from being mere buttresses banks are now becoming the keystone of the economic edifice.

The science of banking arises from the science of economics, of which, however, it is only one branch — though not the least. The art of banking depends closely on progress made in industrial and commercial techniques, and on the circumstances in which it is employed. The evolution of the one thing influences that of the other.

In what direction will the science and art of banking develop? Through what successive phases will they evolve? What transformations, what periods of growth or of sterility will they experience? Prediction is extremely difficult. It is, however, principally on bankers that the solution of the great economic problems of the modern world will in the future depend. If they are to direct the economy and the energies of the nation, they will have to evince a readiness to accept new ideas and take certain risks.

This shows how numerous and how complex must be the qualifications of men holding important posts within the bank. They must have extensive financial, economic and legal knowledge, so that they can make decisions or at least support their opinions with sound and unbiased knowledge. The executives of great banks must have regard not only to their own country but to all the countries of the world, since they must anticipate the main trends and events of the world.

In the following pages I have tried to assemble and to make available to the reader an ordered and accessible body of information which I hope will be useful and instructive to all interested in banking and financial studies or to all who exercise the profession of banker.

It now remains for me only to address to the reader the prayer addressed in ancient days to the departing navigator: *Vale et negotia ex sententia perfice*.

R. O.

I

HISTORICAL SURVEY OF BANKING OPERATIONS

1. Banks in Babylon

In the Near East in pre-Christian times economic activity was highly centralised about the royal house and the priesthood. The royal palace and the temple were the centres to which goods flowed and from which they were then in part redistributed to the people. They were also the places where, since they offered security, the people deposited their wealth, principally their crops. So it was in temples and palaces that the first banking operations — the safeguarding of deposits — took place.

In Babylon by 1000 B.C., private deposit accounts were current practice, as is shown by legal texts in the Code of Hammurabi dealing with deposit accounts; a great number of contracts relating to this type of business have been found. These operations gave rise to the issuing of receipts, and were concerned with goods and articles of all kinds: grain, fruit, cattle, agricultural instruments, eventually precious metals. By a natural process of evolution, the existence of these deposits gradually led to transfers to the order, not of the depositor, but of a third party. This was the way in which loan business originated and reached a high stage of development in Babylonian civilisation.

The palace and especially the temple began by making loans from their own assets, and then from a part of the deposits which had been entrusted to them. Initially such loans were, for example, of seed-grain, to be repaid after the harvest. A receipt would be made out and a rate of interest fixed.

A third category of banking operations carried out by royal

and sacred treasuries in the Babylonian period was that of making or accepting payments on behalf of their clients. They undertook to make payments out of the deposits entrusted to them.

Surviving documents from the period do not allow us to determine if there already existed a system of accountancy allowing one debt to be set off against another, but it is extremely possible that book-keeping was already highly developed. However that may be, it would perhaps be inexact to affirm that true banks in the modern sense of the term were already in existence at this date.

At later and more advanced periods of Babylonian civilisation, for example in the seventh or fifth century B.C., these practices had undergone no sensible modification. It should, however, be noted that alongside kings and priests private individuals were playing an increasingly important part in banking operations, and that private enterprise led to an interesting development in this sphere. Business methods were developed and improved, as is shown by the all-too-rare documents which survive from this period. Deposit business becomes much more flexible and current accounts seem to have been quite common. Moreover, the process of abstraction continues; written documents replace actual objects, an acknowledgement of indebtedness can be used as an instrument of payment.

One also finds groupings in the form of partnerships formed to carry on banking operations. Igibi and Maraschu are the best-known names; they are the names of families of important businessmen, carrying out all the financial operations described above but whom one cannot yet consider as true bankers.

The nature of society, especially the extent of individual liberty, was a very important factor in the development of banking in the ancient world. For example, the Mosaic Law led to a very sharp reaction against banking — and so Hebrew civilisation, although it was strongly and directly influenced by Babylonian civilisation, knew almost nothing of banks.

2. BANKS IN ANCIENT GREECE

The development of banking enterprises in early Greece was conditioned by the level of local economic activity, the severity of local laws and the precarious state of trade and exchange. These are factors of a political nature which certainly hampered the development of banking operations in Greece until the fourth century B.C. It is, in fact, from this period onwards that we can discern with some degree of precision the methods employed in these operations, even though we cannot trace the course of their previous development in this region. It may be presumed that, under the influence of the oriental civilisations, temples were used as depositories for the wealth and possessions of individuals.

However, the invention of coinage and the expansion of its use in Lydia from the seventh century B.C. onwards, must have encouraged the emergence and then the practice of banking operations. Certain traders soon began to specialise in the evaluation and exchange of coinage made from precious metals in various countries. The money-changer became the trusted associate of the merchant and he soon began to extend his activity beyond these simple functions. The trapezites, as the first Greek bankers were called, accepted deposits for safe-keeping and acted as agents in the settlement of claims. They also invested the deposits of their clients in commercial enterprises, this active participation in commercial life resulting naturally from their passive role as guardians of deposits, and the two functions developed together. However, the volume of these transactions remained slight because trade was not yet either very brisk or very extensive, and also because, as a result of severe laws in the city-states, the practice of credit had not yet been expanded sufficiently.

The most characteristic figure among the Greek bankers of the day is Pasion of Athens, known to us through the orators of the fourth century B.C. From their speeches we know that he invested his own funds and those of his depositors to whom he paid interest. The merchant had recourse to his bank to borrow money, usually for financing maritime ventures, or to instruct him to settle accounts. The sums to be transmitted were deposited and paid out in cash; deposit contracts, giro transfers and receipts in writing do not appear to have been known at this period. The items entered by the trapezite in his registers constituted the only documents. As yet there is no question of current accounts or of orders to transfer properly so-called.

Pasion has already ceased to be merely a money-changer but he is not yet a true banker, for he is still a merchant and indeed a manufacturer.

This mixed type of business remained the standard formula for centuries. In the Hellenistic period banks developed fairly rapidly, especially in those centres where business and commercial activity had reached a certain level. One of the most famous establishments seems to have been the 'Bank of Delos', the best example of institutions of this kind in Greece at this period. It is particularly interesting that transactions in cash were replaced by real credit operations with receipts and payments made by simple written instructions, with accounts kept for each client. In the Hellenistic period, personal and oral communications with the banker were replaced increasingly by written documents; and the same is true when instructions for the settling of claims were given.

3. BANKS IN EGYPT

In the development of banking operations in this period, Egypt has a special place. Until the Alexandrian conquest a primitive economic system persisted; but the Ptolemies introduced coinage into Egypt and the same evolution which has been observed in Greece took place here also.

Indeed, trapezites are to be found here, as in Greece, but they are, in some sort, official agents; many of them have Greek names and the earliest of them came from Greece. The operation of these banking agencies was strictly regulated and supervised by the state, which, since the minting of money was a royal privilege, had arrogated to itself also the right to change money. A monopoly of this kind resulted in the trapezites remaining, like the coinage itself, artificial elements with little influence on the economic life of the country. Subjects continued, for example, to pay their taxes in grain, a commonly accepted medium of payment. As in Babylon, however, state depositories were set up in which private individuals could deposit their crops. These depositories ensured that both payments and receipts in kind could be effected by documents authorising either withdrawals or transfers, and resembling cheques and clearing.

These practices reached an especially high stage of development during the Roman period, since Egypt was the source of much of Italy's food supply. On the other hand, the state monopoly in banking was suppressed under the influence of economic conditions and private banks rapidly increased in number and importance. The depositories and the banks became the two centres of economic activity and bankers took on some of the functions of notaries, being competent to draw up legal contracts. But this development, which is apparent only from the fourth century B.C. on, is specifically Roman. The typical Egyptian bank derived in part from the Greek trapezites and in part from the Oriental organisations.

4. BANKS IN ROME

Originally the Roman bank was modelled on those of the East, and especially of Greece. All the earliest bankers have Greek names and it is probable that the Bank of Delos was the model imitated in Rome. Later on, Rome was the banking centre of the Republic and of the Empire: the other Italian cities had only very few bankers and hardly any were to be found in the provinces.

Originally banking services were provided by departments of the state, principally by a college of officials (*viri mensarii*) who accepted money on deposit from the citizens and who were authorised to use it in making loans. When private money-changers set up in Rome during the third century B.C. they were immediately subjected to state supervision, which was never allowed to lapse. However, there were no banking monopolies during the Roman period, and this liberty allowed banking operations to develop and flourish.

Bankers must certainly have been a numerous class in Rome,

considering the number of designations which might be used for them (*mensularii, argentarii, mummularii, fenoeratores*). Moreover their operations were very varied in nature.

At first it was certainly money-changing and the valuation of precious metals which formed the banker's principal business. But as Rome's relations with other nations extended further and further East, the market was invaded by the practices and customs of the Greek bankers. In Rome bankers discharged functions which today are shared between the stockbroker, the auctioneer, agents for public sales (*auctiones*), money-changers, discounters and credit institutions of all kinds.

Roman bankers were then essentially dealers in money in every sense of the word: very many documents are extant which illuminate the functioning of their undertakings and the mechanism of their operations. In Rome bankers exercised many varied functions of which the following were the most important:

(a) Valuation and exchange of metallic currency

The earliest banking operations must have been concerned with metal ingots. At first objects were bartered against objects; in this primitive period banking operations were completely unknown. But copper or bronze began to be used as a standard object of exchange, and at each transaction both the purity of the metal and the weight of the ingot had to be checked. Later on coins imported from Greece were substituted for the primitive ingots and the role of the banker became very important since many foreign coinages were introduced into Rome among which there was inevitably a considerable proportion of coins either unknown or of doubtful value.

Certainly the booty captured in the wars of conquest also increased this flood of exotic currencies and so exchange business became the most important activity of the ancient bankers, along with the valuation of coinage, the determination of rates of exchange, the supervision of weighing and of payments. It will be seen then that the earliest bankers speculated in monetary metal accepted at its real value, rather than in metallic currency accepted at its nominal value. It is therefore not surprising to discover them also trading in metallic objects of all kinds so that their profession approximates to that of the jeweller–money-changer.

(b) *Advances, investments, etc.*

But the activity of the Roman banker was not confined to these operations and he was very soon carrying out transactions which make him seem much more like a modern banker. In fact, when no disinterested friend would oblige one with a free loan, one had recourse to him for a loan at interest. Bankers were sometimes called *fenoeratores*, which indicates that they were in the habit of lending money at interest; various forms of contract were indeed in use. It is, moreover, probable that, since deposits at no fixed term were widely used among them, bankers not only speculated with their own money, but that they also put to work moneys entrusted to them. However, usury appears to have been abused — at least in the earlier days of the Republic — even more by private individuals, and especially by rich patricians, than by bankers.

Doubtless at a very early date Roman bankers ceased to deal exclusively in monetary metal. Among their credit operations properly so-called, the *mutuum*, that is to say a cash advance at a stipulated interest, must have been the most primitive and the simplest; it was an operation open to all, borrowers and lenders, protected by Roman law as a matter of course. But bankers could equally well use other procedures, more characteristic of and more peculiar to their trade. Nevertheless there were numerous incidents, in the Senate, in the Law Courts and in the Forum, occasioned by the computation and determination of interest. At times bankers were free to levy interest; at times they were strictly forbidden to do so; usually, a maximum rate was fixed; nevertheless, the levying of interest gave rise to constant abuse, of such a nature that, even under the Empire, doubts could be raised as to the morality or utility of banking operations.

Be that as it may, bankers survived all the laws and all the regulations and always raised interest on their money whatever method might be used to ensure its collection.

(c) Regular and irregular deposits

At the present time deposits may be broadly classified into three categories: *General deposits*,[1] *Special deposits*[2] and *Specific deposits*.[3]

In Rome regular deposits (general deposits) and also doubtless sequestration with a banker were common practice. But the receiving of irregular deposits — *deposit vel contra* (special deposits) was one of the commonest and most characteristic features of their profession. It was acknowledged that an irregular deposit should be interest-bearing by right, as good faith and custom dictated. Restitution was guaranteed by a special lien, particularly should the banker go bankrupt.

(d) Orders to pay

These deposits could be used in several other ways. Whether the banker were a regular depositary or not, depositors often instructed him to make payments on their behalf, and quite soon it even became accepted practice for the banker to make loans on behalf of the depositor, on an order called a 'prescription'. And so it naturally came about that capitalists adopted the practice of depositing their funds with an *argentarius* under terms which

---

[1] *General deposits* (interest-bearing): consist of money or deposit currency in which the bank becomes the owner of the deposit. Should the bank fail, the general depositor becomes a general creditor.

These deposits are also classified as demand deposits, time deposits, commercial deposits, savings deposits, government deposits, individual deposits which are subdivisible into alternate deposits and joint deposits.

In ancient Rome such deposits were called '*Regular*'.

[2] *Special deposits* (not interest-bearing): consist of property other than money (bonds, stocks, notes, life-insurance policies and other valuable papers, jewellery, silverware, plate, etc.).

Special deposits never become the assets of the bank, and in case of failure are not applicable to the payment of liabilities but must be returned intact to depositors.

In ancient Rome such deposits were called '*Irregular*' (*depositi vel contra*) and, in principle, interest-bearing.

[3] *Specific deposits* (usually not interest-bearing): are those made for specific purpose and consist of property other than money in which the bank acts as baillee, money left to discharge a note, or to purchase securities.

stipulated that they should be interest-bearing while reserving the right to specify how they should be used. However, neither the cheque nor the bill of exchange were known to Roman bankers: in both cases, in fact, the order clause allowing the document to circulate until maturity is missing.

(e) Instruments of transfer

Since bankers normally acted as intermediaries, either to accept or to make payments, this service could easily be used to make a remittance from one centre to another. If a sum paid in at Rome had to be paid out in some other town, this could be done by an exchange of liabilities.

(f) Legal proceedings

In all the branches of his business the banker could protect himself by various legal procedures; other procedures safeguarded his clients. In particular, a banker who had promised to make a payment in another town was indirectly constrained to do so by the indemnity which he might be forced to pay, if he contented himself with making payment at Rome.

(g) Accounts — current accounts

One of the more important techniques used by Roman bankers was the use of account-books analogous to those which all citizens kept with scrupulous care. This account-book was called a Codex and was indispensable in drawing up contracts. Clients' accounts were grouped in a 'journal'. Bankers also kept a special account-book, the *calendarium* or calendar of maturity dates. They were also accustomed to use various forms of documents in actual dealings with their clients. A procedure peculiar to bankers deserves to be noted: the *editio rationum* or production of accounts. Anyone running a bank could be compelled at a moment's notice to produce his accounts for his clients', or even for a third party's, inspection. Arrangements to set off one sum against another were linked with this keeping of accounts; they also were peculiar to bankers and show clearly that current accounts were a common, indeed a normal, practice.

The partnership was the only form of company organisation open to bankers and this probably limited the scope of their operations, preventing concentration of capital. Nevertheless bank partnerships were fairly common in Rome although they were subject to special regulations.

Under the Republic the Roman bankers were bold enough to group themselves together in a professional syndicate, the 'Collegium Argentarium': the Emperors had no objection. They knew that the *argentarii*, private bankers subject to the regulations governing partnerships, would never form a state within the state. On the contrary he encouraged them and granted them the status of a privileged corporation in order to keep them in even stricter subjection. In this way certain *argentarii* became extremely rich, such as Jucundus of Pompeii and Pompeius Trimalcion.

Private individuals but with a semi-official status, the *argentarii* inspired ever-increasing confidence in the Romans who became accustomed to using their services in all circumstances, being themselves timid in business matters.

When Constantine I, called the Great, founded Constantinople Roman banks had already been in existence for five centuries; the body of knowledge inherited from the Greeks had been greatly developed under the influence of the juridical genius of the nation. The distinction between public law and private law, the distinction between the status of persons and the status of things, the institution of strictly personal, perpetual and absolute rights in shared property, the freedom to enter into contracts, these are achievements of Roman law, which will reappear in modern society.

5. BANKS IN THE MIDDLE AGES

The barbarian invasions put a stop to the development of bank operations in the Roman Empire. Afterwards, as late as up to the Crusades, the money-changers alone remained active.

The existence of many small states each producing their own coinage, frequent modifications in money-rates and the in-efficiency of minting methods, all made the specialist, able to determine the weight, the fineness and authenticity of coinage indispensable.

During all this period, therefore, which extends from the end of the Roman Empire to the eleventh century, the banking industry was represented only by the money-changer. The age of the Crusades was the starting-point for the development of monetary and credit operations during the second part of the Middle Ages. Two tendencies are to be noted: the rise of a class of professional money-lenders and the rise of a system of trading by bills of exchange, from place to place.

The first professional money-lenders were the Jews. At first their loans were consumer credits involving considerable risks and therefore high rates of interest. For a long time the Jews had as competitors in this branch of business only the Italians. It was, indeed, in Italy that economic prosperity was most rapidly re-established and to meet its own needs Italian commerce gave rise to the first truly professional organisation devoted to financial and credit operations, even on an international plane. It has been said that in Italy during this period the main features of the modern bank reappeared, after being eclipsed during the early high Middle Ages.

We possess a quite considerable body of information on the genesis and development of banking operations at Genoa. Already in the eleventh century, the money-changers, called *bancherii*, were genuine bankers in the modern sense of the word. They accepted deposits from Genoese merchants, they granted them loans and advances, principally to finance sea-borne ventures; they undertook to make payments on their clients' behalf on the spot by means of orders to transfer and by set off, and through their agents and correspondents abroad they made payments in other towns; that is to say, they drew up bills of exchange. These functions enabled the Genoese bankers to fulfil the pressing needs of commerce.

The expansion in the volume of international payments and in credit operations, the difficulties that merchants experienced in obtaining at any time and at any place the cash needed to settle accounts, the desire to escape constant fluctuations in the exchange rates of the various currencies, the inconveniences of making loans, and the risks involved in keeping and transporting sums of money in cash — such were the principal factors important in stimulating the development of banking business up to the seventeenth century. On the other hand, thanks to the deposits which they received, bankers could meet the steadily increasing demand for credit. To begin with they made interest-bearing loans to merchants, then they carried out various other kinds of credit business, gradually squeezing out the Jews.

Such operations began and developed in the Mediterranean towns, principally in Italy. But from the early years of the twelfth century — and perhaps even before this date — Italian merchants began to extend their financial operations beyond the barrier of the Alps. It was the Lombards, whose name and reputation have remained famous in financial history, who were (except for the Jews) the first professional agents for credit operations in France, in England and in Germany.

In the tenth century the Lombards were Italian merchants who travelled to the Rhineland to sell Byzantine cloth and Asian spices, both bought in Venice. At this time they were few in number; they did not act in concert; the Jews may have cursed their competition but they were not greatly alarmed by it.

It was the revolutionary expansion in trade during the eleventh century and the appearance of industrial undertakings, first in the Netherlands and then in the Italian towns, which made the Lombards influential and important.

The conditions prevailing during that era made team-work inevitable. The Flemish merchants and manufacturers set up guilds. At a very early date in Florence the trades formed corporations. The Lombards must be given credit for realising at once that they would have to close their ranks to face up to their future tasks. They formed companies, private companies. We have no precise information about the legal status of the Lombard companies; they preserved the name of their founder — so they were not limited companies — and must have embodied a structure almost identical with that of a modern partnership.

These first companies had a fixed headquarters in Italy: but the Lombards swarmed into France and into Germany and, from the beginning of the twelfth century, all their advances began to converge on the Flemish cities, their opposing commercial pole. A fair of an international character was held for the first time in Thourout in 1082.

The Lombards naturally made every effort to encourage the recently founded industries of the Italian cities: Milan, where gold and silver thread was spun; Lucca, where gold brocade was made; Venice, whose workmen produced textiles, glassware and lace; Florence, whither immigrants from Sicily had brought the secrets of silk production. . . .

It should be pointed out that the name 'Lombard' was applied not only to natives of Lombardy, but also to Piedmontese and Tuscans. However, they were always Italians.

The most important Lombard companies were those of the Acciaioli, the Bardi, the Boccaci, the Buonsignori, the Frescobaldi, the Guidagni, the Peruzzi, the Tolomei, the Ugolini, the Scali, the Scotti, the Strozzi, etc.

As representatives of their companies, placed under the protection of their consuls, the Lombards rarely appeared as suppliants asking for favours; on the contrary, they would set up in business only where they were granted exemptions from taxation and other privileges. Their boldness was tempered with prudence; the cunning Lombards always kept open a line of retreat; they left their families at home in Italy and kept up a close connection with the parent house.

It will be clear that there can be no comparison between the circumstances of the Jews and those of the Lombards. Competition was keen; to begin with, murderous. But the Jews were beaten from the start; their rivals outclassed them absolutely.

Their first great task was to establish a firm link between the Italian and the Flemish centres of production, and, as soon as that was achieved, they began to practise banking. They soon showed themselves masters in this field. Among the Lombards the financiers became the equals of the merchants, versatile, playing their hunches, ingenious in their planning, international in outlook. And their companies became not merely powerful business houses, but also powerful banks.

The Lombards had flooded into France, where the fertility of the soil, the king's need of funds, the rivalry among the feudal magnates, the growing importance of Paris, all favoured them. They worked hard, trading at the centre they had chosen and spending several months of each year at the fairs in Flanders, in Champagne, in Provence.

To gain a just perception of the scope of the Lombards' business and the extent of their credit, one must remember that they were active at the fairs not only as wholesale merchants and as bankers but also as tax collectors, collecting Peter's pence and despatching it to Rome, that they contributed to the financing of the Crusades, that they had a hand in the manipulation of the currency in the reign of Philip the Fair and co-operated in the administration of the Royal Treasury.

In the thirteenth century the Tuscans, and then in the fourteenth the Florentines, entered into competition with the Lombards, who had set up a close business community in Cahors. These Italians, master bankers, established subsidiary companies in all big towns and their agents travelled throughout Europe, usually under the protection of the Papal diplomatic service, whose financial plans they carried out throughout Christendom. The substantial deposits which they received allowed them from the fourteenth century on to make loans to the kings of England and France and thus to exercise some measure of control over the economy of these countries. The 'Casa dei Medici' at Florence represents the apotheosis of the Italian bank of this period.

Alongside these private bankers, there were in several Mediterranean towns public banks which undertook long-term capital investments, especially in public utilities. An example is the famous 'Casa di San Giorgio' at Genoa. As early as 1401, in Barcelona, a genuine public bank was founded, combining the functions of a discount bank, a deposit bank and a transfer bank: the 'Tabula de Cambi' and similar establishments were also opened in Valencia and Saragossa. These are in some measure the forerunners of the public banks which were to be created in the sixteenth and seventeenth centuries in Venice, Milan, Amsterdam, Hamburg and Nuremberg.

However, France could not remain aloof from this development and improvement of banking activities. First of all one must not forget the services rendered to the monarchy by the Order of the Knights-Templar, created at about 1120 in Jerusalem by French crusaders. Having found it necessary to deal in foreign exchange, since they were the first to negotiate the ransom of Christians of any nationality captured by the infidel, they gradually extended the scope of their activities, accepting many deposits and administering much sequestrated property, since the churches and ecclesiastical establishments where such deposits were stored offered a guarantee of security; they granted important loans not only to governments and princes but even to popes and certain monasteries.

Despite the manifold services which they had rendered to the national economy, the Order of the Templars was suppressed by Philip the Fair, jealous of the influence it had acquired in the Kingdom and of the wealth it had accumulated.

In the Middle Ages fairs played an important part in the economic life of certain European countries and it is incontrovertible that their existence and functioning contributed powerfully to the expansion of trade and also raised a number of financial problems, whose resolution greatly strengthened the position of the banker.

If one is determined to find a precedent for an institution in antiquity, one is rarely disappointed. Herodotus speaks of the Panegyris, a fair which was held in Athens every five years.

Financiers fulfilled a role of considerable importance in the medieval fairs. At first money-changers made it possible, by 'manual' exchange, to settle transactions in cash. All coins were legal tender at the fair, provided they were of standard fineness. But the work of the money-changers was made easier by the existence of a currency which they used as a standard: fair-money. The most famous of these fair-moneys was undoubtedly the pound of Provins, which was decorated with a comb with closely set teeth, a standard tool of contemporary weavers.

However ticklish the money-changer's trade might be, the

bankers needed an even higher degree of ingenuity and adaptability. They dealt with forward transactions, demanding a high degree of accuracy in calculations, combined with judicious planning; with exchange contracts; with the initial drafting of the bills of exchange used at the fair (these bills were drawn up by the fair notaries and carried the chancellor's seal); they were, so to speak, universally current; if a merchant could not meet his obligations, the bill became executory on the goods and even on the person of all his compatriots. They also dealt with credit operations, that is to say, loans to merchants or to noblemen, often living a long way away, who took advantage of this unusual gathering of financiers by sending their stewards to negotiate the advance which they needed.

The bankers also collected the fair-taxes on behalf of the abbot, the count and the king; these taxes were relatively numerous despite exemptions.

The earliest of the medieval great fairs were those of the Netherlands, which can be traced back to the tenth century, the fairs of Ghent and Thourout, followed later by those of Messines, Lille and Ypres. These five alone made possible the setting up of a 'cycle', that is to say, an almost uninterrupted spiral series of commercial operations.

The medieval fairs have a specific character. It is quite impossible to confuse them with some unimportant local market. Their international character, their superior organisation, their privileges, their regular recurrence, their links with other fairs, make them a new institution, without an analogue in the past. They were a market not only for the products of local industry but also for those of the most distant countries.

It could even happen that local production was not such as to justify the holding of a fair and that the fair was held nevertheless. In such cases, the fair had been established in a centre enjoying an especially favourable geographic situation, as was the case with the fairs of Champagne. It cannot be said that the industries of Lagny, Troyes or Bar were negligible, but they do not bear comparison with the output of the weaving towns of Flanders. So Lagny, Troyes and Bar became the sites of famous fairs because these cities were situated at a great crossroads, at the intersection of the North–South European axis with the East–West axis, linking Germany and the Baltic with Spain. One must add that the skilful political manœuvring of the Counts of Champagne gave signal encouragement to their development.

As for the fairs of the South, they were favoured by the nearness of Italy, which sent them her own top-quality products as well as goods imported from the East by the Lombard merchants. The Montpellier fair was the oldest. That of Beaucaire — whose popularity survived till the seventeenth century — owed its existence to the initiative of Count Raymond VII of Toulouse. That of Nîmes was the creation of Philip the Bold.

The fairs of the North and those of the South were like the poles of a magnet, exercising a mutual attraction. As a result there was a balance of forces in Champagne, at a crossing of cardinal routes. Here two worlds met and mingled.

The fairs of Champagne were the best-known and the best-organised and served as models for many other commercial gatherings. To be sure, they did not immediately arrive at such a high degree of harmonious development: their prosperity dates from about 1150 and their apogee is reached about 1250.

Less than a century later Lyons became the true financial centre of the kingdom of France because of its four annual 'settling fairs' which made it a veritable capital market. It will therefore be interesting to examine the conditions under which the banking industry of Lyons worked.

6. Banks in Lyons

Foreign banks, principally German and Italian, became very numerous in Lyons from the end of the fourteenth century. The operations commonly conducted in this town were money-changing, deposits, transfers, settlements and collections, exchange business, loans and borrowings. Despite the suppression of feudal coinages and the increasing use of bills of exchange, the money-changer was still indispensable in Lyons, since debasement of the currency was a frequent happening, and since many foreigners came to do business at the fairs and if they could not use bills of exchange or letters of credit, they could make payments only in the currency of their native country. During the fairs the rate of exchange of all the commercial centres of Europe was quoted daily. Special publications called 'Arithmetics' gave this information and from them one can see how many sorts of coined currency were daily dealt in on the Lyons market during the fairs.

But alongside these quoted currencies, quite a number of others were in circulation and so it was absolutely necessary to have recourse to bankers and money-changers who would change foreign currencies for currencies generally acceptable or who would allow foreign merchants to open an account with them.

Like the Italian bankers, the Lyons bankers would also act as paying agents. They accepted deposits of cash, verified its value, and then credited the depositor in their books with the total of the sums he deposited in this way expressed in currency current on the spot, either écus de change or livres, sous and deniers. The traders not only had their funds in safe-keeping but they could also use, when they needed to, a currency having a generally recognised value, acceptable everywhere. The banker thus became an agent of the depositor and, quite naturally, replaced him when accounts were to be settled or payments accepted. Payments were made by simple transfers, by orders to pay, which could be presented for clearing during the fairs. All traders who frequented the fairs had current accounts of this kind with the principal bankers of Lyons.

This system of accounts tended to reduce to a minimum the circulation of hard cash and the Lyons banks could thus achieve in the sixteenth century an objective identical with that of the contemporary system of cheques and clearing-houses.

The embargo on the export from France of gold and silver bullion and the difficulties offered by the transport of heavy and cumbersome coinage, were the causes of the great expansion in the use of the bill of exchange. As early as the fifteenth century bankers were dealing in this type of business on a vast scale. The first bills of exchange to be used on the Lyons market were called 'Policies of Exchange' and the Medici Bank was, it seems, the first in France to practise this type of transaction on an extensive scale. Dealing in bills, since it gave great encouragement to trade, was always permitted and encouraged in France by the central power and tolerated by the Church.

Lyons was the principal French discount-market and merchants from all other French commercial centres were obliged to deal with the Lyons bankers. The latter not only dealt in bills of exchange, they dealt also in credit. Among the privileges granted by the Crown to the Lyons fairs, one of the most important was that concerning loans at interest. For this reason capital flowed into Lyons from all those countries where loans at interest remained under the ban of canon law. The best clients of the Lyons bankers were the kings of France, who, starting with Charles VIII, borrowed considerable sums on the Lyons market, especially from foreign bankers.

Another method open to merchants and bankers wishing to lay out capital to advantage was discount. Since they had the right to demand interest when they put out their money with a more or less distant maturity date, it was only logical that they should demand remuneration when they settled a debt not yet due. In the case of a debt settled in advance, they deducted from the sum to be paid the interest which the money would have earned, had the debt not been settled till maturity. What must be emphasised is that at this date there was no clear line of distinction between banking and business. Bankers were nearly always merchants equally ready to make a loan in cash or kind.

Bankers still lent money upon pledge. They also bought and sold stocks and shares; not often, it is true, but the development of commercial indebtedness and the creation of several large companies such as the East India Company were soon to augment considerably this type of business. Lastly, certain bankers still bought for cash the rights of various taxes. Others ran lotteries.

To sum up, the following banking operations were practised in sixteenth-century France, almost exclusively at Lyons: money-changing, deposits, transfers and current accounts, foreign exchange and arbitrage, loans and borrowings, discounting.

As it functioned at Lyons, the bank had by the fifteenth century taken a decisive forward step; it was no longer merely a deposit and transfer bank but a true credit instrument, circulating capital in order to encourage and extend commerce.

7. BANKS IN THE SIXTEENTH AND SEVENTEENTH CENTURIES

The important discoveries of the sixteenth century resulted in a shift in world trade from the Mediterranean to the Atlantic. At the same time, credit and financial operations, as commercial traffic increased in volume, developed considerably and soon burst out of the narrow framework within which they had been confined in the Middle Ages.

The evolution of money proper did not, it is true, keep pace with the expansion of trade. Doubtless the mass of money in circulation increased by a considerable proportion, but the increase was less in gold coin which had played the essential role in important transactions in the last centuries of the Middle Ages, than in silver coins. The debasing of currency was practised more and more frequently in Europe and some countries — as, for example, Spain — were eventually reduced to using copper coinage. In addition, the whole mechanism of payment was constantly disturbed by fresh issues of currency and by falls in the value of money already in circulation, not to mention political and social upheavals and wars. Under such conditions the systematic use of substitutes for coinage was bound to develop rapidly, in the form of deposit and transfer operations, and also in the form of negotiable bonds circulating between one town and another and one region and another. But gradually the Italians lost their *de facto* near-monopoly and banking operations became a commonplace of European civilisation.

At the same time the demand for capital on loan greatly increased not only because of the expansion of trade, but also because of the creation of standing armies and the invention of new types of armament. On the other hand, available capital also increased by a considerable extent, at first in those countries which already had strong commercial interests — Italy and Germany, for example; their commercial traffic had declined considerably but they were later to experience a brilliant financial renaissance. However, financial activity was frequently limited spatially by the wars between Habsburg and Valois; German and Viennese financiers supported the house of Habsburg while Florentine financiers preferred to serve French interests. It was during this period that these important men of business ceased to be called bankers and were denominated financiers. They were indeed high-ranking intermediaries, working most of the time with extensive deposits. These deposits transcended more and more their own resources, but, although they were for the most part short-term debts, in transactions offering the highest profits the financiers very often needed several years to recoup the loans which they had made to kings and princes.

Such disregard for rational banking technique did not fail to have grave consequences. Financial operations were developed to an exaggerated degree and the example of those bankers who were growing wealthy led astray a growing number of amateur financiers, all eager to make their fortune in banking operations. Moreover, kings and princes encouraged this tendency since it made it easier for them to borrow capital. And so Antwerp and Lyons acquired a world-wide importance and attracted an enormous volume of capital, on which the kings of France and of other countries drew heavily. As a result there was excessive demand for credit, culminating in tension, and a general European financial crisis developed.

The princely debtors of France had to suspend their repayments. The state became repeatedly bankrupt and this, together with the wars of religion in France and in the Netherlands, destroyed the prosperity of Antwerp and Lyons along with that of the business-men and the capitalists.

The Genoese remained almost the only bankers for some twenty or thirty years, and by developing their technical proficiency with the utmost care, they succeeded in acquiring a near-monopoly of international credit and remittance business. The most remarkable feature of Genoese banking was the institution of exchange fairs which were the first elements of an international credit system of a highly developed kind.

In the meantime most local deposit and transfer banks had fallen victims of the crisis and only a few public banks, for instance at Genoa, Barcelona and Saragossa, had managed to survive.

The Genoese bankers eventually adopted for use at the fairs full-valued gold coinage and at the same time replaced payments in cash with a highly developed system of money substitutes. They were, for instance, bankers to the Court of Spain, which, at this time, needed considerable sums for its armies in the Netherlands and in Italy.

The loans made to Spain by the Genoese bankers were payable in the Netherlands and in Italy. The bankers, true international credit agents, bought at the fairs bills of exchange payable in the Netherlands, and especially in Italy or at some intermediate commercial centre, where they then bought bills of exchange payable in the Netherlands and in Italy, and gave their own bills of exchange payable in Spain in settlement.

Up till now each bill of exchange had been used only once; the Genoese bankers practised endorsement, so that each bill could be used several times; in addition, since all the endorsers became jointly and severally liable, the bill became more trustworthy. One can say that endorsement allowed the bill of exchange to become the most important form of bank paper. Finally the Genoese perfected the system of offsetting debts against each other, which had already been practised in the Middle Ages at the conclusion of the periodic fairs. By perfecting their technique in this way the Genoese largely succeeded in monopolising the system of international payments and international credit.

8. The old public banks in Europe

The numerous bank failures, referred to in the previous section, gave rise to frequent discussions on fundamental questions affecting banking organisation and banking techniques. Such conferences had already been taking place in Nuremberg from 1548 to 1551. They were resumed with especial vigour in Venice, when in 1582 the last of the great private banks, the house of Pisani, fell a victim to the crisis in its turn. After long deliberations, the opening of private banks was forbidden and the foundation of a state bank was resolved upon. It had been agreed in the course of this debate that Venetian commercial interests needed a transfer and credit bank, but that it was dangerous to entrust these operations to private individuals; hence the necessity for a state bank.

The bank was opened in 1587, after two abortive attempts in 1584 and 1585, under the name of 'Banco di Rialto'. It was replaced in 1619 by the 'Banco del Giro' which continued in operation till 1806; similarly in Genoa after 1585 the 'Casa di San Giorgio' became more and more a state bank handling deposits and transfers. Its suppression was decreed in 1797 and it finally disappeared in 1815.

In 1585 the 'Banco di Sant'Ambrogio' was founded in Milan. However, after lively discussions, in the course of which technical expositions of an extremely modern tenor were presented, this establishment, at first prosperous, had cause to rue its financial dealings with the town of Milan; and had to be reconstituted in 1662.

The Bank of Amsterdam, founded on 31 January 1609, guaranteed by the state and administered by the burgomasters, engaged in commercial operations such as foreign exchange and the purchase of precious metals; it soon began to use a money of account or *banco* money in terms of which receipts were handed to depositors in the form of a written title showing the value of the deposits.

Moreover, in order to make the use of the new bank money more general, it was decided that all bills of exchange of 600 florins or more should be paid in this way; in addition, bills of exchange made out in bank money and whose value exceeded 300 florins could also not be paid except through the bank, the result of which was that all merchants were obliged to have an account with the bank. The Bank of Amsterdam rendered very great services to Netherlands trade and subsisted more or less intact till 1795.

In Germany a bank analogous to that in Amsterdam was

founded in Hamburg in 1619, under the name of the 'Bank of Hamburg' to accept deposits of fine silver or of foreign moneys and to run accounts on these deposits. This new establishment also found it advantageous to create a money of account, the 'Mark Banco', which gave the right to the person to whom it was credited to withdraw a certain quantity of fine metal from the bank; moreover, this Mark Banco was used in settling accounts in transactions between merchants and even between countries. In 1873 the Bank of Hamburg was absorbed by the Reichsbank (at that time the bank of issue).

Among the other banks founded at about the same time, one may mention the Bank of Nuremberg, in 1621, and above all, the Bank of Stockholm, founded in 1608; this was the first bank to give each client having a credit of balance receipts which were soon in circulation as hard cash throughout Sweden, being used first for buying goods, then for paying bills of exchange. This new function marked a particularly important stage in the orientation and extension of banking activity.

At first, these banks had been planned to accept deposits and to aid the flow of money. After this, they had been led, in order to make use of the money entrusted to them to work, to launch out actively into credit operations in the form of discounting bills of exchange. This extension of their field of action was justified by the unsatisfactory monetary conditions of the day: and it was to remedy this ill that they created special currencies designed for the financing of large-scale commercial enterprises, and which provided the element of monetary stability which such enterprises needed.

In the Bank of Stockholm contemporaries witnessed the foundation of a true bank of issue, since the receipts handed to its clients were in fact merely promises to pay, guaranteed by the metal deposited with the bank by holders of current accounts. This bank served as a model for the Land Banks which sprang up in Germany in the eighteenth and nineteenth centuries.

The Bank of Stockholm experienced grave difficulties and in 1776 a petition in bankruptcy was filed, and notes were honoured only to 50% of their face value.

2

THE DEVELOPMENT OF BANKING
IN VARIOUS COUNTRIES

1. BANKS IN FRANCE

In the following pages we shall give a brief and inevitably synthetic sketch of the evolution of banks and banking in France.
This subject is very extensive and there can be no question of
treating it at all exhaustively. A new work, at present in preparation, will make a detailed study of the present structure of the
French banking system.

The first French bank of issue was set up on 2 May 1716 by the
Scottish financier John Law, the son of a Scottish jeweller-banker,
and was called the Banque Générale. The capital of the bank was
fixed at 1·2 million écus, that is to say, 6 million livres, the écu
being at that time valued at 5 livres; shares were at a face value of
1,000 écus. Purchase price was accepted at the rate of 25% cash
(livres) and 75% treasury notes. The liquidation of the Public
Debt and the operation of the bank were in this way intimately
connected from the very beginning.

The bank was granted the privilege of issuing notes for a period
of twenty years, called écus de banque, whose value corresponded
exactly to that of the metallic crowns which were at that time in
circulation in France. Thus anyone holding notes was certain of
having an asset of a fixed and invariable value, which offered a
genuine safeguard against fraud and against the errors to which
debasement of coinage could give rise. Consequently, the notes
were immediately in heavy demand.

By a decree of 10 April 1717, in response to general public
demand, it was laid down that the notes would be accepted in

payment of all duties and of all taxes. The notes then stood at a premium in relation to coinage and this soon encouraged the directors of the bank to make further issues. Moreover, the very moderate discount rate of the Banque Générale resulted in an appreciable drop in the rate of interest and greatly contributed to the general esteem which the bank enjoyed.

By an edict of 4 December 1718 the bank became a state institution, under the name of the Banque Royale; the state for the first time became the guarantor of the notes in circulation. The close connection which was thus set up between state and bank could not fail to have a disastrous effect on the confidence enjoyed by the latter, taking into consideration the precarious state of the kingdom's finances.

John Law had made the Banque Royale a bank of issue, pledged to issue notes of a guaranteed value, a deposit bank accepting the funds which its clientele wished to deposit and finally a commercial bank which was to use part of its resources in financing the commercial activity of the India Company (Compagnie des Indes).

These three functions were certainly too vast to be properly discharged by a public institution. Moreover, the interference of the state in the policy of the bank had had the most deplorable consequences; it is beyond the power of the sovereign to determine the value of a currency. Reckless gambling in the shares of the Compagnie des Indes and the conflicting policies which were pursued provoked a panic and a general loss of confidence. The Banque Royale had to suspend payment. On 2 December 1720 John Law had to resign, and fled to Brussels.

The collapse of Law's system was to prevent the establishment in France of any new bank for the greater part of the eighteenth century. Not until 1776 did a decree of the *Conseil du Roi* (Council of the King), dated 24 May, approve the establishment of the Caisse d'Escompte, under the direction of a Genevan banker, a certain Penchaud.

But before long the same errors as before were to be committed. The royal treasury, always short of money, had repeated recourse to the Caisse d'Escompte to procure the funds it needed.

At the close of 1789 the debts of the state to the Caisse d'Escompte amounted to 157 million livres. In the following year the National Assembly decreed forced currency for the assignats whose issue it had already authorised; these were intended to mobilise and set into circulation, in the form of bonds guaranteed by landed property, the riches of the regular and secular clergy which the nation had just appropriated. Issues were soon being made in rapid succession and the Caisse d'Escompte was dissolved by a decree of 24 August 1793, having existed for seventeen years.

France then passed through a period of veritable monetary anarchy and not before 1796 was a new bank of issue established, the Caisse des Comptes-Courants; then a second in the following year, the Caisse d'Escompte et de Commerce, and finally a third in 1800, the Comptoir Commercial.

The monetary confusion which characterises the closing years of the eighteenth century all resulted from a failure to regulate properly fiduciary issues and the inevitable transformation of convertible paper-money into unconvertible paper-money, as the volume of notes in circulation increased while assets guaranteeing them dwindled away.

As a result the First Consul, Napoleon Bonaparte, wishing to re-establish order in the public finances and in the general economy of the country, resolved to centralise in a single institution the operations of the private banks, whose weakness was their lack of unity. On 13 February 1800 a new institution was established with an initial capital of 30 million francs, in the form of 30,000 shares at 1,000 francs, with the object of discounting bills of exchange bearing three signatures, by issuing in exchange notes payable to bearer at sight, a faculty which a law of 24 April 1803 was soon to transform into an exclusive privilege in the Paris district: the Bank of France was founded.

The initiative taken by the First Consul in the domain of banking resulted from his passion for system, centralisation and hierarchical order. Among the original shareholders of the Bank of France were: Napoleon Bonaparte, his brothers Joseph and Jerome, the Consuls Cambacérès and Lebrun, Barbe-Marbois,

Minister of the Treasury, Generals Murat and Duroc, and Hortense de Beauharnais.

Up to 1850 the activity of the Bank of France developed concurrently with the expansion of business, although there were difficult periods in 1805, 1846 and 1848. A decree of the Provisional Government, dated 2 May 1848, granted the bank the exclusive right to issue notes for all French territory and amalgamated the departmental banks of issue with it.

Thanks to a prudent but firm management, the Bank of France has always been able to honour its notes in cash, except during critical periods in the years 1848, 1870 and 1914, and to provide the French economy with the support of its credit.

Towards the middle of the nineteenth century business was increasing very fast, not only because of continuing expansion but also because of the many revolutionary discoveries being made in industrial techniques. In this period there was an increasing utilisation of steam coupled with the development of railways. The expansion of credit, corollary to the increase in economic activity, became an ever more pressing necessity. It was with this in mind that the brothers Isaac and Émile Péreire founded in 1852 the Société Générale de Crédit Mobilier, the first large commercial bank authorised to accept deposits and also to invest funds in the shares of industrial and commercial firms (decree of the Conseil d'État — State Council — of 18 November 1852). But its activity was dispersed in so many different branches of commerce, on no effectively co-ordinated plan, that the Crédit Mobilier had to go into liquidation in 1875, after a mere twenty-three years.

Experience had shown that it was desirable to separate the credit structure from the bases indispensable to its progressive development. Indeed, the three essential conditioning factors, that is to say, the existence of a sound currency, the free availability of a sufficiently high purchasing power and the opportunity to invest capital with the greatest possible degree of security, could not be provided by one type of institution. In the same way that needs create organs, diversity demands specialisation. It is for this reason that in the evolution of banks it has become progressively necessary to distinguish between four great categories of banks, each with their own sphere of activity: banks of issue, deposit banks, commercial banks and institutions of medium- and long-term credit.

In France the modern bank was born of the industrial revolution which characterised the nineteenth century. Capital had to be found to launch new enterprises and then to allow their orderly development.

However, the commercial crisis of 1847 and the political events of 1848 caused a collapse of credit. Discount banks were hastily re-established, but for the most part they had insufficient capital at their disposal and for several years the Press called constant attention to the lack of financial institutions capable of meeting the needs of industry and commerce. This lacuna was partially filled by the establishment of the four first deposit banks: the Comptoir National d'Escompte of Paris (in 1848), the Crédit Industriel et Commercial (in 1859), the Crédit Lyonnais (in 1863) and the Société Générale (in 1864). These banks were constrained to extend their activity over the whole metropolitan territory, but by various methods: the Crédit Industriel et Commercial by the creation of regional affiliates, the others by opening branch establishments. They were then confronted by a further task, that of being the agents for the diffusion of the liquid resources of France.

These great establishments served as models for important regional banks, especially in the north, in the east, and in the district round Lyons; that is to say, in the industrial districts.

The liberty which prevailed up to the outbreak of the Second World War favoured the appearance of a great number of small banks. But such banks, less well equipped to resist competition and at times fairly deeply engaged in local business, were more severely tested by the crises than institutions working with a more diverse clientele of higher financial standing. However, they were still numerous in 1913, especially in agricultural and wine-growing districts and in various other districts where they had succeeded in retaining a business clientele.

In the period immediately after the First World War there was a great development of banking; but this was an inflationary period; the world crisis of 1931, a result of the Wall Street crash and of the moratoriums declared in Central Europe, brought many firms, not all of them small, to bankruptcy. France was not, however, the country most deeply affected, and no important measure was taken at this time to regulate the activity of the banks. In certain other countries (notably the U.S.A., Italy and Belgium) very strict legislation was adopted, decreeing a clear separation between the functions of deposit banks and those of commercial banks.

The shock of the Second World War and the upheaval which it caused in financial methods were needed before it should be considered proper for the French authorities to intervene directly in the process of credit distribution.

Today France ranks as the third most important banking power in the Western World, after the U.S.A. and Great Britain. The great French banks, those which through the intermediary of their branches and their affiliations operate on a world scale, have funds committed in all the five continents; they are the principal agents of French commercial and financial activity in the international field and their efficiency and their dynamism help to make France a nodal point in the network of international finance.

The French institutions, which the statisticians traditionally regard as great international banks, are the following:

> Crédit Lyonnais
> Société Générale
> Banque Nationale pour le Commerce et l'Industrie [1]
> Comptoir National d'Escompte de Paris [1]
> Banque de Paris et des Pays-Bas.

In conformity with their vocation these banks, in order to facilitate the financing of the French economy in its present phase

---

[1] As from 1 July 1966 the Banque Nationale pour le Commerce et l'Industrie and the Comptoir National d'Escompte de Paris have merged to form a new bank called Banque Nationale de Paris, which will be the largest French commercial bank with total assets of 27,662,679,818 francs on 2 August 1966, 2,011 branches and 32,700 employees.

of full expansion, have paid particular attention to their connections in foreign financial centres and on foreign stock exchanges, where they have at their disposal a very extensive network of correspondents spread over the whole world. Moreover, they maintain, not only in London and New York but also in other important financial centres, branch offices, affiliates or agencies, which have become very important elements in their organisation.

On the practical side, another characteristic of these institutions is the extensive scope of their operations. When one considers that on 31 December 1964 the total assets of the five banks mentioned above amounted to approximately 64 milliard francs, one can picture their power and influence in the domain of international finance.

In addition, since they have a numerous clientele, both French and foreign, these institutions have actual control of hundreds of thousands of deposits of securities, whose value is not included in any statistical tables but which certainly amount to some scores of milliards of francs: so that they operate with a higher capital than a perusal of the balance-sheet would suggest.

The diffusion of French liquid capital has been principally the work of the great credit establishments, whose desire to serve their clients has induced them to set up important stock departments. The great French banks therefore play a preponderant role in promoting the movement of capital both directly by operations in which they are engaged on their own account and indirectly by those in which they are engaged on behalf of their clients. In this way they discharge functions important with respect to world economy.

The busy international traffic in securities and in capital, the close connections maintained with foreign banks and the demands of an economy orientated resolutely towards foreign trade, all these things naturally result in great activity in the field of foreign exchange. With the return to convertibility, French banks have resumed their important role in the international arbitration of exchange.

Because of the position which the great French credit institutions have acquired in the course of the last thirty years, they have become essential to the international movement of capital, which is in turn essential to the development of a modern and productive international economy.

As soon as France finally has achieved a currency of undoubted stability and as soon as she raises all restrictions imposed on the transfer of capital, her latent financial possibilities will doubtless come to a full flowering. The new transformation of the political situation will result in France's becoming a financial power that bears comparison with any other in the Western World. What an inspiring prospect for the great French bankers!

If the techniques of banking have developed little in the course of this century, the structure of the banking system in the various countries of the world has, on the other hand, been profoundly transformed. Such a transformation has been carried out also in France.

At the present moment there exist in France three main groups of banks: that is to say:

1. The public sector, comprising chiefly the following institutions:

Banque de France
Banque Centrale des États de l'Afrique de l'Ouest
Banque Centrale des États de l'Afrique Équatoriale et du Cameroun
Institut d'émission des départements d'Outre-Mer
Caisse centrale de coopération économique
Caisse des Dépôts et Consignations
Caisse nationale de Crédit Agricole
Caisse nationale des marchés de l'État
Caisse nationale des marchés de l'État des collectivetés et établissements publics
Caisse nationale de l'Énergie
Caisse nationale d'Épargne (Post Office Savings Bank) (P.T.T.)
Caisses de Crédit Municipal.

2. The semi-public sector, comprising chiefly the following institutions:

> Crédit Populaire de France (grouping 41 Banques Populaires)
> Crédit foncier de France
> Crédit national
> Banque Française du Commerce Extérieur
> Caisse centrale de Crédit Coopératif
> Caisses d'Épargne et de Prévoyance.

3. The private sector, which divides again into two main groups:

> the banks belonging to the Association Professionelle des Banques, a total of 338 on 31 December 1964, and the financial companies belonging to the Association Professionelle des Établissements Financiers, a total of 454 on 31 December 1964.

The four great nationalised deposit banks, the Crédit Lyonnais, the Société Générale, the Banque Nationale pour le Commerce et l'Industrie and the Comptoir National d'Escompte de Paris, belong to the private sector. These four establishments do not, in fact, have a special status granting them fiscal or financial privileges. On the contrary, they are subject to the same directives as private banks, embodied in the commercial legislation and regulations issued by the Conseil National du Crédit. They are members of the Association Professionel des Banques, the corporate association of private banks. Their essential characteristic is that the state holds their total capital as the sole shareholder.

In metropolitan France there are about 7,800 bank branches, of which about 3,800 are permanent; for a population of 48 million this represents an average of 160 branches per million of population and for a surface area of 551,695 sq. km. an average of 114 branches per 1,000 sq. km. This proportion is far from being impressive and is much less than that of other countries: in Belgium the corresponding figures are of the order of 180 and 50, and in Great Britain of 240 and 50 (based on figures obtained some years ago).

This coexistence submits the establishments of credit to the pressure of competition, and this compels them to improve the quality of their services, to the benefit of their clientele.

About 140,000 persons are employed in the French banks.

The banking and commercial importance of Paris has induced many leading foreign banks to set up agencies. In addition to the thirty-three foreign banks listed in the table below there are in Paris forty-one agencies representing foreign credit institutions, having their headquarters in sixteen different countries. These

(a) *Branches in France of foreign banks, having their head office abroad*

Name	Country	Assets in Francs	Number of offices
1 The Bank of Tokyo Ltd. . .	Japan	599,252,604	1
2 Morgan Guaranty Trust Company of New York	U.S.A.	557,030,200	1
3 The Chase Manhattan Bank . .	U.S.A.	545,027,172	1
4 Bank of America N.T. & S.A. .	U.S.A.	510,681,668	1
5 Banco Español en Paris . .	Spain	441,383,554	7
6 Barclays Bank (France) Limited .	England	431,273,992	15
7 Lloyds Bank Europe Limited . .	England	277,087,649	9
8 First National City Bank, New York	U.S.A.	234,264,776	1
9 Ottoman Bank	Turkey	223,992,254	2
10 American Express Company, Inc., New York	U.S.A.	221,053,615	4
11 Westminster Foreign Bank Limited	England	216,414,064	5
12 Bank Polska Kasa Opieki . .	Poland	99,686,732	1
13 Bank of London & South America Ltd.	England	67,849,636	1
14 Société Tunisienne de Banque .	Tunisia	46,942,015	2
15 Intra Bank	Lebanon	45,605,110	1
16 Banque Libanaise pour le Commerce	Lebanon	35,959,178	1
17 The Hongkong & Shanghai Banking Corporation . . .	England	24,522,545	1
18 Banque Italo-Belge . . .	Belgium	20,844,046	1
19 Banco de Bilbao	Spain	19,034,265	1
20 Thos. Cook & Son, Bankers (France) Ltd.	England	5,412,308	1
21 Bank Saderat, Iran . . .	Iran	1,844,931	1
Subtotal		4,625,162,254	58

(b) Banks established under French law but under foreign control

Name	Country	Assets in Francs	Number of offices
1 Banque Commerciale pour l'Europe du Nord	U.S.S.R.	2,811,997,531	1
2 Banco di Roma (France)	Italy	350,559,582	4
3 Banque Jordaan	Holland	273,588,792	2
4 Banca Commerciale Italiana (France)	Italy	187,655,553	7
5 Société Bancaire et Financière	Israel	105,187,948	1
6 Banque Franco-Allemande	Germany	63,738,497	2
7 Banque Franco-Portugaise d'Outre-Mer	Portugal	56,223,869	1
8 Mutuelle Industrielle	Belgium	55,812,458	1
9 The Royal Bank of Canada (France)	Canada	35,774,892	1
10 Banque Canadienne Nationale	Canada	19,503,131	1
11 Banque d'Arbitrage et de Crédit	Sweden	18,953,688	1
12 Crédit d'Escompte	Italy	10,164,056	1
Subtotal		3,989,159,697	23
Total (*a*) and (*b*)		8,614,321,951	81

agencies are not authorised by the Conseil National du Crédit to transact business themselves. Their essential object is to establish relations with financial and economic circles in France, and to provide for an exchange of information between these circles and the general management of the banks which they represent.

In addition, eighteen important American Investment Houses have agencies in Paris. They form a very useful link between French money markets and the great financial centres of the U.S.A.

The above table shows a list of the thirty-three foreign banks, established in France and licensed by the Conseil National du Crédit (National Credit Board, the highest French banking authority) to carry out banking operations of all kinds (listed in order of the total of the balance-sheet on 31 December 1964).

The number of stockbrokers assigned to each of the eight stock exchanges is as follows:

(By permission of *Journal Officiel*, Paris)

The eight Stock Exchange regions of France

The seven underlined cities are, together with Paris, the regional stock exchanges of France.

Paris	86	Bordeaux	8	Lille	5
Lyons	11	Nantes	8	Toulouse	5
Marseilles	9	Nancy	5		

TOTAL 137

The Paris Stock Exchange is the most important in the European Common Market.

On 31 December 1965 there were 989 French or Franc-area shares listed on the official register, and their capital value represented some 93,312,154,000 francs.

The stock-exchange capital (calculated by multiplying the number of listed shares by their value on a given date) represents the value attributed to a company on the stock exchange. This is one of the most significant ways, among all others, of evaluating a business.

Given the difficulties of obtaining exact figures of the total amounts involved in stock-exchange transactions at Paris and at the various regional centres, the only way to compare the relative importance is to compare the amount of stock-exchange tax paid by each centre for the year 1964. The amounts are in thousands of francs.

Paris	129,867
Lyons	809
Marseilles	515
Bordeaux	491
Nancy	480
Lille	460
Nantes	261
Toulouse	82

This table shows that dealings on the Paris Exchange amount to 97·66% of such dealings for the country as a whole. This is, of course, an approximation, if only because dealings in French *rentes* pay no tax.

2. BANKS IN ENGLAND

In a synthetic study, such as the present, it is impossible to give a detailed account of so complex a mechanism as the British banking system. But a brief sketch of the system as a whole from its origins to the present day and a sort of summarised general balance-sheet will not be without interest.

Jews were the first in England to deal in money: and for a long time the Jews alone gave the Norman kings the support they needed in periods of war and of rebellion. But the times were so unsettled and borrowers defaulted so often, and indeed so systematically, that the Jews were obliged to ask for very high rates of interest on the loans which they granted. A charter of Henry III was necessary to limit the permissible interest on loans to twopence in the pound per week, that is to say 43% per annum. These practices and the opprobrium which burdened dealings in money provoked a hatred of the Jews which resulted in 1290, during the reign of Edward I, in an edict of expulsion.

The Jews were succeeded by the Lombards. This collective name was used to refer to the rich Italian merchant-bankers, coming from Milan, Florence, Venice, Genoa and Lucca. In the thirteenth and fourteenth centuries the principal Italian banking houses having branches in London were, at first, the Gualterotti and the Frescobaldi, and later, the Bardi, the Peruzzi, the Acciaioli and the Medici.

The Lombards gave their assistance to Edward I and his successors, who, on the expulsion of the Jews, had been faced by an empty treasury. Their services were dearly bought, but they were so indispensable that the Lombards were almost totally exempt from the strict surveillance to which all foreigners were at that time subjected. The only condition imposed upon them was that of living in a certain street, which even today still preserves their name. A strange quirk of Fate! Lombard Street, at one time a street reserved almost exclusively for foreigners, has today become a street of prestige, a synonym for power, the general headquarters of British high finance.

The Lombard merchant-bankers made it their custom to hold a meeting twice daily in Lombard Street; these meetings seem to be the distant origin of the London money-market. However, transactions of only a few kinds were carried out at these meetings, for the Lombards were simply money-lenders, not even money-changers; the Crown had reserved to itself the privilege of exchanging money; this privilege was leased to a 'Royal Exchanger'. Gradually, however, the custom grew up of entrusting money and valuables to the Lombards for safe-keeping.

It is difficult to decide if the goldsmiths were, to begin with,

Lombards who became jewellers or if Lombards and goldsmiths coexisted before they joined forces. However this may be, the Corporation of Goldsmiths was registered in 1392, during the reign of Richard II, and history even preserves the name of a goldsmith who was Lord Mayor of London from 1189 to 1213.

Three centuries later, in 1556, there were in London 107 goldsmiths, of whom 76 had their place of business in Chepe (Cheapside), the others in Lumberde Street (Lombard Street).

During the reign of Elizabeth I and later, during the Civil War, personal fortunes were composed largely of jewels, plate, and gold and silver coins. All this wealth was entrusted to the goldsmiths or to the Royal Mint. But it happened in 1640 that Charles I, short of money, appropriated £130,000 sterling in the form of bullion, deposited for safe-keeping at the Royal Mint.

This act of violence frightened both public and merchants and, no longer having confidence in the public authorities, from now on they entrusted their liquid assets to the goldsmiths.

In imitation of the Banco del Giro at Venice, the goldsmiths issued depositors with a deposit certificate. Then they devised a refinement: they issued their certificates in denominations of a fixed and equal value: 'goldsmiths' notes', which were soon circulating freely, and were considered more acceptable than cash. The goldsmiths used deposits in making short-term loans, guaranteed by the bills of exchange held by the borrower. These loans were usually made in the form of notes. And so, on the one hand, the goldsmiths' cash and bullion in hand guaranteed both deposits and advances, on the other hand, the issue of notes was in part covered by commercial drafts. An immense step forward had been made in the technique of fiduciary issue.

In 1672 Charles II, having exhausted his treasury in the Dutch War, repeated his predecessor's exploit. He closed the Exchequer and confiscated, purely and simply, £1,328,526 sterling, which the goldsmiths had in deposit with the Treasury, which was paying them 8% interest. This disastrous expedient brought most of the goldsmiths to bankruptcy and a great number of their clients to ruin. The affair took on the proportion of a national bankruptcy.

A few years later the king was obliged to acknowledge his debt and to undertake to pay interest on the whole at the rate of 6%; but in 1683 even the payment of this interest ceased. The debt was to be acknowledged again in 1705; the capital was never reimbursed and even today the 'Goldsmith Bankers' Debt' constitutes the first item of the National Debt.

Among the goldsmiths who survived the crisis of 1672 was to be found Sir Francis Child, who has remained famous as 'the Father of the Banking Profession'. He was, indeed, one of the first to abandon the trade of goldsmith and money-lender, and to become a banker properly so-called.

Never very numerous, the goldsmiths numbered seventy to eighty at the end of the seventeenth century: in 1801 one could count sixty-eight private banks which were their direct descendants. A few are even now still in existence, such as the firm C. Hoare & Co., which already existed under this name in 1683.

In the period of the goldsmiths there existed no public debt in England; only agreements between the state and private financiers. It was to fall to the lot of William III to create it. (William of Orange was Stadtholder of Holland when he was offered the English throne in 1689.) The repeal of the Edict of Nantes had brought many French protestants to England. Cromwell had turned a blind eye to Jewish immigration. And after the change of 1688 many Spanish Jews, settled in Amsterdam, followed the new king to London. These new forces flowed together and a creative flood transformed the world of finance. William III, clinging to the traditions of his country of origin, affirmed that the state would honour its obligations, then, basing his policies on this principle, he gave a free rein to the invention of his advisers, to raise money by all the methods known at that time: short- and long-term annuities, annuity associations, tontines, lotteries, etc. Montagu, Chancellor of the Exchequer, excelled in the invention of ingenious devices. As for the London Exchange, under James I, Cromwell and Charles II, it staunchly fulfilled its duties since its foundation by Sir Thomas Gresham. But the English capital did not enjoy that central importance which had been the lot of Antwerp and which had benefited Amsterdam. Except for merchandise, speculation was for the most part confined to the shares of the great commercial companies at the head of which stood the English East India Company.

After the accession of William III, the character of the Royal Exchange was amended. Dealings in public securities soon began to be practised, and to increase in importance. The year 1695 was particularly lively. In 'Gresham's temple' were to be met all sorts of people: Dutchmen, Frenchmen, Venetians, Spaniards, Italians and even Turks.

Let us now sketch the life of a powerful and fascinating character, one of the financial geniuses of the period, the founder of the London Stock Exchange: Thomas Gresham. A man of destiny, in this sense, that his actions were in intimate harmony with the trend of development in his native country. For, in the fifteenth century, England had remained an ill-starred, unimportant country. But, in the sixteenth century, England was on the march: agriculture, commerce, industry, navigation, all were transformed. Guides and instigators were needed in this creative expansion: Gresham was the most eminent of them.

When Thomas Gresham was born in London in 1519, his father was already head of an important business and banking house in Milk Street. Richard Gresham disdained neither political honours nor political profits. He was Lord Mayor of London in 1537. When Thomas Gresham inherited the business, at his father's death, he transferred the bank to Lombard Street, the very centre of the business world. His ability was such that the Crown, a few years later, sent him to Antwerp with the title of 'royal merchant'. Here his role was to be difficult, complex, multiple. His initial task consisted in raising the large sums of money which English men of business were not able to lend to the king, then to guard against the times of payment of the bills being extended, which would have been very burdensome. He also struggled to maintain a rate of exchange favourable to English currency, always keeping a watch on the money market, pledging his own credit whenever it was necessary. No one knew the Antwerp Exchange as intimately as he did, and no session took place without his receiving a schedule of the position of all accounts. This approximated to a regular information service. And, in fact, Thomas Gresham directed for a long time the English information services in the Netherlands.

Mary Tudor's reign came during the long years spent in Antwerp. She was as fiercely Catholic as Gresham was profoundly Protestant. The banker was initially relieved of all his offices. But who was competent to replace him? The Catholic banker William Dauntsey made vain attempts to do so. Thomas Gresham therefore resumed his work, hampered, however, by the fact that he was employed but his advice was disregarded. Things were different under Elizabeth I. Gresham increased and extended his influence in the business capital of the world, and continued to render service, both financial and political, to his country. Perhaps he would have lived out his life on the banks of the Scheldt, if the rebellion in the Netherlands had not brought financial ruin to Antwerp. Thomas Gresham returned to London and, positively indefatigable, undertook the realisation of a double plan: to make England independent of foreign money, and to endow London with an Exchange comparable to that of Antwerp.

From 1566 on, Thomas Gresham prosecuted both these enterprises simultaneously. He induced the merchant classes to advance considerable sums to the Crown and he devoted much of his time and much of his private fortune to the construction of a building both more imposing and more restrained than the Exchange of Antwerp. This was to be the Royal Exchange, officially opened by the Queen on 23 January 1571. The London Exchange was destroyed by fire in 1666; it was rebuilt and the prime importance of the role it played throughout modern times is well known.

As for Thomas Gresham, his energy, his knowledge, his boldness, his fabulous wealth, his fame make him a heroic figure in the history of finance. Even those who do not know of him, know by heart his famous proposition: 'If good money and bad money are in circulation together, the bad money will tend to drive out the good money from circulation.'

He died in 1579 at the age of sixty.

During all this time, the jewellers continued to operate as bankers. Their organisation, however, remained defective: they

lent at exorbitant rates (33%) and the crisis of 1672 had prejudiced
the public against them. They were grudgingly tolerated. And so
the idea of a bank was in the air, sketched out in a work by Baltha-
zar Gerbier in 1651 and also in a public proposal by Samuel Lamb
in 1658. In 1678 a certain Mr. Lewis revived the project energetic-
ally. At last in 1688 a Scottish gentleman, William Paterson,
elaborated a project having the double advantage of being realisable in practice and in harmony with the political necessities of the
moment. Despite its merits, Paterson's initiative would, perhaps,
like those of Lamb and Lewis, have come to nothing if it had not
coincided with William III's assumption of power.

Paterson's plans were more far-reaching than the articles of
association of the Bank of Amsterdam or of the Bank of Stockholm. The new establishment was expected to provide a higher
degree of security, a reduction in the rate of interest, a true paper
currency. But even if these plans met the wishes of the Government and of commercial interests, they met with furious opposition. They were anathema to the jeweller-bankers. And since the
bank, although it did not yet exist officially, already owned a
provisional Head Office, its enemies referred to it as the 'harpy of
Grocers' Hall'. The opposition was so skilfully conducted that no
less than six years were needed to get the Bill authorising the
creation of the bank through Parliament; and even so, it passed
only because the Government could no longer exist without
borrowing and could not find a lender. Oddly enough, the Act
which created a bank was called a Tonnage Act. In fact, the
association called 'the Governor and Company of the Bank of
England' were authorised to raise by subscription £1,200,000
which was to be immediately lent to the Government, so that the
war against France could be prosecuted; to repay this voluntary
advance, Parliament authorised the Crown to collect various dues
on the tonnage of ships, as well as on beer, ale and other beverages,
in favour of the subscribers.

The subscription list, opened on 21 June, was covered in ten
days. The Charter was conferred on 24 July 1694, and on this date
the Bank of England began its long and perilous existence — the
bank was essentially a private bank of issue, not privileged, and its

capital of £1,200,000 had been entirely subscribed by the public; it was granted no monopoly of issue — the Bank of England may be rightly considered the first modern bank of issue since it was the first to issue true bank-notes and to combine issue with the discounting of bills of exchange.

The bank began business in a modest way. The Head Office had been transferred to Mercer's Chapel and consisted only of a large hall in which directors, secretaries and clerks sat ranged in hierarchical order. Its officers were remarkable men: the governor, John Houblon, great merchants like Gilbert of Heathcote and Michael Godfrey. William Paterson was of course on the Board of Directors. The constitution required a total of twenty-four directors elected by those shareholders who owned shares to the value of at least £500. Paterson resigned after a bare year, because the bank in his estimation was not fulfilling all its objectives.

Less than a century after the foundation of the bank, England already had its great industrialists: Matthew Boulton in metallurgy, Benjamin Gott in textiles, Josiah Wedgwood in pottery, John Wilkinson in engineering. They had built and equipped factories in which they employed thousands of workmen.

All this industrial activity was a source of wealth, which nourished, stimulated and increased trade. Masters of the oceans and of a great colonial empire, the English worked doggedly at improving their roads and waterways, in order to give the greatest possible encouragement to trade. Their breadth of vision and their determination rarely failed them.

As a port, as a commercial centre and as a financial centre, London was definitely beginning to supersede Amsterdam.

This power, both of commerce and industry, was buttressed by an efficient financial organisation based on the Bank of England and the Stock Exchange and by the unshakeable confidence of the citizens — of all classes — in the destiny of their country.

The Bank of England was fully prepared to meet the tasks which awaited her. It had been in existence for a century and had not spared its support to the Government during the wars with Revolutionary France.

England's expenditure was enormous because she was subsidising the continental nations, fighting against Napoleon. The subsidies paid to her allies necessitated considerable transfers of capital in extremely difficult conditions. In carrying them out, the British Government relied on an international syndicate of bankers, which included Baring Brothers & Co., Hope & Co. and Fries & Co.

The bank Baring Brothers & Co. had been founded by Francis Baring, son of a Bremen pastor, and was at this time directed by Alexander Baring. His brother-in-law, Labouchère, was head of the banking house Hope & Co. of Amsterdam. As for the firm Fries & Co., it was under the direction of David Parish, a citizen of Hamburg, of Scottish extraction, an intimate friend of Talleyrand, and one of the most picturesque and daring figures in modern finance.

The Rothschilds will appear later; they did not belong to the syndicate, but their role will nevertheless be of capital importance.

On this plane, Napoleon was outclassed by his opponents. His staff lacked vision. In this financial battle the last word was to be with the manufacturers of Manchester, the merchants of Liverpool, and, above all, with the bankers of the City of London.

Today the Bank of England, the nerve centre of the City of London, maintains the equilibrium of the delicate and complicated apparatus, constituted by the financial, commercial and banking network, all of whose threads converge upon her. The Bank of England has its Head Office in the City of London in Threadneedle Street, and eight branches situated in Birmingham, Bristol, Leeds, Liverpool, Manchester, Newcastle, Southampton and near the Law Courts in the Strand in London. It has no branches outside England properly so-called. This is in part due to the fact that the Scottish and Irish banks issue their own notes, which, however, are not legal tender and are covered almost entirely by means of payment in legal tender deposited in London at the Bank of England.

The bank is administered by the Court of Directors which is composed of the Governor, the Deputy Governor, and sixteen directors, who are now appointed by the Crown. The Chief Cashier ranks highest in the hierarchy of permanent officials of the bank; his department is the vital department of the bank, which is responsible for the issue of notes and for all banking transactions.

The Bank of England carries out all normal banking operations but only to a deliberately restricted extent, which no longer has any great practical importance. On the other hand, the bank is charged with the administration of the public debt. Since national-isation (1 March 1946) its principal function has been to act as financial adviser to the Government, to determine in conjunction with the Government a monetary policy and to put it into execution. It is not only the Bank of the Government but also the Bank of the banks.

The Act nationalising the bank authorises the Government to give directives to the bank, which, for its part and acting in con-junction with the Exchequer, can give instructions to the banks of the kingdom. Its preponderant influence is reinforced by the fact that it operates as the agent of the Exchequer in the control of exchange.

The severe crisis of 1793 occasioned a return to a rigorous adherence to the principle of note issue which was to find its authoritative formulation in the Joint Stock Bank Act of 1844. According to this Act, the decisive event in the history of the Bank of England was the clear-cut separation between the issue of notes (Issue Department) and other financial affairs (Banking Department).

New regulations dealing with the covering of notes were intro-duced. Above a certain limit, called the fiduciary issue, the notes issued have to be entirely covered by gold. This limit was initially £14 million, but was raised in successive stages; eventually reach-ing the figure of £1,575 million, authorised by the Currency and Banknotes Act of 1954.

In 1958 a resolution adopted by both Houses of Parliament authorised the Bank of England to exceed this ceiling for periods of two years and by stages of £50 million, so that today (5 January 1966) the figure of £2,900 million has been reached.

In Scotland the first banks of issue were founded by landed proprietors in free association. A certain number of proprietors formed an association to establish a bank. The capital was made up either by contributions of cash or by transfer of landed property. These banks issued notes payable to bearer at sight and which came into circulation either when deposits were withdrawn in cash or when bills were discounted or when money was borrowed on a mortgage.

In 1695 the Bank of Scotland was founded at Edinburgh and for the first time the Scottish Parliament granted this bank the exclusive privilege of issuing notes. The bank's privilege expired in 1717 and was not renewed. From then on, until an Act of 1845, all Scottish banks were at liberty to issue notes.

In 1760 seven Edinburgh banks established the first clearing-house in the United Kingdom, an organisation similar to that used at the former fairs at Lyons. So it was at Edinburgh that the organisation and functioning of the clearing-house took on the definitive form which they still retain.

In 1773 the London bankers followed the example of their Scottish colleagues and founded the London clearing-house.

The City, which enjoys administrative autonomy and which can be crossed on foot in half an hour, is as busy as a beehive on week-days from 9.30 a.m. to 5.30 p.m. Outside these hours it is almost entirely deserted. The City provides employment for several hundreds of thousands of people, but has a population of only about 5,000 permanent inhabitants.

Because of its geographical situation, London was predestined to be a great financial centre. It possesses a rich hinterland and controls navigation on the Thames. The river makes it inevitable that London should be an important trading centre and it is the Thames, affording a direct outlet to the sea, which, from the Middle Ages to the present day, has formed the ideal route for communication with the Continent. The history of London as an international financial centre goes back to antiquity. From Roman days, except for a few brief interruptions, money has been minted here, an accurate barometer of economic life for two thousand years. The decline of European financial centres, such as Amsterdam, Antwerp and other towns, facilitated the rise of London to that financial hegemony which she has exercised in recent centuries.

The City has not failed to profit from the dominant position which England has acquired in international markets. She put at the disposal of the whole world a complete highly developed financial and banking system, which facilitated with a high degree of flexibility the execution of all possible commercial, industrial and maritime transactions.

One of the sturdiest pillars of the financial edifice of the City to-day is formed by the great deposit banks, which are subject to very stringent measures of control by the public powers.

The dominant and preponderant position of the great British banks is founded above all on the high degree of confidence with which the public favours them; which has allowed them to accumulate a mass of deposits from their clientele of steadily in-creasing importance.

The five banks, known as the 'Big Five', alone acknowledged deposits amounting to £7,966 million on 31 December 1964, to which should be added about £1,300 million deposited with other banks, in which the 'Big Five' are directly interested.

The table below shows the distribution of these deposits among the 'Big Five' (31 December 1964).

Title	Head Office	Founded	Deposits	Branches	Share-holders
1 Barclays Bank Ltd. .	London	1694	2,147	2,421	89,000
2 Midland Bank Ltd. .	London	1836	1,927	2,533	92,000
3 Lloyds Bank Ltd. .	London	1765	1,618	2,110	79,000
4 Westminster Bank Ltd.	London	1834	1,224	1,340	68,000
5 National Provincial Bank Ltd. . .	London	1833	1,050	1,610	70,000
		TOTAL	7,966	10,014	398,000

Deposits are given in millions of pounds.

It is in the five great banks that are accumulated as high a proportion as 75% of the liquid reserves and means of pay-ment of the economy, of local authorities and of the public at large. This enormous mass of deposits gives them effective control of the distribution of credit, which allows them to play a decisive role in all sectors of British economic life.

The proverbial security which the Big Five enjoy, their almost limitless capacity to grant short-term credits (middle- and long-term credits are excluded from their operations), their vast field of action at both national and international levels, all these factors contribute in making the City the great financial capital of the world.

The concentration of banking affairs in a few houses is an essential feature of contemporary England. In 1899 there were still 106 joint-stock banks: in 1918, only thirty-four were left: today, only five, whose joint power is truly formidable.

English banks are characterised by the degree of specialisation of their business. In principle the English use the term 'bank' only to mean banks of deposit, making short-term advances. Outside the banks properly so-called, various firms carry out transactions which in other countries form an essential part of the operations of true banks.

The specialisation of banking business in England has given rise to and kept in operation various institutions peculiar to the English banking scene.

Special mention must be made of the merchants' banks. These are important banking houses belonging to the Accepting Houses' Committee. Among the oldest and enjoying an international reputation the following deserve mention:

Arbuthnot, Latham & Co. Ltd.
Baring Brothers & Co. Ltd.
Wm. Brandt's Sons & Co. Ltd.
Brown, Shipley & Co. Ltd.
Antony Gibbs & Sons Ltd.
Guinness Mahon & Co. Ltd.
Hambros Bank Ltd.
Hill, Samuel & Co. Ltd.
S. Japhet & Co. Ltd.
Kleinwort, Benson Ltd.
Lazard Brothers & Co. Ltd.

Samuel Montagu & Co. Ltd.
Morgan Grenfell and Co. Ltd.
N. M. Rothschild & Sons
J. Henry Schroder Wagg & Co. Ltd.
S. G. Warburg & Co. Ltd.

The merchants' banks are firms specialising in the acceptance of bills of exchange. Many of them are old commercial houses which, having acquired a reputation for soundness and integrity, came to back the signature of other firms of lesser standing; then the day came when, as this subsidiary branch of their business brought in large profits, they abandoned commerce and devoted themselves exclusively to the acceptance of drafts. Their clientele is scattered over the whole world and as London is the principal trading centre for many raw materials the merchant bankers are able to gather exact information about the affairs of all firms which trade at London: in this way they know the real value of the paper offered them and their operations are carried out with a minimum of risk.

These merchant bankers have sometimes extended their business. Some of them have become representatives of foreign governments or of great foreign firms and assume responsibility for the service of securities issued at London. Most of them are now organised as private or limited liability companies.

Their close and extensive relationship with international finance allowed them to accept bills of exchange drawn by their correspondents; often they will discount such bills. Their signature makes a bill of exchange acceptable at other banks, and bestows, if the need should arise, the right to rediscount at the Bank of England.

The merchants' banks assume additionally a very important role, both on the national and on the international level, as intermediaries and fiduciary agents when capital issues are made. They are members of the Issuing Houses' Association, in which about sixty banks and Investment Trusts are grouped, and play a predominant role in its affairs. With the exception of British Government Loans and of certain municipal issues, all other new issues are floated by the merchants' banks, often with the support of underwriters' syndicates comprising other London financial institutions. They also act as agents in the direct investment of capital and in launching issues of stocks and shares on the London Stock Exchange.

Another group are the Discount Houses whose business is confined to the discounting of commercial paper. Some are grouped in large Joint-Stock Companies (three of the most important are the Union Discount Company, the National Discount Company and Alexanders Discount Company); the Discount Houses are members of the London Discount Market Association. They procure capital for discounting either by borrowing from banks or by accepting deposits from the public against interest. Bill brokers are private firms; they work with capital provided by the banks either by straightforward loans or by rediscounting bills not due. Thanks to these brokers, English banks accept only paper whose soundness is guaranteed by the knowledge and ability of the broker. Some of these brokers, called 'Running Brokers', are merely intermediaries who do not put their own signature on the bill and are paid on a commission basis.

Finally we must mention the Issuing Banks, grouped together in the Issuing Houses Association, which specialises in the issue of long-term securities; the Finance Houses, grouped together in the Finance Houses' Association, who finance hire-purchase transactions by industrial and commercial enterprises, and the bullion brokers, who deal in precious metals. Discussions have been taking place which could lead to the merger of the Finance Houses' Association and the Industrial Bankers' Association. The two bodies together would represent the vast majority of hire-purchase interests in the country: the Finance Houses' Association members include sixteen of the biggest groups accounting for over three-quarters of total business, while the Industrial Bankers' Association has a membership of over twenty-five of the smaller companies.

The cornerstone of the British banking empire in other parts of the world is formed by a certain number of banks whose business extends to the Commonwealth countries and the various

Latest situation of the fifteen British banks engaged particularly in overseas banking transactions.

Name	Head Office	Date	Deposits £ million	Branches	Country
1 Barclays Bank (D.C.O.), affiliated to Barclays Bank Ltd.	London	31.3.65	1,000	1,416	45 countries
2 Australia & New Zealand Bank Ltd.	London	30.9.64	666	1,046	Australia and New Zealand
3 The Standard Bank Ltd.	London	31.3.65	549	1,100	South Africa
4 The Chartered Bank	London	31.12.64	490	111	30 countries
5 Bank of London & South America Ltd.	London	31.12.64	410	85	22 Latin American countries
6 National & Grindlays Bank Ltd., affiliated to Lloyds Bank Ltd.	London	31.12.64	317	190	10 countries of Asia and Africa
7 English, Scottish & Australian Bank Ltd.	London	30.6.64	194	507	Australia
8 The British Bank of the Middle East	London	31.12.64	1,111	33	12 countries of Middle East and Morocco
9 The Eastern Bank Ltd., affiliated to The Chartered Bank	London	31.12.64	106	22	11 Asian countries
10 Lloyds Bank Europe Ltd., affiliated to Lloyds Bank	London	30.9.64	89	15	France and Switzerland
11 Bank of West Africa Ltd.	London	31.3.65	85	80	South Africa
12 Mercantile Bank Ltd.	London	31.12.64	84	41	9 Asian countries
13 Westminster Foreign Bank Ltd., affiliated to Westminster Bank Ltd.	London	31.12.64	48	7	France and Belgium
14 Barclays Bank (France) Ltd., affiliated to Barclays Bank Ltd.	London	31.12.64	22	13	France
15 The Hongkong & Shanghai Banking Corporation	London	31.12.64	$HK 4,298 million	78	20 countries in Asia, Europe and U.S.A.

continents. They are grouped in the British Overseas Banks' Association.

The table on p. 52 gives a survey of the vast ramifications of this group of banks, ranged in order of the amount of deposits held on 31 December 1962. Important subsidiary and affiliated companies of the banks mentioned therein:

1. Barclays Bank (D.C.O.)

Barclays Overseas Development Corporation Ltd., London
Barclays Export Finance Company Ltd., London
Barclays Bank of California, San Francisco (U.S.A.)
Bank of Trinidad (Gordon Grant) Ltd., Port of Spain (Trinidad)
Crédit Congolais, Kinshasa (Congo)

3. The Standard Bank Ltd.

The Standard Bank of South Africa Ltd. (operates in South and S.W. Africa)
The Standard Bank Ltd. (operates in Central and East Africa)

Arrangements have now been made to merge the interest of the Bank of West Africa Ltd. with the Standard Bank Ltd.

4. The Chartered Bank

The Eastern Bank Ltd.
The Chartered Bank of London, San Francisco (U.S.A.)
Allahabad Bank Ltd., Calcutta (India)
The Irano British Bank, Tehran (Iran)
The Commercial Bank, Tripoli (Libya)
The Mutual Acceptance Company Ltd., Sydney (Australia)

5. Bank of London & South America Ltd.

Bank of London & Montreal Ltd., Nassau (Bahamas)
Banco La Guaira Internacional C.A., Caracas
Compania Financiera de Londres S.A., Buenos Aires (Argentine)
Banco de Comercio S.A., Mexico City (Mexico)
Balfour, Williamson & Co. Ltd., London

10. Lloyds Bank Europe Ltd.

Lloyds Bank (Cannes) S.A., Cannes (France)
Lloyds Bank (Belgium) S.A., Brussels

15. The Hongkong & Shanghai Banking Corporation

The Hongkong & Shanghai Banking Corporation of California,
San Francisco (U.S.A.)
Hongkong & Shanghai Bank (Trustee) Ltd., Hong Kong
Hongkong & Shanghai Bank (Malaysia) Trustee Ltd., Singa-
pore
Hongkong & Shanghai Bank (Trustee) Ltd., London
Wayfoong Finance Ltd., Hong Kong

The Mercantile Bank Ltd. in London and The British Bank of
the Middle East Ltd. in London belong to the group of the
Hongkong & Shanghai Banking Corporation.

The City of London can proudly say that the sun never sets on
its financial empire.

All these powerful groups of banks bring a great flood of business to London, and in return the highly developed credit organisation of the City is at the disposal of the countries involved. On
the other hand, many banks having their headquarters in the
various Commonwealth countries are, in their turn, represented
in London by important branches and direct financial operations
of great scope towards the British capital. The importance of
London as a banking and commercial centre has induced many
foreign banks to open branches and agencies in the City.

It should be noted that the London branches of foreign banks
are authorised to conduct business on exactly the same footing as
British banking establishments. They have the same rights as
British banks and are treated in exactly the same way by the Bank
of England. Following the example of the great British banks,
they put their surplus liquid assets at the disposal of the discount
market and also discount bills themselves.

At present seventy-five important foreign banks are represented at London; among them are eight French banks, listed
below:

Banque de Paris et des Pays-Bas Ltd.
Banque de l'Indochine
Crédit Lyonnais
Société Générale
Crédit Industriel et Commercial
Société Centrale de Banque
Banque Nationale de Paris (through its affiliate, the British and French Bank Ltd.)
Banque de Suez et de l'Union des Mines (through its affiliate, the British and Continental Banking Co. Ltd.)

If the City of London has in recent years regained all its prestige, this is largely because competition from other great international financial centres has met with little success.

In the United States foreign trade is conducted entirely in dollars and the New York banks find too many opportunities to invest their excess of liquidity at home: they are not greatly interested in international commercial transactions which involve much careful detailed work, not to mention the risks involved in foreign exchange. On the other hand, the British banking system, because of its specialisation, is better adapted to the financing of international trade and has at its disposal a much more extensive network of foreign branches. The close relations which the English banks maintain with the commercial, maritime and assurance interests of the City give them an unfailing advantage over other important centres of international finance.

3. BANKS IN GERMANY

In the financial history of Germany, the period between 1367 and 1680 is dominated by a colossus: the Fugger family. Their bank was the most powerful credit institution, owing its long-standing importance to the scope of its operations which covered all Europe and Spanish America. For more than two centuries the Fuggers were the greatest financiers of their time. Never before had a banker manipulated such a mass of capital, or possessed so much wealth. During all the sixteenth, and part of the seventeenth

century, the course of European history was determined by the
Fuggers in their bank at Augsburg. In their hands and at their
mercy lay the fate of imperial dynasties. In 1535 they obtained the
right to mint money.

In the period of the Fuggers, other bankers had their offices in
Augsburg. The best-known are: Gossembrot, Haug, Herbrot,
Herwarth, Höchstetter, Manlich, Meuting, Neidhart, Seiller, and
above all the Welsers, in importance second only to the Fuggers.
Concurrently with the Fuggers and often in association with
them, the Welsers participated in the great credit operations of
the imperial house of Habsburg. The Welsers also lent to the
kings of France, a thing to which the Fuggers would never consent.

Nuremberg was the most important German town which com-
peted with Augsburg as a banking centre. The Nuremberg
bankers were less influential, less daring and less distinguished.
Among the most important were the Tuchers, the Imhofs and the
Klebergs. In 1619 the Bank of Hamburg was founded and in
1621 the Bank of Nuremberg. Some account has been given of
these two banks in Chapter 1 (Section 8 (p. 22)).

Towards the end of the eighteenth century the first Land Banks
were established. In 1770, to alleviate the destruction caused by
the Seven Years War, landed proprietors began to form associations, with the aim of setting up credit institutions, which would
facilitate the raising of loans on landed property. Brandenburg
soon followed suit in 1777, Pomerania in 1781, Hamburg in 1782,
Prussia in 1787, Saxony, etc. The object for which these associations were founded was to issue mortgage bonds (*Pfandbriefe*),
which circulated like a kind of bank money and passed from hand
to hand in many transactions. Some of these banks even issued
bank-notes.

To be sure, credit in Germany was not, at this period, available
only at Land Banks. Other private banking-houses established at
Hamburg, Cologne and Frankfurt were doing extensive business,
especially with foreign countries. One might mention the Hamburg establishments, Joh. Berenberg Gossler & Co., Brinckmann
Wirtz & Co.; at Cologne, the firms Sal. Oppenheim Jr. & Co.,
J. H. Stein; at Frankfurt the firms B. Metzler seel Sohn & Co.,

Bethmann Gebrüder, Koch Lauteren & Co. All these names still appear in the records of the great German bankers.

In Germany, as in all countries in the middle of the nineteenth century, the construction of a railway system provoked the genesis of modern industry. Indeed, railways did in Germany cause the development of metallurgy and mining. So it became necessary, as in all countries which were setting up a railway system and transforming their industries, to create credit institutions, designed for business on a much extended scale and directed according to new methods, so as to be adapted to the new needs. This movement, which gathered strength from 1850 onwards, led to the banks — formerly private banks — being reformed into public companies, a change encouraged by the modification of certain laws dealing with commercial and financial matters: the same thing was happening in England and France. The following are the three great banks, still in existence today, which were founded in the second half of the nineteenth century: Deutsche Bank (1870), Commerzbank (1870) and Dresdner Bank (1872).

Oddly enough, it was from France that the founders of these earliest modern banks took the bold concepts which they embodied in their organisation of credit for industrial undertakings and developed on a large scale. The banking-house Sal. Oppenheim Jr. & Co., of Cologne (one of the most influential, founded in 1789 and still in existence today), had participated in the foundation, in 1852, of the Crédit Mobilier of Péreire Bros. at Paris. It was likewise the house of Oppenheim which participated in the foundation in Germany in 1853 of the Bank of Commerce and Industry, later to become the Darmstädter und Nationalbank, which in turn was absorbed in 1932 by the Dresdner Bank. In Germany it was also the house of Oppenheim which developed and rendered fruitful the ideas of the Brothers Péreire.

By 1879 financiers had begun to group banks together or to amalgamate them. The Deutsche Bank alone absorbed forty-three banks, the Dresdner Bank forty-one and the former Disconto-Gesellschaft twenty-eight. This latter bank amalgamated in 1929 with the Deutsche Bank.

At the time of the German Confederation, there were as many as thirty-three banks of issue, more than the number of states forming the Confederation. The bank-notes they issued were not identical; difficulties were experienced in sending them from one state to another. When the war of 1870-1 had created a unified Germany, Bismarck, who realised clearly that the shreds and patches which he was trying to stitch together might one day pull apart, had the idea of creating a single bank of issue. The tendency in German politics at the time was to make Berlin not only the political capital of Germany but also the centre of financial power, a policy whose eventual culmination was the centralisation of all banks of issue in one single bank, the Imperial Bank or Reichsbank, the supreme regulator of German finance.

In 1876 the Reichsbank was founded. A strenuous task awaited it, that of acting in support of all joint-stock banks which might require assistance in times of crisis. Soon the Reichsbank had extended its branches throughout the Empire and become the financial citadel of Germany.

In 1945 the Nazi régime was in collapse. The victorious allies were firmly resolved to dismantle the economic and financial power of the Third Reich. The Reichsbank was condemned and disappeared at the end of 1946 after seventy years of existence.

After its disappearance there came the successive creation of eleven regional banks of issue, the *Landeszentralbanken*, distributed among the eleven provinces (*Länder*) of the new Federal Republic of Germany. The Allies' desire for decentralisation was evident but they were not blind to the rationale nor to the necessities of German life.

When the suppression of the Reichsbank was resolved at the Potsdam Conference of 1945, provision had also been made for a monetary reform and the establishment of a new central bank. This reform took place in June 1948, and was preceded on 4 March 1948 by the establishment of a bank of issue for all West Germany; the Bank deutscher Länder.

This was not sufficient to cause the disappearance of the eleven provincial central banks (*Landeszentralbanken*): they were proving too useful. Therefore the Central Council of the Bank deutscher

Länder was composed of the President of the Bank and of the eleven Presidents of the provincial central banks, the technical direction being undertaken by a managing Committee (*Direktorium*).

As the ascendancy of the allies diminished and the industrial power of the new Germany grew, the tendency to reunification became more marked. By a law of 26 July 1957, passed by the Bundestag, the eleven *Landeszentralbanken* were amalgamated with the Bank deutscher Länder in a new institution called the Deutsche Bundesbank (German Federal Bank) whose Head Office was fixed at Frankfurt (Main) as long as the Federal Government should not be established in Berlin. The Federal Republic of Germany had thus established a true central bank of issue.

The eleven *Landeszentralbanken* established in the *Länder* (provinces) of Bäden-Württemberg, Bavaria, Berlin, Bremen, Hamburg, Hansestadt, Hessen, Niedersachsen, Nordrhein–Westfalen, Rheinland–Pfalz, Saarland and Schleswig-Holstein continue to exist and their branches and agencies continue to function as regional offices of the Deutsche Bundesbank in the eleven provinces.

A law dealing with credit was voted on 10 July 1961 and came into operation from 1 January 1962. This very important law contains sixty-five articles and covers the whole field of banking. This law delegates the surveillance of credit to the Bundesaufsichtsamt für das Kreditwesen (Federal Office for the Surveillance of Credit) with headquarters in Berlin, and to the Deutsche Bundesbank at Frankfurt. Authorisation to operate a banking establishment is granted by the Federal Office for the Surveillance of Credit, which has very wide powers which seem almost dictatorial.

The Federal Republic of Germany is a young state: but the Germans were quick to see the importance of control over the banks and the apparatus of credit.

The division of Germany into two parts and the isolation of Berlin have shifted the centre of gravity of the country. After 1945 Frankfurt could resume its great historic role and rapidly regained its place in the first rank of the financial world, which, since 1875, it had gradually been losing to Berlin. Today Frankfurt is the centre of the economic development of Federal Germany. It is indeed in Frankfurt that the Deutsche Bundesbank has its headquarters, from which it controls the whole apparatus of credit and assures the return to Frankfurt of its former supremacy.

The financial history of Frankfurt goes far back into the Middle Ages. For centuries the bankers of Frankfurt have formed a class apart, faithful to an unblemished tradition of respectability which is still intact today. At present Frankfurt is like a magnet from which all the financial lines of force of the country radiate, and a characteristic proof of its importance is given by the fact that more than ninety banks and private banking houses are established there. Among the great banks which have their Head Office in Frankfurt are to be counted not only the important Deutsche Genossenschaftskasse, which is the central bank of all the popular banks and working-class credit associations, but also the agricultural banks.

Faithful to its former position, Frankfurt, the seventh largest city in Germany with 750,000 inhabitants, continues to become steadily more cosmopolitan. Her Exchange (founded in 1797) is one of the oldest in Europe and she wants to include new foreign stocks in her official list. After the débâcle of 1945 the Frankfurt Exchange was the first to reopen its doors.

A considerable volume of business has been created by the establishment of numerous foreign banks in Federal Germany. In 1961 foreign banks established in Germany were put on a footing of exact equality with German banks; they may be obliged to deposit with the German Bundesbank the minimum legal reserve, but in return they have the right to accept deposits from German customers in German currency and they are making strenuous efforts to achieve a more important position in the market.

At present 18 foreign banks have a branch in Federal Germany: 4 English, 5 American, 2 Japanese, 1 Belgian, 1 Swiss, 1 Dutch, 1 Spanish and 3 French (Crédit Lyonnais, Banque Nationale pour le Commerce et l'Industrie and Société Générale Alsacienne de Banque).

In addition, thirty-two foreign banks maintain resident correspondents who do not have the right to carry out banking transactions themselves; their essential object is to establish contact with German financial circles and act as an information service both towards the latter and towards the bank they represent.

After the Second World War the structure of the German banking system underwent extensive changes, and now the state exercises a tight control over and dictates policy to the banks. What progress has been made since the collapse of the Third Reich! Germany was then without a government, prostrate, its institutions, the very framework of society in total disarray. Today Federal Germany has rediscovered the formulae for efficiency and constructive development.

It was doubtless a proud moment for German bankers when in 1959 the Federal Republic raised its contribution to the International Monetary Fund in Washington from DM. 1,500 million to DM. 3,507 million. Another proud moment came with the issue of a loan to the Anglo-American Corporation of South Africa Ltd., made by the Deutsche Bank, since this was a decisive turning-point, the first foreign loan for fifty years on the German market.

Also under the auspices of the Deutsche Bank, in 1961, a foreign loan at $6\frac{1}{2}\%$ to the Republic of Argentina and in February 1962, a loan at $6\frac{1}{2}\%$ to the Prefecture of Osaka and the Municipality of Osaka of DM. 100 million. This issue was the first Japanese borrowing in Germany and the first Japanese borrowing in Europe since the war. The Union of South Africa obtained a loan from the same bank of DM. 40 million in 1962.

In the course of 1962, the shares of important foreign companies, of world reputation, began to be introduced on German exchanges. The number of foreign stocks quoted on German exchanges has risen to twenty-four, of which three are American. And in 1960 at the time of the dollar crisis one could even see the loser in the last world war offer support to the most powerful currency of the universe!

The three most important German commercial banks, the Deutsche Bank, the Dresdner Bank and the Commerzbank, are

remarkably well organised for the launching of industrial undertakings and for the establishment of enterprises of all kinds.

The shrewd financiers from beyond the Rhine are not more
highly talented than the rest of the human race, but they have
the imagination and self-confidence to play for high stakes and
throw massive amounts of capital into the great melting-pot of
industry; on the financial plane they are like a Macedonian phalanx
on the battlefield. In speaking of Germany one must not forget
that the foundation of its power and of all its miraculous achievements is the tight cohesion and strict discipline of its people.

The financial empire of Germany has today been rebuilt. The
few figures quoted below are enough to give almost tangible form
to the power of this empire.

These are the principal items in the balance-sheet of the
Deutsche Bundesbank (bank of issue), dated 31 December 1964:

In thousands of
German Marks

Gold coin and bullion	16,730,819
Money at call in foreign banks and investments on foreign money markets	10,769,620
	27,500,439
Notes in circulation	27,691,750
Advances to the Federal State, to allow participation in international organisations	3,016,042
Advances to international organisations and consolidated loans	2,683,532

including (a) to the World Bank . . . 1,343,080
(b) to the International Monetary Fund 720,000
(c) liquidation of the European Payments Union 614,613

Various deposits	18,610,521
Capital	290,000 [1]
Reserves	775,800
Various provisions	1,475,086
Total of the balance-sheet	49,561,803

[1] The capital belongs to the Federal State.

German private investments abroad between 1952 and the end of the first
half-year 1965 are estimated to total about DM. 7·81 billion, equivalent of
$1·950 million.

At the same date, the foreign private investments in Germany are estimated
to total about DM. 6·5 billion, equivalent of $1·625 million.

These few figures speak volumes. Germany continues to fulfil her historic destiny. Gold and foreign funds have repeatedly flowed into the country and have contributed to increase the liquid assets of German credit institutions.

So that the mass of money in circulation and the granting of credit might be brought under proper control, the Deutsche Bundesbank has been accorded all appropriate and necessary

Type of bank	*Number of banks*	*Number of branches*	*Total of banks and branches*
1 Important banks and their affiliates	6	1,539	1,545
2 Regional and local banks . .	80	1,659	1,739
3 Private banking houses . .	212	176	388
4 Banks specialising in a particular branch of the economy . .	36	8	44
5 Branches of foreign banks . .	18	7	25
6 Public credit institutions . .	16	12	28
7 Mortgage banks and land banks .	29	9	38
8 Central transfer banks (*Girozentralen*)	13	21	34
9 Savings banks	865	12,089	12,954
10 Central offices, granting popular credit	6	6	12
11 Popular banks and working-class credit co-operatives . . .	736	1,992	2,728
12 Central offices for agricultural credit	13	95	108
13 Co-operative banks for agricultural credit	9,991	3,470	13,461
14 Credit institutions attached to co-operative organisations . .	24	9	33
15 Specialised credit institutions .	18	28	46
16 Institutions financing instalment sales	228	476	704
17 Investment houses . . .	11	1	12
18 *Kassenvereine*	7	1	8
19 Various credit institutions . .	47	..	47
TOTAL	12,356	21,598	33,954

The *Kassenvereine* are organisations effecting transfers of stocks and shares; they exist in all large towns which have stock exchanges. In France the SICOVAM is equivalent to the German *Kassenvereine*.

powers to control the currency, in accordance with modern theory and practice in monetary matters. All that the central bank has to do is to choose the appropriate devices for realising its policy, set them in operation at the opportune moment and suitably to regulate their application.

The supreme guiding organ of the Bundesbank is the *Zentralbankrat* (Central Council). This council has the final word in deciding the monetary and credit policy of the bank. The central executive organ is the *Direktorium* (Board of Management), which has provincial counterparts in the Boards of Management of the eleven *Landeszentralbanken*.

On 31 December 1964 the German banking system included a total of 12,356 institutions, divided into nineteen categories as shown in the table on p. 63.

According to the Credit Law, which has operated since 1 January 1962, the creation of a new bank does not depend upon its fulfilling a need. The Bundesaufsichtsamt für das Kreditwesen is obliged to give its authorisation if sufficient capital is proved and if the new bank has recruited personnel worthy of trust and qualified to direct the bank's operations. Agencies may be opened without previous authorisation. It is sufficient to notify their establishment to the Bundesaufsichtsamt in Berlin and the Deutsche Bundesbank in Frankfurt.

On 31 December 1964 about 435,000 people were employed in the 12,356 credit institutions listed on p. 63.

4. BANKS IN AUSTRIA

Within the framework of this study of the Austrian banks, it seemed interesting to indicate also the principal landmarks in the banking history of the former Austro-Hungarian Empire. The following pages contain a brief factual account.

Austria is the heir of an impressive historical tradition. Austria of today is a Federal Republic made up of the following nine Federal Provinces, given in the order of size of their respective population: Vienna, Lower Austria, Upper Austria, Styria,

Carinthia, Tirol, Salzburg, Burgenland and Vorarlberg. Her constitution is that of a Republic, with a Federal President elected for a six years' term of office by direct popular vote. The Austrian Parliament has two chambers, the *Nationalrat* and the *Bundesrat*. General election to the lower chamber, the Nationalrat, takes place every four years.

The country covers an area of approximately 32,000 sq. miles, and has a population of 7,215,300 (31 December 1964). Of this total, no less than 1,650,000 live in the Federal capital of Vienna, which has the rights and status of a Province. Other large cities are: Graz, the capital of Styria (240,000 inhabitants), Linz, the capital of Upper Austria (200,000 inhabitants), Salzburg, the capital of the Province bearing the same name (110,000 inhabitants), Innsbruck, the capital of Tirol (102,000 inhabitants) and Klagenfurt, the capital of Carinthia (71,000 inhabitants).

The unit of the Austrian currency is the Schilling, which is divided into 100 Groschen, and has a fine gold parity of 0·0341796 gramme. At par, therefore, 26 Schillings equal 1 US Dollar.

Nearly 90% of the population is Roman Catholic, and about 6% is Protestant. Recent information analysing the population by occupation shows the following pattern: Industry 47·5%, Agriculture and Forestry 22·7%, Trade and Communications 15·9%, Free professions 6·8%, Government Service 5·2%.

Before 1914 Vienna, at the zenith of its splendour and power, was not only the capital of a vast empire but also one of the greatest financial centres of the world. About fifty banks had their head office there and their branches were to be found in all Central European countries.

On 28 June 1914 the Archduke Franz Ferdinand, the heir to the throne, and his wife were assassinated in Sarajevo and a world war began which was to prove disastrous for the Austro-Hungarian Empire.

Although the Habsburg state was divided on the great questions fundamental to its existence, it showed remarkable financial and economic power during the last decisive struggle in the years 1914 to 1918.

On 21 November 1916, after a reign of sixty-eight years, the

Emperor Franz Josef I closed his eyes for ever. At the commence-
ment of hostilities against Serbia, on 28 July 1914, his authority
had allowed him to unite the peoples of the old Empire again,
despite the nationalist feelings which divided them. From 1917,
and especially after the United States of America entered the war,
the military, economic and financial situation of the Central
Powers became more and more desperate and in this crisis the
symptoms of decadence in the internal situation of the Empire
also began to increase. The old Habsburg state finally crumbled
away, despite its favourable geographical position, its economic
unity and the long evolution which had made it an important
element in the political and economic life of Europe. In the year
1918 the seven-hundred-year-old Austrian state came to an end.
A balanced economic territory with a population of 56 million
and an area of 676,250 sq. kilometres, composed of eleven different
nationalities, was dismembered; and all that was left to the
new Republic of Austria was a population at that date of 6·6
million.

In 1918 approximately seven-eighths of the former territory
was distributed among six successor states (Czecho-Slovakia,
Hungary, Yugoslavia, Poland, Rumania and Italy).

After the war, branches of Viennese banks outside Austria
found themselves dealing with six new currencies and subject to
six new governments who had no respect for Austrian interests
and were prepared to consider only solutions which favoured
their own economic plans. Above all they were intent on making
themselves economically independent of Vienna. Measures taken
with this end in view were the organisation of stock exchanges in
the new states and the consequent elimination of the Viennese
Stock Exchange, the re-routing of roads to avoid Vienna, the
transferring of companies which had head offices in Vienna and
factories within the boundaries of the new states, and so on.

The effect of the dismemberment of the economically unified
territory of the former Empire upon the Viennese banks can be
judged by the following figures: in 1918 the Österreichische
Credit-Anstalt für Handel und Gewerbe (one of the largest Austrian banks of the period) maintained eighteen branches outside

the boundaries of the new Austria, the Anglo-Österreichische Bank thirty-four and the Wiener Bankverein twenty-nine.

After the political reorganisation of the former Imperial territory, it was no longer possible to maintain this network of branches which were gradually incorporated into banks native to the new states. In 1923 there had been seventy-six banks but in 1925 this number had been reduced to fifty-one.

In the course of the following years circumstances compelled a considerable measure of centralisation among banks of top and medium importance. In this process the following banks disappeared either by amalgamation or by liquidation. (Only the most important are listed.)

Allgemeine Österreichische Boden-Credit-Anstalt
Anglo-Österreichische Bank
Niederösterreichische Escompte-Gesellschaft
Allgemeine Verkehrsbank
Union-Bank
Mercurbank
Zentralbank deutscher Sparkassen.

Most of these banks were absorbed either by the present Creditanstalt-Bankverein (formed on 31 December 1933 by the amalgamation of the Österreichische Credit-Anstalt für Handel und Gewerbe, founded in 1855, and the Wiener Bank-Verein, founded in 1863), or by the present Österreichische Länderbank, founded in 1880.

These two banks are today by far the largest commercial banks in Austria.

The following table lists the eight most important Austrian banks and will give a more exact idea of the importance of these two banks. (Listed in order of total assets on 31 December 1964, in thousands of Austrian Schillings. 26 Schillings equal 1 U.S. Dollar.)

	Name	*Head Office*	*Total assets*
1	Creditanstalt-Bankverein	Vienna	16,687,615
2	Österreichische Länderbank	Vienna	11,641,414
3	Genossenschaftliche Zentralbank . . .	Vienna	5,559,516
4	Bank für Arbeit und Wirtschaft . . .	Vienna	4,093,813

Name	Head Office	Total assets
5 Österreichisches Credit-Institut . . .	Vienna	3,243,610
6 Zentralkasse der Volksbanken Österreichs .	Vienna	2,682,456
7 Österreichische Kontrollbank	Vienna	1,741,421
8 Österreichische Investitionskredit A.G. . .	Vienna	1,209,519

The Creditanstalt-Bankverein also controls three important regional affiliated companies:

Bank für Oberösterreich und Salzburg (Linz) . .	*Total assets*	2,313,185
Bank für Kärnten (Klagenfurt)	*Total assets*	1,171,182
Bank für Tirol und Vorarlberg (Innsbruck) . .	*Total assets*	1,131,438

The Österreichische Länderbank also controls a regional bank:

Eisenstädter Bank (Eisenstadt)	*Total assets*	67,344

On 31 December 1964 the total Austrian bank organisation was comprised of twenty-five joint-stock banks, eighteen private banking-houses and ten mortgage banks.

Austria's credit mechanism is very highly developed. The Creditanstalt-Bankverein, the Österreichische Länderbank and the Österreichisches Credit-Institut were nationalised in 1946. The legal form of a private company has been preserved, and the members of the board have in no way altered the general policy under which banking transactions are carried out. All three of these banks are typical general banking institutions although, of course, each bank has its own policy regarding credit transactions. In 1957, 40% of the share capital of the Creditanstalt-Bankverein and of the Österreichische Länderbank was returned to private ownership by sales in the domestic capital market.

In addition to the twenty-five commercial banks in the form of joint-stock companies, there are also eighteen private banking-houses, most of them of small size. A special position is held by the Österreichisches Postsparkassenamt (Austrian Post Office Savings Bank). Founded in 1883, it is the central clearing-house for all postal cheques and post office savings account transactions. Other special credit institutions include the Österreichische Investitionskredit A.G. (founded in 1957), whose principal task is to negotiate loans from international finance institutions for Austrian private industry, and the Österreichische Kommunalkredit

A.G. (founded in 1958), which provides credit for industrially less-developed parts of the country in order to finance the development of industrial estates and other facilities to attract the establishment of local industries. The financing of instalment buying is carried out by four institutions. Further groups of credit institutions which should be mentioned are: the Provincial Mortgage Banks, the Savings Banks with the Girozentrale der Österreichischen Sparkassen (total of balance-sheet as at 31 December 1964, 11,602,702,000 Schillings) as the main clearing-house, the Agricultural Credit Co-operative Societies, with the Genossenschaftliche Zentralbank as the head office, and the Volksbanken with the Zentralkasse der Volksbanken Österreichs acting as the head office for the credit associations.

The relative importance of the various groups of credit institutions within the entire Austrian credit system may be seen from the following table, which shows the division of the total deposits and outstanding credits as of 31 December 1962:

| | Deposit balances of the credit institutions | | | | Increase in volume of credit | |
| | Current account deposits | | Savings account deposits | | Commercial credit granted by | |
	Mill. schillings	%	Mill. schillings	%	Mill. schillings	%
Joint-stock companies .	12,307	44·7	6,623	15·8	19,834	34·7
Private banks . .	1,357	4·9	462	1·1	1,435	2·5
Savings banks . .	5,162	18·7	18,524	44·3	16,139	28·2
Agricultural credit co-operatives . .	1,859	6·8	7,636	18·2	8,091	14·1
Trade credit associations	1,552	5·6	3,222	7·7	3,996	7·0
Other credit institutions	5,332	19·3	5,391	12·9	7,701	13·5
TOTAL . .	27,569	100·0	41,858	100·0	57,196	100·0

The bank of issue developed in the same way and arrived at the same form as in other European countries.

The Wiener Stadtbank (Bank of the City of Vienna) was modelled on the old Italian Monte. It was responsible for receiving and safeguarding the security furnished by the borrower, while it also distributed the interest from the loan among the stockholders. Later on it began to accept deposits and to grant loans to the state. This bank obtained the right to issue bank-notes, called *Bancozettel*. In 1811 there was an official devaluation of the *Bancozettel*, which were reduced to a fifth of their face value: they were replaced by a new currency, called *Wiener Währung*. In 1816 there was a second devaluation; 250 paper gulden came to be equalled to 100 silver gulden.

Not until after the Napoleonic Wars was the idea conceived of founding a true private bank of issue in the form of a joint-stock company. The articles of this new bank were drawn up by the then Minister of Finance, Count Stadion.

1 June 1816 saw the foundation of the 'Privilegierte Österreichische Nationalbank', with right of issue. In 1878 Hungary ceased to be a province of the Austrian Empire and became a second independent state within the framework of the Austro-Hungarian Monarchy. The bank changed its name to become the Österreichisch-Ungarische Bank.

After the First World War the Treaty of Saint-Germain prescribed the liquidation of the Österreichisch-Ungarische Bank, which the new Republic of Austria replaced on 22 December 1922 with the Österreichische Nationalbank, still existing today.

From March 1938 until 3 July 1945 — that is to say during the seven years of the German Occupation — the Österreichische Nationalbank disappeared and was replaced by the 'Hauptstelle Wien der Deutschen Reichsbank'.

After the liberation of Austria by the troops of the Allied Powers, decrees were issued on 3 July 1945 authorising the reopening of banks and the re-establishment of the Österreichische Nationalbank. The so-called 'Schillinggesetz' of November 1945 withdrew Austria from the monetary zone of the Reichsmark and reinstituted the schilling as legal tender.

Today the Austrian National Bank, in carrying out its duties in safeguarding the Austrian currency, is empowered to lay down the minimum reserves to be held by credit institutions (at the present time between 8% and 10% according to the nature and amount of the deposits), and can also directly influence the volume of credit under the so-called restrictions agreement (determining a fixed relationship between the increase in deposits and new loans). Under the National Bank Law of 1955, the issuing bank also has the authority to operate an open-market policy. This policy was operated for the first time in 1962 when the Austrian National Bank, with a view to reducing excessive liquidity, directed the credit institutions to purchase treasury bills and other fixed in-terest-bearing government securities which were not to be sold by them for a certain period of time.

On 31 December 1964 total assets of the Österreichische Nationalbank amount to Schillings 42,114,835,850, of which these are the principal items:

	Schillings
Gold, coin and bullion	15,459,451,531
Foreign exchange, foreign notes and coin	16,761,579,354
	32,221,030,885
Bank-notes in circulation	25,740,352,210
Capital	150,000,000
Reserves	3,081,448,216
Deposits	38,406,898,883

Gold and currency provide a cover of 125% for the fiduciary issue.

The Vienna Stock Exchange was founded by Empress Maria Theresa in 1771 as a public institution. At that time it enjoyed a monopoly for dealings in government bonds, thus protecting the country's creditors and promoting national credit.

Today the Vienna Stock Exchange is under the management of an independent corporation, the Council of the Vienna Stock Exchange (Wiener Börsekammer) consisting of twenty-two representatives of Austrian finance who are partly delegated by credit institutions and partly elected.

The Vienna Stock Exchange is the only securities exchange in Austria. The general public is not admitted, and business on the exchange can be transacted only by members. Applications for membership are carefully checked by the Stock Exchange Council and granted at its discretion. Almost all the credit in-stitutions in Vienna, and some in the Austrian Provinces, are represented on the stock exchange, as well as the private banks, savings banks and other credit institutions. The private bankers and authorised banking officers attend the stock exchange meetings to transact business.

Securities transactions in Austria need not necessarily be effected on the stock exchange. Each credit institution, executing customer's orders as trading agent, carries out mainly those transactions on the stock exchange which it cannot settle itself by compensation.

At present the stock exchange has about seventy members, the majority being banks and other credit institutions, and the rest made up of brokers. The official brokers (*Sensale*), who can be compared with the 'specialists', fulfil an important function. These are public officials nominated by the management of the stock exchange after passing an examination; after ratification of their appointment they are sworn into office by the government authorities. Their sole function is to act as agent in dealings in officially quoted securities between the exchange members. There are also brokers dealing in securities on the stock exchange, the so-called free brokers. They execute clients' orders on the stock exchange and act as intermediary between other exchange members. Their status corresponds approximately to that of 'floor brokers'.

About 80 stock and 300 fixed-interest-bearing securities are at present admitted to trading on the Vienna Stock Exchange and quotation on the official List. The Federal Ministry of Finance determines which securities may be officially quoted, after having received a report from the Council of the Stock Exchange. Application for listing must be filed by the issuer and countersigned by a credit institution represented on the stock exchange. This corresponds roughly to the 'listed securities'.

5. BANKS IN ITALY

The Italian bankers held a near monopoly of international finance for several centuries, and from the twelfth century onwards extended their restless and rewarding activity to all the countries of Europe.

Very long — and certainly very incomplete — would be any list which one might draw up today of the bankers, money-changers and merchants who emigrated from Florence, Venice, Genoa, Siena, Piacenza and Lucca to settle in France, Belgium, Spain, England and other countries. Among the throng of ancient Italian banking houses, famous names stand out which cannot be omitted from the financial history of the Middle Ages. These are the best-known:

Acciaioli, Alberti, Albizzi, Altoviti, Anguissola, Bardi, Boccaci, Bonaccorsi, Buonsignori, Cacciaconti, Cerchi, Chigi, Folcacchieri, Fornaci, Fornari, Frescóbaldi, Grimaldi, Gualterotti, Guidagni, Medici, Mozi, Peruzzi, Pisani, Piccolomini, Scali, Scotti, Strozzi, Tolomei and Ugolini.

But the extent and the long-uncontested supremacy of the Italian bankers' empire began to decline in the closing centuries of the Middle Ages, and gradually dwindled away as modern states were formed and grew strong.

From the thirteenth century onwards the Italian city-states frequently had recourse to forced loans. The method employed was to compel all citizens to pay in a deposit to a special institution, called a 'Monte' (plural 'Monti'); in addition, the Monte collected the revenues from duties and taxes, set aside as a guarantee of the loan, and distributed the profits among the forced depositors. The most famous of the Monti was that organised by Florence in the thirteenth century to meet the expenses of its war with Pisa.

The Monti multiplied; cities used them to sell annuities to voluntary purchasers. Later Monti were set up by all communities in need of capital. Now, these Monti were subject to a double law of growth. On the one hand, having considerable capital, and enjoying the confidence of the public, they assumed the right to accept and to administer private deposits; this is the starting-point of the great state banks, which were to flourish in the following centuries. On the other hand, the original depositors shared in the profits of the bank, but their losses could never be larger than their initial deposit: and so the first joint-stock companies were born.

On 2 November 1624 the Monte dei Paschi di Siena was set

up, the Grand Duke Ferdinand II of Tuscany having granted it a privilege which enabled it to assemble its initial capital. The Monte was charged to collect the revenue from the annual leasing of the pastures (in Italian *paschi*) of the Maremme de Grosseto, a state property.

In order to mobilise this revenue shares were issued, which were subscribed by those wishing to contribute capital; each share conferred the right to a proportion of the revenue; the capital thus assembled was used to make loans to farmers and merchants.

The Monte dei Paschi di Siena makes its appearance then with a singularly modern formula for success: it issues shares in order to build up a capital, which it then lays out to advantage by making loans at interest. Through the centuries banking institutions of this kind were exceedingly prosperous.

The Monte dei Paschi di Siena is always in existence and is the fourth oldest bank in the world and still ranks with the greatest contemporary Italian banks.

The three other oldest banks, still in existence, are also Italian: the Banco di Napoli at Naples (founded in 1539), the Istituto Bancario San Paolo di Torino at Turin (founded in 1563) and the Banco di Santo Spirito at Rome (founded in 1605).

From the Middle Ages onwards the word 'Monte' is often to be encountered and takes on many meanings, all of which, however, contain the concept of 'accumulation'.

The problems of credit and of deposit had also had to be faced in Venice in the thirteenth century: Venetian bankers, although they had not acquired the European reputation of their Florentine colleagues, had developed ambitious undertakings, usually bound up with the purchase and resale of merchandise. This close connection between trade in goods and trade in money entailed such disadvantages that in the fourteenth and fifteenth centuries the Senate of the Republic had to take steps to safeguard the deposits. Unfortunately the need for money had induced the same Senate to regard the bankers as the state's own money-lenders and the results of this policy were lamentable: nearly all Venetian bankers went bankrupt in the middle years of the sixteenth century. During the debate in the Venetian Senate on the establishment of the

Banco di Rialto, it was stated that of 109 private banks which had been in business in Venice, 96 had gone bankrupt: the failure of the Banco Pisani in 1581 was particularly disastrous.

As, however, it was essential that the business of banking should be carried on in so busy a commercial centre as Venice, the Senate decreed in 1587 the creation of a public bank, to be called the Banco di Rialto, and to have a monopoly of banking operations. The state itself turned banker: it would accept and safeguard deposits; but it renounced all right to appeal to the bank for its own needs and to carry on commercial operations of all kinds. So this was to be exclusively a deposit and transfer bank, not even authorised to invest the moneys deposited with it.

In 1619 a second public bank was created, the Banco del Giro with the same functions as the Banco di Rialto. In 1637 the latter was absorbed by its younger rival. The Banco del Giro was to develop considerably the use, standard in Venice, of *contadi di banco*, ancestors of the cheque and the bank-note.

As early in their history as the twelfth century, the Venetian banks had adopted the practice of handing the depositor a receipt, confirming the deposit he had made. These receipts, called '*contadi di banco*', took two forms; either they carried a simple promise to pay a certain amount or they were an extract from the banker's records, establishing that the depositor was credited with a certain sum. These documents were made out in the depositor's name; but nothing forbade the latter's giving up his credit with the banker by handing the evidence of indebtedness to a third party; in this way the depositors were using the receipts as instruments of payment. In the fourteenth century, this was common practice; it even happened that, in consideration of the risk of non-payment due to the financial situation of the banker, the assignee was allowed to benefit by a note's being reckoned as less than its nominal value. The use of these receipts was greatly extended in the course of the following centuries; they were the origin of the bank-note and the cheque.

The reasons which caused the Venetian reform in 1587 led to identical results in the other Italian towns.

In 1686, after an interval of a century and a half, the Casa di

San Giorgio at Genoa began again to carry out banking operations. It accepted deposits and effected transfers; thanks to wise
and prudent direction, it became extremely influential and was a
financial power of the first rank until the day in 1766 when in
order to save the Republic of Genoa it paid Austria £14,820,000;
and this payment ruined it. The Republic disappeared in 1816,
absorbed by the state of Sardinia.

In 1593 a cunning Milanese named Zerbi founded the Banco di
Sant'Ambrogio at Milan; this bank, like its neighbours, was a
deposit and transfer bank. But its affairs were imprudently
conducted and it granted loans to the state; and in 1630, finding it
could no longer reimburse its depositors, it transformed itself into
a simple association of state creditors; it survived in this form
until 1805. From this date the bank, rechristened 'Monte Napoleon', used its resources to pay gratuities to former soldiers of the
French imperial armies.

Public banks in Italy were born of a double phenomenon: the
disastrous history of the private banks and the development of the
'Monti di Pietatis'.

The private bankers of the Middle Ages, whatever may have
been their professional ability, had completely failed to recognise
the rules which should govern the use of deposits; they had used
money at call to finance commercial enterprises with long-term
profits or they had made long-term loans to the state. Their
failure had disastrous consequences. Hence the intervention of the
state in an endeavour to organise official banks which would give
more solid guarantees to the depositor.

On the other hand, it had become plain in Italy in the course of
the fifteenth century that it was extremely difficult for private individuals to obtain credit; the only method open to them was to
apply to the Jews, who made loans on security at very onerous
rates of interest; and even so, Jews had not been able to set up in
business in all the cities of the peninsula.

This gave birth to the idea of setting up institutions which
would make loans against security to private individuals: since
these establishments were to carry out the same sort of operation
which the former 'Monti' had carried out on behalf of the city-

states, it seemed sensible to base their organisation on that of the 'Monti'; they were called 'Monti Pietatis'.

The first Monte di Pietà was founded at Orvieto in 1463; it seemed an institution of such general utility that numerous institutions of the same kind were set up at the end of the fifteenth century and at the beginning of the sixteenth; one of the most famous was that founded by the Dominican Girolamo Savonarola at Florence in 1495.

The Popes were greatly in favour of these Monti di Pietà which assumed the role of charitable institutions open to all whose modest situation in life made it difficult to borrow from bankers.

The success of these Monti di Pietà was so considerable that their operations were extended; they began to accept deposits on which they paid interest just as they required interest on their loans; when they had acquired loyal depositors, they became true banks. And so the banks at Naples were produced by the fusion of several institutions which had begun life as Monti di Pietà: the Monte Sacro della Pietà, founded in 1573, the Monte di Ave Gratia Plena of 1575, and the Monte di San Elegio, of 1592.

In the seventeenth century the example of the Italian Monte di Pietà became widespread in Germany, in Belgium and in Austria; in contrast, they had only a modest success in France.

Public banks in Sicily also prospered in a double form: 'La Tavola di Palermo', which commenced operations in 1552, and 'La Tavola di Messina', which dates from 1587. Both these institutions disappeared in the course of the nineteenth century.

Before the formation of the kingdom of Italy, there were three banks of issue in the peninsula: the Sardinian National Bank in Piedmont, the Tuscan National Bank in the Grand Duchy of Tuscany, and the Papal State Bank in the Papal States. In the other states of the peninsula other banks issued certificates of credit, deposit receipts, bonds and notes, but not bank-notes.

When the kingdom of Italy was established in 1861, the Sardinian National Bank, transformed into the National Bank of the Kingdom of Italy, was authorised to extend its operations over the whole peninsula, since it was intended to grant it the sole

privilege of issuing bank-notes. However, the economic crisis of
1866 and the heavy charges of the war against the Austro-
Hungarian Empire did not allow this project of unification to be
realised. Instead, the two banks of issue which were already
operating in the kingdom, the National Bank of the Kingdom of
Italy and the Tuscan National Bank, were joined by the Banco di
Napoli, the Banco di Sicilia and the Banca Toscana di Credito;
and at last, after the capture of Rome in 1870, there was a new
institute of issue: the Papal State Bank, which took the name of
the Banca Romana.

In 1893 the Banca Romana ceased to exist and the National
Bank of the Kingdom of Italy, the Sardinian National Bank and
the Banca Toscana di Credito amalgamated to form the present
Banca d'Italia; from then on this bank had a preponderant posi-
tion and took general control of the whole monetary currency.
It was the first step towards unification of the privilege of issue.

Italy was making progress, its economic life was becoming
healthier and more complex and unification in all sectors of
national life was making great progress. Alongside the Banca
d'Italia two other banks, both in the south, the Banco di Napoli
and the Banco di Sicilia, continued to operate as institutes of issue.

By a law of May 1926, the Fascist Government completely
centralised the function of issue in the Banca d'Italia. This measure
finally gave Italy a single bank of issue, while the Banco di Napoli
and the Banco di Sicilia, abandoning their former prerogatives,
devoted themselves to the economic problems of the southern
regions and of the islands, which had been their traditional domain
for centuries.

We pass now to ordinary banks of credit. We must first note
that in the first thirty years of the kingdom of Italy, credit was not
yet efficiently organised, and credit operations of a normal kind
were usually carried out by the banks of issue. In this period, two
credit institutions only can be considered national banks: the
Società Generale di Credito Mobiliare, founded in 1863 and
modelled on the Crédit Mobilier Français, and the Banca Generale.
These two banks had chosen as their principal activity the placing
of commercial and industrial shares with the public and the

financing of undertakings of the most varied kind. At first, they had a difficult time; however, thanks to the funds which they succeeded in accumulating by means of large issues of debentures (bonds), they knew a fair degree of prosperity for a certain period.

It was the collapse of the Banca Romana in 1893 which by causing a panic among Italian savers put these two institutions in such a situation that their continued functioning became impossible and so forced them to go into liquidation. What was, it seemed, bound to cause a complete breakdown of the banking system of newly born Italy opened on the century a new era, giving healthy encouragement to banking activity. In fact, after the collapse of the Società Generale di Credito Mobiliare and of the Banca Generale, two other credit organisations arose.

The influx of German capital (Deutsche Bank, Dresdner Bank and Berliner Handels-Gesellschaft) gave birth in 1893 to the Banca Commerciale Italiana. In 1895, again with the help of German capital (Nationalbank für Deutschland), the Credito Italiano was founded, incorporating the Banco di Genova, established in 1870. The Banco di Roma was already in existence, having been founded in 1880.

It was these three establishments, Banca Commerciale Italiana, Credito Italiano and Banco di Roma, which, favoured by a new freeness in the market, successively came to rank as important credit institutions conducting business on a national scale and even extending their interests into the international domain.

The cornerstone of the Italian banking system is the law of 12 March 1936; this law lays down a sharp distinction between banks dealing in middle- and long-term credit. In addition this law centralises the control of all banks in a single specialised state body, an *ad hoc* creation called Ispettorato per la difesa del risparmio e l'esercizio del credito (Inspectorate for the safeguarding of savings and the exercise of credit), and headed by the Governor of the Banca d'Italia. Set thus at the summit of the banking hierarchy, the Banca d'Italia acts as moderator and regulator of the banking activities of the nation.

At present the Italian banking system is organised in the following way:

establishments dealing in short-term credit; to this category belong

(*a*) Credit institutions (*de droit public*):
   Banca Nazionale del Lavoro
   Banco di Napoli
   Banco di Sicilia
   Monte dei Paschi di Siena
   Istituto Bancario San Paolo di Torino
   Banco di Sardegna.

(*b*) Banks of national standing:
   Banca Commerciale Italiana
   Credito Italiano
   Banco di Roma

(these are banking companies which have a national standing and operate in at least thirty of the Italian provinces).

(*c*) Ordinary credit banks, including popular co-operative banks.

(*d*) Savings banks: these are flourishing and influential credit institutions, the most important of which is the Cassa di Risparmio delle Provincie Lombarde, in Milan, which alone administers deposits of more than 1 billion lire, worthy to rank with the best institutions of this kind in the world.

(*e*) Monti di Pietà of the first rank: they grant loans against security and are subject to special regulations as well as the banking law.

(*f*) Rural and artisan banks: these also are subject to special laws as well as to the banking law. Their importance is not very great and in practice they grant small loans in rural communities and make advances for specifically working-class purposes.

Only those establishments which offer short-term credit are authorised to accept deposits.

Institutions offering middle- and long-term credit, which deal in what is called 'financial credit', comprise public institutions such as:

   Istituto Mobiliare Italiano
   Consorzio di Credito per le Opere Pubbliche
   Istituto Nazionale di Credito per le Imprese di Pubblica Utilità

Istituto Nazionale di Credito per il Lavoro Italiano all'Estero
as well as private establishments, such as:
Banca di Credito Finanziario (Mediobanca)
Ente Finanzario Interbancario (Efibanca)
Banca Centrale di Credito Popolare (Centrobanca)
Credito Industriale Sardo.

In addition, to meet the capital needs of small- and middle-sized firms, numerous regional institutions have been set up, as well as a special body called 'Mediocredito' (Central Institution for middle-term credit for small- and middle-sized firms) whose function is to mobilise middle-term credits granted to small- and middle-sized enterprises.

There are also numerous specialised establishments for dealing with agricultural credit and credit based on real property, as well as for granting loans to the building industry, the tourist industry, shipbuilding, the film industry, fishing and mining: loans subject to numerous regulations, which ensure particularly favourable conditions.

Worthy of special note is the Cassa del Mezzogiorno (Southern Bank); its headquarters is in Rome; it was created by the state in order to further the industrialisation of the backward regions of the south of Italy and in the islands of Sardinia and Sicily.

It is principally American and Swiss interests which have invested foreign capital in Italy. Financial aid from the United States is dealt with through the agency of the Istituto Mobiliare Italiano in Rome. The interests of the Bank of America in San Francisco (California) are represented by its affiliate the Banca d'America e d'Italia in Milan, and Swiss interests by the Banca Vonwiller in Milan. It should not be forgotten that there is also a branch of Crédit Commercial de France in Milan.

The participation of Switzerland in the Italian money-market has been of great assistance to the Italian economy and has greatly increased since the end of the Second World War. There can be no doubt that the Italians, having safeguarded their personal future by transferring their capital to Switzerland, have invested considerable amounts in Italian industrial debentures such as

Montecatini, Olivetti, Pirelli, Italcementi, Selt-Valdarno, etc.,
issued in Switzerland; in this way their capital has returned to
Italy in the guise of foreign capital. The Italian authorities are
not opposed to this practice and have prepared, as one may
imagine, to welcome capital even if offered under the protection
of anonymity.

The law of 12 March 1936, called the 'Banking Law', decreed
radical reforms in the financial structure of the country and
brought an eventful period to a close. Its eventual objective was
the total centralisation and nationalisation of credit. Indeed, it
should not be forgotten that the Institute for Industrial Reconstruction (I.R.I.), a holding company owned by the Italian state
holds the total capital of the Banca Nazionale del Lavoro, 98%
of the capital of the Banca Commerciale Italiana and of the
Banco di Roma, and 78% of the capital of the Credito Italiano;
these are the four most important Italian banks.

There are ten stock exchanges in Italy, in Milan, Rome, Turin,
Genoa, Florence, Naples, Trieste, Venice, Bologna and Palermo.
Incontestably the most important is at Milan. The value of the
stocks dealt in at this exchange exceeds that of all the other
Italian exchanges together. It is, for instance, six times more
important than that of the second-ranking of these exchanges, at
Rome. And it is again in Milan that the only Italian produce
exchange is to be found, dealing in cereals and grain, not only in
the service of trade and industry, but also having an options
market with its own clearing-house.

The triangle Milan–Genoa–Turin contains two-thirds of the
productive capacity of Italy. Milan (1,700,000 inhabitants) is
the economic and financial capital of Italy. Its supremacy is
largely due to the very lively and often audacious spirit of initiative of its business community, which has skilfully exploited the
industrial potential of the Milanese region; similar expertise
has not been available in any other Italian province. Innumerable
industrial enterprises have been formed in this district and have
prospered sufficiently to win a world-wide reputation. Important
industrial groups such as Edison, Montecatini, Pirelli, Snia-
Viscosa, Breda, Falck, Marelli, Innocenti, Tecnomasio Brown

Boveri, Alfa Romeo, Motta, Carlo Erba, etc., have given Milan and the province in which it is situated a developing industrial and commercial prosperity which, it goes without saying, is reflected in banking activity, on the exchange and in trade in general. To all these factors must be added the organisation of one of the most important annual fairs in the world. Of the 1,240 banks established in Italy, with an approximate total of 130,000 employees, 65 have their head office in Milan, with approximately 20,000 employees.

The Bank of Italy (bank of issue), founded in 1893, has its head office in Rome. At the end of 1963 its organisation comprised thirteen regional headquarters, eighty branches, fifteen agencies and seven delegations in other countries. The legal status of the Bank of Italy is that of a public company and its fully paid-up capital stands at 300 million lire, divided into 300,000 registered shares of 1,000 lire each, which may be held only by persons of good reputation and establishments (*de droit public*). The state holds, it will be seen, none of the capital of the bank.

On 31 December 1964 the capital of the bank was held as follows:

Institution	Number	Shares in thousands	Per-centage	Votes
1 Savings banks . . .	77	178·0	59·3	468
2 Public credit institutions .	8	54·5	18·2	141
3 Banks of national standing .	3	21·0	7·0	54
4 Social security organisation .	1	15·0	5·0	34
5 Assurance companies . .	9	31·5	10·5	99
Total	98	300·0	100·0	796

The High Council is the elective administrative body. The governor is the head administrator. He is appointed and dismissed, as are the director-general and the deputy director-general, by the High Council. The approval of the Cabinet is required and the decision is formally sanctioned by a decree of the Head of State, on the advice of the President of the Council.

6. BANKS IN THE VATICAN

The area of the Vatican City is 108 acres and its population consists of 904 inhabitants, of whom 620 are citizens and 284 residents. The monetary unit is the Vatican Lira, quoted at the same rate as the Italian Lira. Although the Vatican City is a sovereign state, it issues no bank-notes and allows those of the Italian Republic to circulate; in contrast, the monetary law of 31 December 1930 prescribes the minting of gold, silver, nickel and bronze coins.

The Istituto per le Opere di Religione (Institute for the Works of Religion), which has its headquarters in the City of the Vatican, is the pontifical institution of credit. This Institute, however, does not issue notes or mint currency; these rights are reserved to the Government of the Holy See.

In passing, there are about 540 million Catholics in the world, representing about 18% of the population of the world. The number of its adherents makes the Catholic Church the most important religion of the world.

The Ecclesiastical Government consists of twelve Ministries, called Sacred Congregations, which are listed below:

> The Congregation for the Doctrine of the Faith (formerly the Holy Office)
> The Congregation of the Consistorial
> The Congregation of the Oriental Church
> The Congregation of the Discipline of the Sacraments
> The Congregation of the Council
> The Congregation of the Religious
> The Congregation of the Propaganda Fide
> The Congregation of the Rites
> The Congregation of the Ceremonial
> The Congregation for the Extraordinary Ecclesiastical Affairs
> The Congregation for the Seminaries and Universities
> The Congregation for the Basilica of St. Peter.

At the head of each of these Congregations stands a Cardinal — with the exception of the Sacred Congregation for the Doctrine of the Faith, the Consistorial and the Oriental Church, the presidency of which is traditionally reserved for the Pope.

Below the Congregations are the Offices. Among the latter are the Apostolic Chancellery, which composes and despatches Decretals and Papal Bulls; the Apostolic Datary; and above all the State Secretariat, the most widely known administrative body of the Holy See. It combines the functions of a private secretariat to the Pope and of a Ministry of Foreign Affairs. This Secretariat is divided into three important sections:

ordinary business
extraordinary business
composition of briefs.

This completes our rough sketch of the organisation of the Government of the Catholic Church. Will the recent decisions of the Vatican Council bring about a reorganisation of the Sacred Congregations? We must wait and see.

It is plain that a state governed in this way can exercise no power without considerable financial resources.

The Holy See has its budget, like any other sovereign state. The Vatican, the smallest state in the world, is still today one of the greatest financial powers in the world; but its finances are so complicated and mysterious that no exact appreciation of them has hitherto been possible. One thing is certain: the wealth of the Vatican is skilfully administered and carefully distributed. In their work the financiers of the Vatican have at their disposal an exceptional information service such as no banker has ever known or probably will ever know; nuncios, apostolic delegates, cardinals, bishops and faithful Catholics who hold key appointments in foreign governments; in addition, they have the diplomatic privileges of the Vatican.

A Commission headed by a Cardinal controls the day-by-day administration of the wealth of the Holy See, while a Special Administration manages the 1,750 million lire paid in June 1929 by the Italian Government, at the time of the Lateran Treaty and Concordat, as compensation for the loss of temporal power. Under the direction of able and well-informed financial experts, the Special Administration has successfully executed important financial transactions, on a world scale. Thanks to judicious and profitable investments, the initial capital has been multiplied more than once.

Since no balance-sheet has ever been published, and since all operations are carried out in the utmost secrecy, it is impossible to give even an approximate estimate of the present value of the funds of the Special Administration. In international banking circles the figure of $500 to 600 million has been offered as an estimate. No portion of this capital is in the Vatican. It is invested in Italy and in other countries, principally in the United States, in Great Britain and in Switzerland. A large proportion of the Vatican assets are deposited with the soundest and most important banks: the Chase Manhattan Bank in New York, the Morgan Guaranty Trust Company in New York, Hambros Bank Ltd. in London and the Crédit Suisse in Zürich.

As for gold reserves, they are stored with the Federal Reserve Bank of New York and it appears that the Special Administration has received exceptional authorisation to deposit a very large reserve of gold in Fort Knox, the American golden citadel.

In Italy large sums are invested in innumerable banking, commercial and industrial enterprises. Whole Roman districts belong to the Vatican and revenue-earning premises are constantly under construction. Many of the Chianti vineyards are on estates which belong to the Church.

Seven or eight milliard lire are deposited each year in the vaults of the Banco di Santo Spirito in Rome (Bank of the Holy Ghost, founded in 1605 and controlled by the Vatican), earmarked for the countries in which the Holy See has to incur considerable expenses in the fight against communism.

Other important banks owe direct obedience to the Vatican, such as the Banco Ambrosiano and the Banca Provinciale Lombarda in Milan, the Credito Romagnolo in Bologna, the Banca Cattolica del Veneto in Vicenza, the Banco San Geminiano e San Prospero in Modena, the Banco San Paolo in Brescia and the Banca Piccolo Credito Bergamasco in Bergamo.

The central Vatican bank is the Istituto per le Opere di

Religione (Institute for the Works of Religion) founded in June 1942 and having its head office within the walls of Vatican City. The Institute is controlled by a Committee of ten Cardinals. Unlike other banks, its clients are selected. The only people who may open an account with the Institute are those who reside in Vatican City: diplomats accredited to the Holy See, some high-ranking officials of the Vatican, the members of the Roman Curia, the Religious who administer the schools, orders, hospitals, etc., and a small number of Italian citizens to whom this privilege has been granted because of their commercial relations with the Vatican or because of good services rendered to the Church. The advantages of having an account with the central Vatican bank, in addition to the prestige it confers, are complete exemption from all the regulations of the Italian state and the power of transferring money to any country in the world.

Since no balance-sheet nor inventory have been published, what estimate could one make of the real wealth of the financial empire of the Vatican? What value could one set on the artistic treasures of St. Peter's, on the thousands of masterpieces in the Vatican museums, on the magnificent palaces scattered about Rome, or on the others which the Holy See possesses in its own right in the various quarters of the globe? It would be difficult, if not impossible, for those not in the confidence of the Vatican to make such an estimate.

Doubtless the Church, a spiritual institution, has been reproached with sullying its hands in financial matters. But one must remember that this massive religious machine cannot function without the support of the enormous financial resources required to meet the needs of many apostolic missions in all quarters of the globe. The size of its revenues allows the Papal State to offset the expenses which the Catholic Church is obliged to incur in the accomplishment of its duties and of its mission in the world — aid for the leper hospitals of Africa, for missions, for refugees, for the education of priests, etc. No Pope could ever take a vow of poverty.

The Vatican financial administration is efficient and the resources available are exploited to the utmost. It is master of the art of economising; it seems to have the gift of foreseeing the future, and its financial organisation could serve as a model to many governments. Catholics all over the world feed the treasure-chests of the Vatican with their offerings, but the sums which come in soon go out again to do God's work. This is the daily miracle of divine bounty and Catholic generosity.

7. BANKS IN BELGIUM

The Belgian credit reform came into operation on 1 September 1935. The bank law created at the same time a 'Bank Commission' responsible for supervising the strict application of this reform. This Commission is composed of a President and six members, appointed and dismissed by royal decree. Both President and members are appointed for six years: two members are replaced every two years. The Bank Commission has authority to control and co-ordinate all Belgian banks, and its work is done in the name and on the behalf of the public power of which it is a branch. The Bank Commission is, however, not a section of the administration, in the usual sense of the word; it is subject neither to direction nor even in certain matters to supervision from a minister. It has been endowed with a very peculiar legal status.

The reform of 1935 ordained for the first time in Belgium a strict cleavage in banking affairs between the deposit bank and the commercial bank. The disappearance of the all-purpose bank marked the end of a chapter in the financial history of Belgium. It would be unjust not to mention the immense services which banks ready to finance industrial enterprises have rendered to the country and to its colonies during more than a century of pro-digious industrial development.

In compliance with the royal decree of 22 August 1934, dealing with the protection of savings and with banking opera-tions, every all-purpose bank split into two distinct bodies. For example the Société Générale de Belgique, founded in 1822, retained for itself its traditional role of a financing company and founded the Banque de la Société Générale de Belgique which continued its banking activities.

The Banque de Bruxelles, founded in 1871, continued to operate as a holding company under the name of 'Société de Bruxelles pour la Finance et l'Industrie' (Brufina) while setting up a new separate company which revived the name of 'Banque de Bruxelles' and continued its work as a deposit bank.

After the promulgation of the bank law, bank deposits were protected against all circumstances and the banking system became such as to encourage the development and expansion of the national economy.

The following public institutions are not subject to the control of the Bank Commission:

> Banque Nationale de Belgique (bank of issue)
> Institut de Réescompte et de Garantie
> Société Nationale de Crédit à l'Industrie
> Caisse Générale d'Épargne et de Retraite
> Crédit Communal de Belgique
> Caisse Nationale de Crédit Professionel
> Office Central de Crédit Hypothécaire
> Institut National de Crédit Agricole.

In contrast to what has happened in other countries, the Banque Nationale de Belgique (a bank of issue, founded in 1850) has escaped nationalisation, although 50% of its capital is in the hands of the state and its governor is appointed by royal decree.

At the same time as the credit reform came into force, an accelerating tendency towards centralisation made itself felt in the banking system: the great banking-houses rapidly extended their network of branches by absorbing regional banks. So it has come about that the three banks with a wide network possess a total of 1,785 branches scattered through all Belgian territory. They play a preponderant role in the distribution of credit and control two-thirds of the resources of the banking system.

The table on p. 90 shows the position of the three banks in question.

The Extraordinary General Meeting of shareholders in the Banque de la Société Générale de Belgique, which was held on

30 November 1964, approved the merger of the Société Belge de Banque and the Banque d'Anvers with the Banque de la Société Générale de Belgique.

As from 1 January 1965 the bank is called 'Société Générale de Banque' and in Flemish 'Generale Bank Maatschappij'. It will have 740 branches and offices throughout the whole of Belgium. Also belonging to the group of banks affiliated to the

Name	Head Office	Year of foundation	Total assets in thousands of Belgian francs	Number of branches
1 Banque de la Société Générale de Belgique S.A. . . .	Brussels	1934	77,365,878[1]	641
2 Banque de Bruxelles .	Brussels	1935	65,912,986[2]	681
3 Kredietbank . .	Brussels	1935	41,811,296[2]	463
		TOTAL	185,090,160	1,785

[1] Balance at 31 December 1964.
[2] Balance at 31 March 1965.

Société Générale de Banque in Brussels is the Banque Générale du Luxembourg in Luxembourg.

After the three important ones come the following, in order of importance:

Banque Italo-Belge (Brussels; 150 million Belgian Francs)
Banque van Roeselare en Westvlaanderen (Roulers; 75 million Belgian Francs)
Banque de Commerce (Antwerp; 60 million Belgian Francs).

One must also mention the Banque Lambert in Brussels (capital and reserves 620 million Belgian Francs) and Nagelmackers Fils & Cie in Liège (founded in 1747), both of which are limited partnerships.

On 31 December 1964 banks in Belgium fell into the following groups:

Banks incorporated in accordance with Belgian Bank Laws
Limited Companies . . 56
Limited Partnerships . . 16
—
72

Banks incorporated in accordance with foreign law
French 4
American 3
English 1
—
TOTAL 80
—

The French banks are:

Banque de Paris et des Pays-Bas
Comptoir National d'Escompte de Paris
Crédit Lyonnais
Société Française de Banque et de Dépôts (affiliated to the Société Générale in Paris).

The American banks are:

American Express Company
Morgan Guaranty Trust Company of New York
First National City Bank of New York
Bank of America (established in 1965).

The English bank is:

The Westminster Foreign Bank Ltd.

In addition, the following foreign banks, incorporated according to Belgian law, have their head offices in Belgium:

Banque d'Amsterdam pour la Belgique (affiliated to the Amsterdam–Rotterdam Bank in Amsterdam)
Banque Europeénne d'Outre-Mer (affiliated to the Nederlandse Overzee Bank in Amsterdam)
Crédit du Nord Belge (affiliated to the Crédit du Nord in Lille)
Lloyds Bank (Belgium) Ltd. (affiliated to Lloyds Bank Ltd. in London)
Banco di Roma (Belgique) (affiliated to Banco di Roma, in Rome)

Banco Español en Bruselas (affiliated to the Banco Exterior de España in Madrid).

On the other hand, the following Belgian banks have branches in foreign countries:

Société Générale de Banque, a branch in Cologne, Germany.

Banque Belge pour l'Étranger (Extrême-Orient), all of whose business is conducted abroad, maintains a branch in Hong Kong with four sub-agencies. This bank also possesses two important foreign affiliations: the Banque Belge Limited, in London, and the Belgian American Banking Corporation, in New York.

Banque Italo-Belge, head office in Brussels and one branch in Buenos Aires (Argentine), one branch in Montevideo (Uruguay), five branches in Brazil, one branch in London and two branches in France (Paris and Le Havre).

The Banque Italo-Belge was founded in 1911 by the Société Générale de Belgique in collaboration with the great Italian bank, Credito Italiano in Milan.

The professional association which links all Belgian banks is the Association Belge des Banques (Brussels).

Foreign and Belgian establishments have the legal status of banks on exactly the same footing. In contrast to the laws obtaining in many countries, the royal decree of 9 July 1935 contains no nationalistic clauses. Foreign banks wishing to extend their operations to Belgium are free to set up branches or to incorporate affiliated companies in accordance with Belgian law. The branches are, on the whole, subject to the same laws as Belgian banks. Affiliated companies of foreign banks which have adopted the form of company organisation prescribed in Belgian law are in all respects on the same footing as Belgian banks. Anyone is at complete liberty to set up a bank in Belgium. The capital assigned may come in its entirety from foreign sources. No law and no regulation prescribes that directors or principal officials should be of Belgian nationality. No pressure of any kind is exerted in this respect.

Control of foreign exchange is vested in the Institut Belgo-Luxembourgeois des Changes, a dependency of the Banque Nationale de Belgique. One must remember that in 1921 a monetary union was established between Belgium and Luxembourg and because of this the Institut's control extends equally to the Grand Duchy of Luxembourg.

An extremely favourable geographical situation has made Brussels one of the most important financial centres of Europe: today it has a population of 1,300,000, including the suburbs. The most important stock exchange in the country is that of Brussels. It is administered by the Commission de la Bourse and a Government Commissioner sees that the regulations are observed.

The second most important exchange is that of Antwerp. The Antwerp Exchange is considered to be the oldest in Europe, no doubt rightly: already in the fifteenth century two annual fairs were held in the city. Opened in 1531, its importance and its cosmopolitanism justified the inscription on its façade: 'At the service of merchants from all nations and of every tongue.' Contemporaries must have found it quite surprising.

Since the devaluation of 1949, the metallic content of the Belgian franc has been defined as 19·748241173 milligrams of gold, of a purity of 900 thousandths; and this definition can only be modified by a special law, voted by Parliament. The obligation on the Banque Nationale de Belgique to honour its notes in gold is currently suspended but can be reimposed by a simple royal decree. 33% of the daily maturing obligations of the bank must be covered in gold.

The balance-sheet of the bank, dated 31 December 1964, showed:

Belgian francs

Notes payable to bearer in circulation . . 160,286,697,400
Gold coin and bullion 72,554,849,139
The proportion of cover on this date was 44·56%.

The Banque Nationale de Belgique has two branches, of which one is in the Grand Duchy of Luxembourg, and forty agencies situated in the more important towns of the country.

8. BANKS IN HOLLAND

An extremely favourable geographical position, near the mouth of the Rhine, together with an immense colonial empire and the intense commercial activity to which it gave rise, made eighteenth-century Amsterdam the most important financial centre in the world. This supremacy was destroyed during the Napoleonic period: and Amsterdam's downfall was London's opportunity. However, in the second half of the nineteenth century, the Amsterdam money-market again became extremely active; and after the First World War, principally because of the influence of the German banks established there, it became an international centre of the first importance.

The confidence which the florin inspired enabled Amsterdam not only to function as a clearing-house for many international financial transactions, but also to attract important amounts of foreign capital to Holland. On the other hand, the position of Amsterdam was greatly strengthened by the absence of any bank failures during the bank crises of 1929–31.

It is true that the general trend towards protectionism and economic nationalism, not to mention political insecurity, was a grave hindrance to the continuing development of commerce, but this did not prevent Amsterdam from being considered the fourth most important financial centre in the world, ranking only after London, New York and Paris, at least until the outbreak of the Second World War.

The disastrous material consequences of the Second World War, the loss of the immense Dutch colonial empire, the regulations imposed on foreign exchange and economic restrictions of all kinds, have gravely prejudiced Amsterdam's prestige, although it still remains one of the most important European financial centres.

The financial structure of Holland has been gradually modified in the course of this century until it is not unlike that of Great Britain. Specialised establishments undertake different categories of business; for example, commercial banks, savings banks, agricultural banks, mortgage banks; an official bank for local authorities (Bank for Netherlands Municipalities), a bank for the middle classes, guaranteed by the state (Nederlandsche Middenstandsbank), a semi-public establishment for the export trade, a semi-nationalised company for investments and for financing participation in industrial and commercial undertakings, etc.

In Holland the multi-purpose bank has always remained a standard type and commercial banks have complete freedom of investment, even though their resources consist largely of deposits at call. In addition, it is the commercial banks which play the most important role in the money-market. Their business is based principally on current accounts, short-term credits, dealings in securities, foreign exchange — to which must be added issues on which specialised establishments would not offer the necessary return.

On 31 December 1964, 116 commercial banks were entered on the register of the Nederlandsche Bank (bank of issue) and in the table below the four most important are listed (position on 31 December 1964):

Name	Head Office	Founded	Total assets on 31/12/64 in thousands of florins	Number of branches
1 Amsterdam–Rotterdam Bank . . .	Amsterdam	1863	5,953,251	460
2 Algemene Bank Nederland . . .	Amsterdam	1824	5,672,184	400[1]
3 Nederlandsche Middenstandsbank . .	Amsterdam	1927	1,763,764	178
4 Hollandsche Bank-Unie	Amsterdam	1914	1,158,426	26[2]
		TOTAL	14,547,625	1,064

[1] 22 in foreign countries.
[2] 23 in foreign countries.

It is estimated that these four great banks discharge by themselves about 70% of the total banking business of the country.

Other credit institutions have an important place in the economy of the nation, such as the Coöperatieve Centrale

Raiffeisen-Bank (Utrecht), the Coöperatieve Centrale Boeren-leenbank (Eindhoven), the Nationale Handelsbank, the Neder-landse Overzee Bank and the Kas-Associatie.

On 31 December 1964 the register of the Nederlandsche Bank (bank of issue) gave the following list of all credit institutions:

	Number	Combined balance-sheet (in millions of guilders)
Section I		
Commercial banks	114	
Central credit institutions	2	
	— 116	
		17,604·0
Section II		
Co-operative Central Farmers' Credit Bank at Eindhoven		
Agricultural credit banks	600	
Affiliated savings banks	606	
	— 1,206	
Co-operative Central Agricultural Credit Bank at Utrecht		
Agricultural credit banks	688	
Affiliated savings banks	688	
	— 1,376	
Unattached agricultural credit banks		
Agricultural credit banks	16	
Affiliated savings banks	10	
	— 26	
	2,608	
		8,905·1
Section III		
Security credit institutions	63	
	—	221·1
Section IV		
Associated savings banks	235	
Unattached savings banks	19	
	254	
	—	5,103·4
GRAND TOTAL	3,041	31,833·6

There is in Holland a class of bankers who compel respect by their adherence to the traditions of their long-established firms. A few are listed below:

Vlaer & Kol (Utrecht; founded in 1691)
R. Mees & Zoonen (Rotterdam; 1720)
A. C. Fraser & Co. (Rotterdam; 1736)
F. van Lanschot (s'Hertogenbosch; 1737)
Hope & Co. (Amsterdam; 1762)
A. van Hoboken & Co. (Rotterdam; 1774)
H. Oyens & Zoonen (Amsterdam; 1797)
Vermeer & Co. (Amsterdam; 1839)
Teixeira de Mattos Brothers (Amsterdam; 1852)
Lippmann, Rosenthal & Co. (Amsterdam; 1859).

All these names appear, moreover, on the list of the oldest private banks in the world, which is to be found in Chapter 6.

All Dutch banks are members of the Nederlandse Bankiers-vereniging (Association of Dutch Banks) in Amsterdam, which is the professional association linking the diverse institutions together.

The bank of issue is the Nederlandsche Bank (Bank of the Netherlands), with its head office in Amsterdam. It was founded in 1814 by William I and is thus one of the oldest banks of issue in the world. It remained a private bank until 1948, but the law of 23 April 1948 transferred all its shares to the state. Other legal measures have further extended the prerogatives of the state, although, in practice, little use appears to have been made of them up till now.

The law made the Nederlandsche Bank responsible for maintaining the value of the florin, in conformity with the interests of the country, and insuring that the currency remains as stable as possible. At the same time the bank has had to become 'lender of the last resort' in relation to the state, a task which has not failed at times to cause the directors a certain degree of anxiety. In fact, the bank holds at the Government's disposal, in the event of its being in the lowest possible financial water, credits with a limit of 150 million florins; but the state is entitled, in cases of urgent

need, to exceed this limit considerably. Apart from the conventional activities of a bank of issue, the Nederlandsche Bank is
authorised to intervene in the foreign-exchange market and
money-market, by means of operations on the open market and
to exercise a certain measure of control over the banks themselves.
Indeed, a law of 1952 delegated to the Nederlandsche Bank the
surveillance and control of credit, and the bank applies this law
very rigorously, especially with respect to the legal standards
of liquidity.

Although determining the parity of the florin is the responsibility of the Government, the latter comes to an agreement with
the bank before taking a decision. The Government has in fact
the power to change the parity, without having recourse to
legislation or consulting Parliament, within the limits imposed
by membership of the International Monetary Fund. Since 1936
the florin is no longer a gold currency in the strict sense of the term.
It is at present linked to the United States dollar on a basis of
parity between fl. 3·62 and $1. Since 1956 the daily maturing
obligations of the Nederlandsche Bank must have a minimum
cover of 50% in gold and currency.

Balance-sheet 31 December 1965	*Million florins*
Gold coin and bullion	6·327
Foreign exchange	1·216
Bank-notes in circulation . . .	7·753
Notes backed by gold and convertible currencies 91%.	

In the Netherlands there are three stock exchanges, in Amsterdam, Rotterdam and The Hague. Under the present law, dealings
in stocks and shares may only be effected through the agency of a
member of one of the three associations which form the Nederlandsche Organisatie van het Effectenbedriji (Netherlands
Organisation for the Trade in Stocks and Shares). The three
associations in question are:

the *Vereeniging voor den Effectenhandel* (Committee of the
Amsterdam Stock Exchange)
the *Vereeniging van Effectenhandelaren* (Committee of the
Rotterdam Stock Exchange)

the *Bond voor den Geld- en Effectenhandel in de Province* (Committee of the Stock Exchange of The Hague).

Contrary to the custom in many other countries, where dealings in stocks and shares take place only between brokers, on Dutch exchanges transactions are carried out by banks as well as by brokers. Indeed, banks carry out a considerable proportion of the dealings.

The share market is concentrated in Amsterdam. The Amsterdam Exchange, established in 1606, four years after the foundation of the Dutch East India Company, is one of the oldest in the world. Since 1876 it has been managed by the Vereeniging voor den Effectenhandel, whose members — numbering 510 — are the brokers, the issuing houses, the banks and their directors.

At the end of 1962, 2,247 stocks were quoted in the daily official list of the Amsterdam Stock Exchange. Stocks not included in the official list (unquoted or supplementary list) are called in Dutch 'incourante fondsen'. The term 'incourante' — not current — does not mean that dealings in these stocks are uncommon. Quite on the contrary, dealings in some of them occur more frequently than in stocks included in the official list.

For some years Amsterdam has been gaining in importance as a financial centre, above all, on a national level and within the framework of Benelux. However, the position which this town occupied before the Second World War in international finance has not yet been recovered.

9. BANKS IN SWITZERLAND

The organisation of the Swiss banking system will be easier to understand if we first give a brief sketch of the political structure of the Confederation. Switzerland has an area of 41,295 sq. kilometres and a population of 5,600,000. There are four linguistic groups: 72.7% of the population are German-speaking, 20.8% French-speaking, 5.3% Italian speaking and 1.2% Romansh-speaking. Switzerland is divided into nineteen cantons and six sub-cantons. The capital is Berne (180,000 inhabitants), seat of the Federal Government.

On 14 December 1907 an association called the Union of
Swiss Cantonal Banks was founded at Basle; its members were
the state-guaranteed cantonal banks, and eventually those other
cantonal banking-houses whose share-capital is for the most part
held by the canton. Today twenty-eight establishments belong
to the Union and all cantons are represented in it. Each cantonal
bank has its own character and its own peculiar tasks, depending
on the importance and the economic structure of the canton in
which it is situated. However, all these banks have so many
common interests that the need for the association is easily under-
stood. This association has strengthened the bonds between the
various cantonal institutions, so characteristic of the Swiss
banking scene.

Among the member-institutions of the Union are some banks
of a very high standing as the following table makes clear (situation on 31 December 1964):

Name	Head Office	Founded	Total assets on 31 December 1964 in thousands of Swiss francs
Zürcher Kantonalbank	Zürich	1869	5,266,840
Banque Cantonale de Berne	Berne	1834	1,986,277
St. Gallische Kantonalbank	St. Gall	1868	1,570,531
Banque Cantonale Vaudoise	Lausanne	1845	1,565,684
Thurgauische Kantonalbank	Weinfelden	1871	1,335,837
Basellandschaftliche Kantonalbank	Liestal	1864	1,325,963
Banque Cantonale Lucernoise	Lucerne	1850	1,294,751
Banque Cantonale de Bâle	Basle	1899	1,102,894
Aargauische Kantonalbank	Aarau	1854	958,495
Graubündner Kantonalbank	Chur	1870	892,326

In 1912 the Swiss Bankers' Association was founded in Basle;
all Swiss banks are members of this Association, including cantonal banks and private banks. At the time of its foundation it
included 316 members, representing 159 establishments, whose
combined balance-sheet totalled 9 milliard Swiss francs. On
31 March 1962 the Association celebrated the fiftieth anniversary
of its foundation; its membership then totalled 1,087 mem-

bers, representing 322 banks, and their combined balance-sheet amounted to 60 milliard Swiss francs.

The exiguity of Swiss territory and its economy has not prevented the birth and growth of banking institutions universally famous, and enjoying great prestige. Four banks have a preponderant position in the economy of the country and their activities spread to the international field.

The following table will give some idea of the importance of these four establishments:

Name	Head Office	Founded	Total assets on 31 December 1965 in thousands of Swiss francs
Swiss Bank Corporation (Société de Banque Suisse) . . .	Basle	1872	10,137,624
Union Bank of Switzerland (Union de Banques Suisse) . . .	Zürich	1912	9,574,253
Swiss Credit Bank (Crédit Suisse) .	Zürich	1856	9,375,434
People's Bank of Switzerland (Banque Populaire Suisse) . .	Berne	1869	3,938,283

The Swiss money market is characterised by a marked degree of decentralisation, a result of the federal structure of the country and the strongly local character of the banking system. The financial power of contemporary Switzerland is embodied in the trio Zürich–Basle–Geneva. They are the three most important Swiss towns as well as the three most important banking and financial centres. Of the three, Zürich (550,000 inhabitants, the largest Swiss town) is incomparably the most important; this town is not only the principal Swiss banking centre but also one of the principal financial centres in the world. Zürich's endeavour to establish its financial supremacy and to become the most important economic centre in the country is relatively recent. In the middle years of the nineteenth century Zürich lagged behind Basle and Geneva. Its dominant position began to be apparent in the course of the twentieth century. At the end of 1961, of 550 banks and finance companies subject to federal law, about 100 had their head office in Zürich. Another statistic: of about 30,000 Swiss bank employees, about 8,000 work in Zürich.

The Swiss National Bank has its head office in Berne but has recognised the importance of Zürich by establishing there its policy-making departments. Two of the great Swiss banks, the Union de Banques Suisses and Crédit Suisse, have their head offices in Zürich and the Société de Banque Suisse and the Banque Populaire Suisse have their most important branches there.

The Zürich Cantonal Bank, whose balance-sheet shows assets of 5,267 million Swiss francs, that is to say about one-fifth of the total assets of all cantonal banks, has no near rival among banks of this kind.

Also at Zürich is the head office of one of the oldest banks in the world, Leu & Co.'s Bank Ltd., founded in 1755, whose total assets amounted — on 31 December 1965 — to 842 million francs.

Three foreign banks have branches at Zürich: the Société Générale Alsacienne de Banque (Strasbourg), Lloyds Bank Europe Ltd. (London) and the American Express Company Inc. (New York). In addition, fourteen great foreign banks have correspondents in Zürich:

Italy: Banca d'Italia (bank of issue)
    Banca Nazionale de Lavoro
    Banco di Napoli
    Banco di Sicilia
    Credito Italiano
    Istituto Bancario San Paolo di Torino
Canada: Canadian Imperial Bank of Commerce
U.S.A.: Bank of America N.T. & S.A. (San Francisco)
England: Barclays Bank Ltd.
    Hambros Bank Ltd.
    Bank of London & South America Ltd.
    Bank of London & Montreal Ltd.
    J. Henry Schroder, Wagg & Co. Ltd.
Turkey: Central Bank of the Republic of Turkey (bank of issue).

On 17 June 1966 a Soviet bank called Wozchod Commercial

Bank Ltd. was established in Zürich with a capital of 10 million Swiss francs and registered as a Swiss company.

The financing companies, often founded by banks, can equally well be classed as commercial banks. Of thirty-five such companies in Switzerland thirteen have their head office in Zürich, and of sixteen investment trusts, five have their offices in Zürich.

Finally, this brief sketch of Zürich as a financial centre would be incomplete if one failed to mention the assurance companies, which maintain close relationships with the banks and the money-market. The great Swiss assurance companies in addition to home business are very active abroad. It is estimated that 90% of the revenue from premiums comes from abroad. Of eighty-eight Swiss assurance companies, twenty-three are situated in Zürich.

Zürich is also the most important centre in the foreign exchange market, with about 50% or 60% of the total turnover in this field, while the proportion for Geneva is only 20% and only 15% for Basle.

After Zürich, the most important financial centre in Switzerland is Basle (300,000 inhabitants). The financial history of Basle goes back to the thirteenth century. The town owes its commercial importance to its geographical situation, at the crossing-point of great highways. Already in the Middle Ages its favourable situation on the banks of the Rhine allowed the town to extend its influence into Austria, Germany and France. Even today one finds on the list of private banks in Basle names which are the heirs of a long tradition, such as La Roche & Cie (founded in 1787), Les Fils Dreyfus & Cie (1812), A. Sarasin & Cie (1841) and Heusser & Cie (1855).

Private bankers of this kind, whose field of action has been somewhat reduced by the establishment of the great credit institutions, are particularly concerned with the administration of private fortunes, with deposits of securities and such stock-exchange transactions which this entails.

Among the other banks in Basle there are a certain number of establishments of varying importance. A characteristic institution is the Bank of Maritime Mortgages, founded in 1943 under the auspices of the Crédit Suisse, whose business is the registration of mortgages on Rhine shipping.

The Société de Banque Suisse has its head office at Basle and plays a preponderant role in the banking life of this region. This bank was the first Swiss bank to establish a branch in London (1898; Swiss Bank Corporation). A second branch was established in New York in 1939 and a third in Canada, under the name of the Swiss Corporation for Canadian Investments Ltd., in Montreal. Finally, in collaboration with the Crédit Commercial de France (Paris), the Banque Franco-Suisse pour le Maroc was founded in Casablanca.

Within Basle's walls are to be found only two branches of foreign banks: the Crédit Industriel d'Alsace et de Lorraine (Strasbourg) and the American Express Company Inc. of New York. Since 1930 the Bank for International Settlements has had its offices in Basle. The choice of this town was determined not only by the political structure and neutral status of Switzerland, but also by the central geographical and economic situation of Basle.

The third most important financial centre of Switzerland is Geneva (200,000 inhabitants). The reputation of Geneva goes back several centuries. In 1798 Geneva had a population of about 30,000, and thanks to the diversity of its industry — clock- and watch-making, jewellery, tanning, fabric printing, printing and publishing, etc. — was already an important business centre. The prosperity of the Genevan bankers soon caused the town to become the most important Swiss financial centre of the period. Its reputation extended well beyond the frontiers, and the French kings were always ready to turn to the Geneva banks when they were in need of funds or needed to put their finances in order.

In 1800 Monsieur Henri Hentsch, head of the banking-house of Hentsch & Cie, was summoned by Bonaparte, who wished to obtain credits for the Army. Henri Hentsch refused, but agreed to distribute the cash which would be provided for him; and carts full of crowns were seen in the Rue Corraterie, where Hentsch & Cie had their offices.

A simpler and clearer picture is presented if one classifies the Genevan banks in four groups:

1. Credit establishments (*de droit public*)
2. Branches of other Swiss banks
3. Private banks
4. Branches of foreign banks.

In the first group are the Mortgage Bank of the Canton of Geneva, founded in 1848, and the Savings Bank of the Republic and Canton of Geneva, founded in 1816. These two banks fill the role of a cantonal bank and they are members of the Union des Banques Cantonales Suisses.

In the second group are the branches of the four great commercial banks: Union de Banques Suisses, Société de Banque Suisse, Crédit Suisse and Banque Populaire Suisse. The following banks also have branches: Schweizerische Hypotheken- und Handelsbank, the Banque Centrale Coopérative de Bâle and the Crédit Hypothécaire pour la Suisse Romande.

In the third group are the private banking-houses, of which the seven oldest and most important are:

Ferrier Lullin & Cie (founded in 1795)
Hentsch & Cie (1796)
Lombard, Odier & Co. (1798)
Pictet & Cie (1805)
Mirabaud & Cie (1819)
Darier & Co. (1837)
Bordier & Cie (1844).

These seven houses are in the hands of some thirty families, for the most part related. These banks are, above all, the administrators of private fortunes and administer the deposits of a numerous clientele, principally foreign, and as a result are active dealers in securities and on the stock exchange. Since they dispose of a high investment potential, these houses participate to a considerable extent in the issues of the money-market. In 1931 these seven houses formed the Groupement des Banquiers privés. These banks, the aristocracy of the Genevan banking world,

are organised as limited partnerships or general partnerships, the
partners being personally liable.

In the fourth group are the branches of foreign banks, which are
very much more important at Geneva than at the other Swiss
towns. The two oldest are the branch of the Banque de Paris
et des Pays-Bas (opened in 1872) and that of the Crédit Lyonnais
(1876). One must also mention the Banque Industrielle et Commerciale de Crédit (affiliated to the Banque Parisienne de Crédit),
Lloyds Bank Europe Ltd., the Ottoman Bank, the American
Express Company Inc., the First National City Bank of New
York. The Banque d'Indochine maintains a branch at Lausanne.

Numerous foreign banks have established subsidiaries at Geneva,
of which the most important are:

the Bank for Swiss-Israeli Trade (founded in 1950 by the
Foreign Trade Bank of Tel-Aviv)

the Discount Bank (Overseas) (founded in 1952 and in which
Israeli interests predominate)

the Intra Bank (founded in 1958 by the Intra Bank of Beirut,
Lebanon)

the Banque Scandinave en Suisse (founded in 1965 by the
Skandinaviska Banken, Stockholm, Sweden)

Compagnie de Gestion et de Banque (affiliated to the Société
Générale de Banque in Brussels).

There are also about a dozen agencies of American and
Canadian Issuing Houses.

There are in Switzerland three stock exchanges, at Zürich
Basle and Geneva. The Zürich Stock Exchange, founded in
1876, is the most important in Switzerland and one of the most
important on the European continent. The Geneva Stock
Exchange, founded in 1850, comes in the second place and the
Basle Stock Exchange, founded in 1876, in third.

The Swiss National Bank opened its doors on 20 June 1907;
at that time there were in Switzerland thirty-six banks of issue
and the notes issued by these various banks were all taken up
by the Swiss National Bank in the course of the three following
years. The Swiss National Bank has two offices, one in Berne

and one in Zürich. The head office is at Berne and the management at Zürich.

As well as these two offices, the bank has branches in Aarau, Basle, St. Gall, Geneva, Lausanne, Lugano, Lucerne and Neuchâtel. In three other towns the bank has its own agencies, and in twelve others it has agencies managed by the cantonal banks.

The Swiss National Bank is a joint-stock company. The nominal capital, whose amount has not been varied since the bank's foundation, is 50 million francs; half of this capital is paid up.

The majority of the shares have been held since the foundation of the bank by the cantons and the cantonal banks (58%). The remainder (42%) is held by 6,083 private shareholders, of whom 4,811 own between 1 and 5 shares (as at 31 December 1962). The Swiss Confederation possesses no part of the capital.

The supreme body of the Institution is the Council of the Bank, responsible for general surveillance of the nation's economic affairs. It has forty members, of whom fifteen are elected by the shareholders, and the twenty-five others, among whom are the President and Vice-President, are chosen by the Federal Council.

The chief executive body of the bank is the General Management, organised on the collegiate principle: it is composed of three members, appointed by the Federal Council for a period of six years. The Federal Council appoints President and vice-president from the General Management.

The strong position of the Swiss franc is demonstrated by the importance of its gold cover.

On 31 December 1965 the assets of the Swiss National Bank totalled (in millions of francs)		15,262·6
Notes payable to bearer in circulation		10,042·5
Gold and bullion	13,164·2	
Foreign currency	852·6	
		14,016·8

The Swiss National Bank can defend itself only with great difficulty against undesirable influxes of gold and currency. Although the bank is under no obligation to buy gold, it is forced to accept foreign currency and gold offered to the extent necessary to discharge its obligation to maintain the currency at par.

10. BANKS IN SPAIN

Spain is the heir of a great and exceptionally impressive historic past. If one wishes to understand contemporary Spain there is no better way than by a brief sketch of the main periods of her history.

In antiquity and in the Middle Ages the Iberian peninsula was invaded by Phoenicians, Greeks, Carthaginians, Romans (200 B.C.), Visigoths (fifth century) and the Mussulmans (eighth century).

In A.D. 711 Tariq, the leader of the Moors, brought the whole peninsula under Arab domination. (Gibraltar perpetuates his name — Jebel Tariq.)

Spain saw a splendid flowering of Greco-Roman civilisation. The Germanic domination brought in fresh elements. The Arab invasion provoked the *Reconquista*: eight centuries of struggle to win back the national territory. This continued cultural contact and ethnic interbreeding have had a lasting effect on Spanish manners and customs; and so it is that at the dawn of the modern period there appears the Spanish race, with its own strongly marked character.

A long and brilliant pre-history, an especially fruitful period of romanisation, active participation in the formation of Christendom: among all the nations of the Mediterranean, all of whom have enjoyed so favourable a human development, the Spanish nation is unequalled in the antiquity and continuity of its civilisation.

In the Middle Ages there was a Spanish Islam, living and inventive, whose wealth, intellect and complexity, as much as the Christian Reconquest, prepared the great future advances of Spain.

From 711 to 1492 Spain — and within Spain particularly Castile — was a community continually at war. The warrior class naturally seized a dominant position. The great nobles were here more powerful, the lesser nobles more numerous, than anywhere else.

In the thirteenth century Spain lived through her finest hours. Islam retreated, the Moors were expelled, the great cathedrals were built. Christian civilisation triumphed all along the line and Spain became the most powerful nation of Christendom.

1479–1598. Three reigns — little more than a century. This period was enough to bring Spain one of the most splendid triumphs in the annals of history: a success too rapid to be built on firm foundations.

In the seventeenth century France, and in the eighteenth century England, wrested its European hegemony from Spain. Latin America seized the opportunity to establish her independence. Her colonial illusions destroyed, Spain saw what her real problems were: land unjustly distributed and inefficiently exploited. A period of profound decadence followed, during which, however, there subsisted a natural pride, still sensible in contemporary political sentiment, in having been not only a great power in the world but also the first in date and the first in importance of the nations to found a great colonial empire.

Spain created an empire, with a common language, a common religion, common manners and customs, and a total lack of colour prejudice. The existence of this empire was a fundamental element in Spanish life for three centuries; it created nations which bear her stamp.

The Spanish Colonial Empire is a fact of capital importance for contemporary times. That it bore the stamp of greatness cannot be denied, which is not without importance for the Spanish consciousness.

Economically and strategically contemporary Spain cannot shut out the harsh realities of the modern world. She has again become one of the danger points of the world: all men today feel that they are in some measure involved with the fate of Spain.

A country of proud traditions and ancient culture, Spain —

who at the dawn of the Renaissance brought western culture to two continents — is at present on the threshold of a new economic development. Thanks to the progress made in industrialisation and to the tentative movements made towards liberalising the economy, the country is at present engaged, after having surmounted the difficulties caused by civil dissension, in gradually bringing her economy into line with that of the industrialised countries of Europe.

Since July 1959 two essential facts have contributed to bringing Spain into harmony with the broad lines of European economy, which is all the more welcome because geographically this country is a natural bridge between Europe and Africa and a gateway open towards Latin America.

First, Spain has become a member of the Organisation for Economic Development and Co-operation, of the International Bank for Reconstruction and Development and the International Monetary Fund, which has offered Spain new opportunities for expansion. Second, the simultaneous implementation of a plan (decree of July 1959) which permitted a successful stabilisation of the currency, after the country had suffered for years from more or less inflationary tendencies.

One of the guiding principles in drawing up this plan was an improvement in the system for foreign capital. It is indeed logical that, if a plan for expansion for the Spanish economy is to be put into operation, capitalisation — on which its structure is based — be firmly maintained by means of a series of productive investments. This undeniable fact opens wide and attractive perspectives in the field of investment, not only as far as national capital is concerned but also for foreign capital.

In October 1964 an international congress took place in Madrid, sponsored by the Ministry of Finance; this congress was concerned with capital investment in general and more especially the investment of foreign capital in Spain. Banks, financial groups and important companies from all over the world were invited to send representatives. This initiative gave further proof of the determination of Spain, which for twenty years had been part of Europe only in a geographical sense, to break out from its isolation, abandon dictatorship and to become a nation wholly integrated into the economy of Europe.

In July 1962 the Spanish Government asked to be admitted to the Common Market, another proof of its desire to belong socially and economically to the Western European Club.

Although Spain has hitherto been an essentially agricultural country, natural conditions would favour its industrialisation. Minerals of various kinds are present in quantities and of a quality which would make their exploitation profitable. The delay in industrialisation is to be plainly seen in the figure for average earnings, which amounts to only $360 annually per head of the population.

The country has an area of 504,748 sq. kilometres, and a population of 32 million which has more than doubled in the course of the last hundred years; the people are hard-working, thrifty and extremely adaptable. By the use of rationalised means of production, agriculture, which provides employment for 40% of the population, would be in a position to provide a stock of food and raw materials which even if not sufficient would at least be susceptible to development and would thus contribute to the development of the Spanish economy.

But the important fact is that Government and people are resolved to embark upon a liberal economy and therefore to expose the products of Spanish labour to the invigorating atmosphere of free international competition.

Even if there are no grounds for speaking of an 'economic miracle', since 1959 Spain has made great economic strides. Tourism has more than tripled and today Spain holds second place among the European touring countries, Italy coming first. The table on p. 112 gives some idea of the importance of this economic sector.

The other economic sectors also show an expanding tendency. The output of electricity increased in 1963 by 12·7% and that of industry by 10%. Industrial production as a whole has increased in recent years by an average of about 6%.

Today Spain is embarking on a veritable economic revolution which is having a profound effect on the national psychology.

	Number of tourists					Revenue in millions of dollars
1959	4,194,686	.	.	.	.	149·9
1960	6,113,255	.	.	.	.	316·5
1961	7,455,262	.	.	.	.	376·7
1962	8,668,722	.	.	.	.	473·4
1963	10,931,626	.	.	.	.	704·6
1964	14,102,888	.	.	.	.	932·1
1965	14,720,000	.	.	.	.	1,157·0

A development plan is being put into operation, which should be realised in four years; that is to say it runs from 1964 to 1967. The plan predicts an annual total increase in the national product of 6%.

Between 1954 and 1962 the increase was only $4\frac{1}{2}\%$, giving at the end of this period, that is to say in 1962, a national income of 670,000 million pesetas. The objective for 1967 is the attainment of 905,000 million. The increase will be 17% in agriculture, 39% in industry and 25% in power production.

The economy will receive vigorous support from a programme of public investment which in the period 1964–7 will cost 334,597 million pesetas; in comparison during the period of four years 1959–62 public investment did not exceed 171,000 million pesetas.

In order to avoid inflation, the investments foreseen will be carefully selected. In Spain an influx of foreign capital is expected, amounting to 15% of the total volume of investment in the course of the four years of the plan.

This enterprise should not encounter too many difficulties in obtaining credit. The Spanish banks have at their disposal abundant idle assets. Further, the Banco de España, the bank of issue, has been endowed with all the necessary powers of control.

All this does not mean that the plan will be realised without difficulties. Among these there is the need for a sufficient number of technicians and of trained workmen. To meet this an appeal has been made to the universities and colleges of the country and vigorous efforts are being made to increase the number of colleges of engineering.

At present the fundamental problem of the Spanish economy is the same as that of other countries: it consists in developing the economy of the country to the utmost possible degree without threatening the monetary stability necessary to conserve the gains made. From this point of view, Spain at present is of great interest in that she displays several symptoms of a transitional phase, which makes total collaboration from the banks indispensable.

Monetary stability and its two essential bases (a balanced budget and a favourable balance of payments) are at present not threatened in Spain, but it was necessary to co-ordinate it with the process of development at which the country is aiming.

In order to guarantee an adequate and providently planned response to the demand for credit, a thorough but gradual reform of banking institutions has been instituted.

The fundamental law for the reform of Spanish banks was passed by the Cortes on 14 April 1962. This was a basic law, later to be extended by the decrees of 7 June 1962, dealing with the nationalisation and reorganisation of the Banco de España, with the creation of the Instituto de Credito a Medio y Largo Plazo and with the reorganisation and functions of the Instituto de Credito de las Cajas de Ahorro.

A justification of the reform has been given: it is that institutions of a financial and economic nature ought to be subject to periodic reform, so as to ensure that they are always adapted to their responsibilities and to the circumstances of the moment. This statement is profoundly true and of general validity.

The first article of the law says expressly that authority in matters of currency and credit belongs to the Government, which, through the intermediary of the Ministry of Finance, will transmit to the Banco de España and to the various institutions of credit directives which they will be obliged to follow.

The Banco de España has been reorganised, and a clear separation set up between the departments responsible for policy and administration on the one hand and those with purely consultative functions on the other. These latter are assured the necessary degree of independence by the presence of representatives of the various economic interests conjointly with representatives appointed by the Government, on the recommendation of the Ministry of Finance.

Within a framework flexible enough to allow the formulation of a financial policy, the creation of money by the bank of issue has been regulated and norms have been established for operations on the open market, rediscount to private banks, loans to banks on hypothecated securities, private banks' obligatory deposits with the central bank and other necessary mechanisms of control.

The inspection and supervision of private banks has been entrusted to the Banco de España on the basis of norms determined by the Ministry of Finance. The transfer of foreign payments and the centralisation of foreign-exchange reserves have been entrusted to the Banco de España by the Instituto Español de Moneda Extranjera.

Since June 1962 the Banco de España has abstained from making any loans to private individuals. The new law expressly forbids such loans and instructed the bank to liquidate all existing loans within a period of five years.

Technically the Banco de España is an autonomous institution. It is controlled by a Governor, three Vice-Governors and an Executive Council composed of the above and of three members of the General Council. The General Council is purely consultative, and consists of the Governor and Vice-Governor, a group of five members appointed by the Minister of Finance, to which must be added two delegates proposed by the private banks, a representative of the Instituto de Credito a Medio y Largo Plazo, a representative of the Instituto de Credito de las Cajas de Ahorro, four from the syndicalist organisation and one of the officials of the Banco de España. Following the example of other countries, Spain has set up a true central bank, a genuine banks' bank.

The new law lays down that the high-level direction, co-ordination and inspection of Savings Banks are to be carried out by the Instituto de Credito de las Cajas de Ahorro, which is also to act as liaison organisation with the Banco de España and the Instituto de Credito Medio y Largo Plazo. The Instituto de Credito de las Cajas de Ahorro is presided over by the Governor of the Banco de España and contains representatives of the Savings Banks, of economic interests and of the state.

The operation of the Savings Banks has been revised so that these institutions may grant more generous credits for socially desirable purposes to landowners, to workmen, to small commercial and industrial enterprises, to small savers and to facilitate the granting of credit to agriculture.

On 30 April 1965 the total deposits in all Savings Banks amounted to 192,284 million pesetas, of which 178,140 million pesetas were in ordinary Savings Banks and 14,144 million pesetas in Post Office Savings Banks.

The group of official credit institutions, called 'Entidades Oficiales de Credito', is composed of the following banks:

> Banco de Credito Agricola
> Banco de Credito a la Construccion
> Banco Hipotecario de España
> Banco de Credito Industrial
> Banco de Credito Local de España
> Caja Central de Credito Maritimo y Pesquero.

In order to co-ordinate their activity all the above-mentioned institutions have been placed under the general direction of the Instituto de Credito a Medio y Largo Plazo, which has appointed representatives of the state and of economic interests to their governing bodies.

The Governor of the Banco de España presides over the Instituto de Credito a Medio y Largo Plazo.

According to the new law, the Instituto de Credito a Medio y Largo Plazo has the following functions:

1. It is the permanent liaison organisation between the Government and the official credit institutions, and transmits to the latter general directives from the Government and sees that they are carried out.

2. It is responsible for the general direction and inspection of these institutions and ensures that they have at their disposal sufficient funds to participate effectively in the economic development of the country.

3. It has at its disposal assets which the Ministry of Finance

secures for it as advances from the Treasury or as certificates of investment (*cédula para inversiones*), subscribed by companies or individuals, or by special means.

4. It is permitted to acquire securities if circumstances require and if such acquisitions come within the framework of the general credit policy.

5. The total volume of credit to be distributed annually by the Institute is fixed by the Ministry of Finance after consultation with the Council of National Economy.

The new structure of the Spanish banking system contains three main divisions, all subject to Government direction:

1. The private banking sector, headed by the Banco de España.
2. The Savings Bank sector, headed by the Instituto de Credito de las Cajas Ahorro.
3. The official credit institutions sector, headed by the Instituto de Credito a Medio y Largo Plazo.

Co-ordination between these three sectors is ensured, on the one hand, by the directives of the Ministry of Finance and, on the other, by the fact that the Governor of the Banco de España is simultaneously President of the Instituto de Credito de las Cajas Ahorro and of the Instituto de Credito a Medio y Largo Plazo.

The official banks, although they are represented on the Consejo Superior Bancario, have their own organisation, called the 'Comisaria de la Banca Oficial', subordinate to the Ministry of Finance. The Governor of the Banco de España is 'Comisario de la Banca Oficial'.

The Consejo Superior Bancario is a consultative organ of the Ministry of Finance dealing with the private banking sector, and all Spanish private banks are entered upon its registers.

Private deposit banks in Spain are at present mixed banks. The character of these establishments in fact corresponds to the state of development of the country. Spain is a nation whose savings are deposited in modest amounts — at all events, lower amounts than the volume of investment which she hopes to realise.

Although no premature attack is to be made on the system of mixed banking still in operation at present, the new law looks forward to a time when institutions will be specialised, having, however, regard to the fact that certain banking establishments are already predominantly orientated towards the industrial sector.

Private banks are regulated in various ways:

1. By decree of 29 November 1962 promulgation of a legal status for industrial and commercial banks, whose object will be to launch new industrial undertakings, to promote private initiative and to collaborate in long-term financing. Their capital is not to be less than 100 million pesetas and they may have up to three branches only.

2. By a decree of 6 December 1962 regulation of the securities held by the deposit-banks, determining the nature and amount of the securities which may be held and the maximum amount of shares held.

3. As deposit-banks launch new companies, determination of the maximum percentage which their participation may be allowed to reach, in relation to their own funds on the one hand and to the capital of these new companies on the other.

4. Determination of norms, designed to prevent an extension of the influence of existing mixed banks over private enterprises and especially over other banks.

5. Determination of limits on rediscount, of advances and deposits with the Banco de España.

6. Introduction of incompatibilities in the exercise of directive banking functions.

7. The proliferation of branches and agencies is to be avoided.

8. Flexible formulas will have to ensure the equality of the chances of all banking enterprises.

9. The establishment of foreign banks has been regulated by the Government, having regard to possible reciprocal arrangements.

10. A delay of five years has been granted the banks during which they may bring their affairs into line with the new bank legislation.

11. By a decree of 5 June 1963 the foundation of new commercial banks has been facilitated, on the condition that any new banks authorised will have to have a minimum capital, determined by the locality in which they are established:

towns of up to 10,000 inhabitants	.	.	.	.	10 million pesetas
towns of 10,000 to 50,000 inhabitants	.	.	.	.	25 ,, ,,
towns of 50,000 to 100,000 inhabitants	.	.	.	.	50 ,, ,,
towns of 100,000 to 250,000 inhabitants	.	.	.	75 ,, ,,
towns of 250,000 or more inhabitants	.	.	.	.	100 ,, ,,

and the capital must be entirely paid up when the bank is established.

12. By decree of 30 April 1964 legislation dealing with investment-houses has been revised, so that they may promote savings without allowing private interests to control certain financial sectors. For investment-houses with fixed capital, as well as investment-houses with variable capital, minimum capital is fixed at 50 million pesetas.

13. By a decree of 27 December 1962 the financing of the acquisition by hire-purchase of industrial plant and of consumer durables has been facilitated by the creation of specialised establishments; state representation within these establishments guarantees adherence to the norms determined for this sort of transaction; the volume of credit granted is controlled in order to avoid excessive pressure; finance bills may be rediscounted within limits fixed by the Ministry of Finance.

The considerable importance of the role of private banks in Spain is clearly seen, if one remembers that for the period 1940–59 they provided more than 60% of the financing in the private sector, while the percentage was only about 25% between 1920 and 1935 (by granting credit or adding shares to their portfolio).

According to the Ordinance of 5 February 1947 there are three categories of bank in Spain:

1. National banks, whose paid-up capital, reserves and deposits must total at least 500 million pesetas and who carry on business in at least three banking zones (Spain is divided into nine banking zones), or in ten provinces.

2. Regional banks whose own funds and deposits must exceed

100 million pesetas and who own several branches in one or several banking zones.

3. Local banks which fulfil none of the above conditions. To these three categories must be added two others of recent creation:

1. Bancos industriales y de negocios,
2. Bancos comerciales;

and finally, foreign banks considered as a class apart.

On 31 December 1964 the private banking sector contained 118 banks, listed below:

Category	Number	Capital	Reserves	Deposits	Total assets
	31 December 1964: in millions of pesetas				
1 Banca Nacional .	14	7,066·9	15,732·2	398·247·0	724,009·3
2 Bancos industriales y de Negocios .	11	3,602·9	175·7	5,416·2	11,909·9
3 Banca Regional .	19	1,747·8	3,961·0	54,784·9	102,202·8
4 Banca Local .	67	1,202·0	991·0	25,626·7	42,713·6
5 Bancos Comerciales . .	3	90·0	0·3	84·8	185·1
6 Foreign banks .	4	140·5	52·5	3,971·2	8,998·1
TOTAL . .	118	13,850·1	20,912·7	488,130·8	890,018·8

The eleven bancos industriales y de negocios as well as the three bancos comerciales are of recent foundation.

The following table gives the twenty most important private banks, listed in order of total assets in millions of pesetas, on 31 December 1964:

Name	Head Office	Founded	Deposits	Total assets
1 Banco Español de Credito	Madrid	1902	79,503·5	164,498·5
2 Banco Hispano Americano	Madrid	1900	73,563·1	116,254·7
3 Banco Central . .	Madrid	1919	51,155·5	89,851·3
4 Banco de Vizcaya . .	Bilbao	1901	40,723·4	71,958·5
5 Banco de Bilbao . .	Bilbao	1856	46,568·4	71,689·7
6 Banco de Santander .	Santander	1857	27,008·1	51,774·5

Table continued overleaf

Name	Head Office	Founded	Deposits	Total assets
7 Banco Popular Español .	Madrid	1926	20,474·1	39,832·4
8 Banco Exterior de España	Madrid	1929	17,532·9	36,929·1
9 Banco Urquijo . .	Madrid	1918	9,088·9	19,807·1
10 Banco Pastor . .	Corunna	1776	8,963·0	15,822·9
11 Banco Iberico . .	Madrid	1946	7,118·1	12,294·1
12 Banco Zaragozano .	Saragossa	1910	6,031·8	11,741·3
13 Banco Comercial Trans- atlantico . . .	Barcelona	1904	5,305·6	11,361·8
14 Banca March . .	Palma de Mallorca	1926	4,820·9	11,300·2
15 Banco de La Coruña .	Corunna	1918	5,200·0	11,185·9
16 Banco Guipuzcoano .	San Sebas- tian	1899	4,967·6	10,442·1
17 Banco de Aragon . .	Saragossa	1910	5,752·9	9,864·8
18 Banco Rural y Medi- terraneo . . .	Madrid	1953	4,182·6	8,745·6
19 Banco Coca . . .	Salamanca	1893	4,126·2	7,855·6
20 Banco Mercantil e In- dustrial . . .	Madrid	1931	4,238·2	7,406·1

The four foreign banks established in Spain are:

Name	Deposits	Total assets
1 Crédit Lyonnais, with branches in Madrid and Barcelona	1,473·7	3,508·0
2 Bank of London & South America Ltd., with branches in Madrid, Barcelona, Valencia and Seville	1,438·9	2,976·6
3 Société Générale de Banque en Espagne, affiliated to the Société Générale (Paris) with branches in Barcelona and Valencia . .	917·8	1,962·7
4 Banca Nazionale del Lavoro (Rome) with a branch in Madrid	140·8	550·9

In November 1965 contacts were made with the Banco
Hispano Americano and the Banco Central in order to negotiate
the merger of both banks. However, this project was not achieved
due to the heavy taxes claimed by the public treasury.

The Banco Exterior de España (Spanish Foreign Bank), a state
institution created by a royal decree of 26 March 1929, is part of

the group 'Entidades Oficiales de Credito'; it appears, however, on the Superior Banking Council's list of private banks, and is in practice regarded as an ordinary bank, since it works with deposits. It has no special charter granting fiscal privileges or financial support. On the contrary, it is subject to the same laws as private banks. Its object is to encourage foreign trade, and for this purpose it controls a network of affiliated banks, such as:

Banco Español en Paris (Paris; branches in Marseilles, Perpignan, Hendaye and Le Perthus);
Banco Español en Londres (two branches in London, one in Liverpool);
Banco Español en Alemania (Frankfurt; branches in Hamburg and Munich);
Banco Español en Bruselas (Brussels);
Banco Español en Marruecos (Casablanca; branch in Tetuan).

The bank also has branches in Asunción and Encarnación (Paraguay), and agencies in Mexico City and Buenos Aires.

According to the previous table, on 31 December 1964 there were in Spain fourteen national banks, whose assets amounted to 724 milliard pesetas, that is, they control about 80% of the total assets of all Spanish private banks. Among the nineteen regional banks, five stand out: the Banco Pastor, the Banca March, the Banco La Coruña, the Banco Guipuzcoano and the Banco Coca, all included in the table.

In Spain most great industrial undertakings are controlled by banks; nearly all of the leading banks are at the head of large-scale industrial groups.

On 30 June 1965 there existed fourteen industrial banks (eleven on 31 December 1964), situated as follows:

six with head offices in Madrid:
Banco Urquijo, the greatest industrial bank in Spain,
Banco de Desarrollo Economico Español, founded 1 August 1963 by the Banco Español de Credito,
Banco de Fomento, founded 6 August 1963 by the Banco Central,

Banco de Financiacion Industrial, founded 1963 by the Banco de Vizcaya,

Banco Europeo de Negocios, founded 20 November 1963 by the Banco Popular Español,

Banco Occidental, founded 29 November 1963;

three with head offices in Barcelona:

Union Industriale Bancaria, founded 9 August 1963 by the Banco Atlantico,

Banco Catalan de Desarrollo, founded 4 January 1964,

Banco Industrial de Cataluña, founded 19 October 1964;

one with head office in Bilbao:

the Banco Industrial de Bilbao, founded 21 December 1963;

one with head office in Santander:

the Banco Intercontinental Español, founded 1964 by the Banco de Santander;

one with head office in Granada:

the Banco de Granada, founded 18 November 1964;

one with head office in Corunna:

the Banco del Noroeste, founded 3 January 1964;

one with head office in Leon:

the Banco Industrial de Leon, founded 2 August 1963.

It is principally the bancos industriales y de negocios which, from 1963 on, have attracted foreign investment in the form of direct participation in these banks. Very considerable amounts of capital have been invested in this section by great foreign banks.

In the course of the last two years foreign investment in Spain has reached a considerable volume. According to statistics issued by the Instituto Español de Moneda Extranjera, foreign investors brought to Spain $173,920,000 in 1963 and $209,300,000 in 1964, a total of $383,220,000. The American share in this influx of capital is by far the largest, as can be seen by the table on p. 123 which lists the four leading investors.

The other investing countries are, in order of importance, the United Kingdom, Belgium, Holland, Sweden, the Philippines and Venezuela.

Year	U.S.A.	Switzerland	Germany	France	Total
1963	100,786,000	27,809,000	18,557,000	6,452,000	153,604,000
1964	109,045,000	34,450,000	21,432,000	8,078,000	173,005,000
	209,831,000	62,259,000	39,989,000	14,530,000	326,609,000

Apart from this private investment, Spain has been granted important loans by the following international organisations:

$100 million by the European Fund of the Organisation for Co-operation and Economic Development.

$75 million by the International Monetary Fund in Washington.

$130 million by the Export–Import Bank in Washington.

$33 million, a loan granted on 25 October 1963 by the International Bank for Reconstruction and Development in Washington for the complete renovation and modernisation of 745 kilometres of roads.

$65 million, a loan granted on 31 July 1964 by the International Bank for Reconstruction and Development in Washington, for the modernisation of 13,000 kilometres of railway line, controlled by RENFE (Red Nacional de los Ferrocarriles Españoles, a state undertaking founded in 1941).

$150 million, a credit put at Spain's disposal by France, under the terms of the Franco–Spanish protocol of 1963 for the purchase of industrial plant.

$40 million, a loan granted on 25 September 1965 by the International Bank for Reconstruction and Development in Washington for the modernisation of twenty-one Spanish ports.

TOTAL $593 million: the list is of value, even though it is perhaps incomplete.

Spain has three stock exchanges (*Bolsas*) — in Madrid, Barcelona and Bilbao. The one in Madrid is undoubtedly the most important. Beside these three principal exchanges, there are also thirteen local exchanges (*Bolsines*) of modest importance, in Burgos, Gijon, Corunna, Oviedo, Pamplona, San Sebastian,

Santander, Saragossa, Seville, Valencia, Valladolid, Vigo and Vitoria.

All exchanges are subject to the regulations issued by a central organisation, the Consejo Superior de Bolsas in Madrid.

Share transactions on the three principal exchanges during 1964 amounted to an actual value of 24,577 million pesetas, distributed as follows:

Madrid Exchange	. . .	9,675 million (63 brokers)
Barcelona Exchange .	. .	3,775 million (45 brokers)
Bilbao Exchange	. . .	2,089 million (30 brokers)
TOTAL . . .	.	15,539 million
Corredores (brokers) .	. .	9,038 million
GRAND TOTAL .	. .	24,577 million

This grand total was made up as follows:

Public securities.	. . .	3,751 million
Shares . .	. .	17,970 million
Debentures	. . .	2,856 million
TOTAL . .	. .	24,577 million

On 31 May 1965 the balance of the Banco de España amounted to 235,332,907,234 pesetas; gold reserves totalled 4,029,938,279 pesetas; currency held by the Instituto Español de Moneda Extranjera amounted to 82,043,140,501 pesetas; notes in circulation amounted to 138,037,989,404 pesetas.

On 17 July 1959, in collaboration with the International Monetary Fund, parity was fixed at 60 pesetas to the dollar, and since this date the price on foreign markets has not dropped.

So far no inflationary pressure has been felt; however, when the presidents of the more important banks surveyed the economy at shareholders' meetings in 1965, nearly all laid emphasis on the progress made in industrialisation on the one hand, and on the difficulties being experienced by agriculture on the other. However, all these important bankers were worried by the steep rise in domestic prices, by the exaggerated increase in wages and the consequent danger of inflation. This shows that the Spanish economy is still in need of strict protection.

Spain has not yet tried her strength on the international market; the test is only beginning. The challenge makes an increase in productive investment necessary. In a competitive economy more plant and more reserves are needed for production than in a protected economy.

Madrid (2,800,000 inhabitants) is not only the political capital of the country but also the chief centre of state capitalism, of the great banks and of the great financial and industrial companies. The banking and commercial importance of Madrid has induced many foreign banks to set up agencies, and several big American investment-houses have an agency there; among the most important is the Merrill Lynch, Pierce, Fenner and Smith Agency of New York.

Also in Madrid is the head office of the influential Instituto National de Industria (I.N.I.) or National Institute of Industry, a state enterprise that enjoys an immense power. Established in 1941, it undoubtedly performed a valuable task during the hard years that followed in helping to revitalise the economy. Its original charter was to serve the needs of defence and economic self-sufficiency, and it was to enter spheres not essential to these purposes only in cases where the large amount of capital required, or the low rate of profit to be expected, discouraged private enterprise. In fact, however, its holdings today extend over practically the whole range of industry — iron and steel, engineering, electricity, transport, and automobile and aircraft industries, naval construction, chemical, textiles and paper, refrigeration and canning of foodstuffs, and telephone and radio companies. The total value of these holdings was estimated in 1964 at 96,000 million pesetas or some $1,600 million. Formerly subsidised from the state budget, it has for the past six years — since the new economic policy — been required to raise the funds it needs in the capital market. This has presented little difficulty. Market issues made by the I.N.I. are classed as 'public securities', in which savings banks are obliged to invest, and on which interest is tax-free, while it operates with a number of advantages that makes it a safe investment.

The development plan, revolutionary, modern, efficient, dynamic, comes at a point in history when everything is stirring and changing, in Europe and in the whole world. No past century offers the example of so passionately interesting a transformation. Time will show what gigantic tasks face the whole ruling class as Spain is transformed into a great industrial power.

11. BANKS IN THE UNITED STATES OF AMERICA

Three and a half centuries ago, in 1624, at the southern tip of Manhattan Island, there existed a tiny establishment of the Dutch West India Company, called New Amsterdam; here were to be found colonists, soldiers, fur-traders, adventurers and simple farmers; in all, about a thousand people. The streets and squares of the little town were surrounded by wooden houses and modest stone buildings; they bore such names as Battery Place, Market Place, New Street, Water Street, State Street, Main Street, Broad Street (the famous Broadway of today) and to the north, Wall Street. This street marked the end of the town. Beyond lay virgin forest, the unknown, danger. Wall Street ran across the island and, as a defence against Indian attacks, palisades and block-houses were built along it in 1653. Two years later the Indians attacked the little town, killing 100 people and carrying off 150 prisoners. After this last attack they withdrew to the north and left the colony in peace.

In 1670 a British fleet under the command of the Duke of York captured the growing township; it became a British possession and the name of New York was imposed upon it. Later it passed to the Federal American Government which made it the capital from 1785 to 1790.

Wall Street, formerly the frontier with the Indians, the watch-tower of the hard-pressed colonists, the bulwark of civilisation, the last outpost of culture, has today become the financial centre of the world, the street where the most tremendous fortunes are won and lost. It is not very imposing, this Wall Street, a mere

200 yards long and 6 yards wide, but what other street in the world can approach the fame of its gigantic financial empire?

Wall Street is the general headquarters of international high finance; its name means power, a power which can make all other great financial centres tremble. Today the little street is lined, left and right, by the cold impassive façades of gigantic skyscrapers and, peering up between these giants, the passer-by glimpses a tiny patch of blue sky.

In the immense buildings of Wall Street and of the neighbouring streets, the world-famed mammoths of American finance have their offices: the Chase Manhattan Bank, the First National City Bank, the Federal Reserve Bank, the Morgan Guaranty Trust Company, the Manufacturers Hanover Trust Company, the Chemical Bank New York Trust Company, the Bankers Trust Company, the Irving Trust Company and many more. Here towers the majestic skyscraper of the famous Standard Oil Company, the most important producer of petrol in the world.

All the great lawyers of New York and America have their offices or their representative in Wall Street. In this meeting-place of international finance all the great banks of the world, of a certain reputation and a certain standing, have a branch or an agency. The geographic centre of all the banking and business activity of the immense conurbation of New York, which has about 15 million inhabitants, is Wall Street. Here beats the pulse of the financial life of New York, of America, of the whole world.

In New York there towers a skyscraper built in white marble, whose façade is modelled on a Greek temple. This architectural monstrosity is called the New York Stock Exchange: it is the heart of world economy, the source of wealth for millions of winning fighters, the source of misery for innumerable losers. Its walls form an arena where every day epic battles are fought, in which millions of dollars are tossed in as a mere tactical move, battles without truce and without mercy, between the most powerful. Here every day millions of shares change hands.

The United States of America is considered to be the home of free economy. Compared with Europe this flattering appellation is not without justification. This reputation has not, however, prevented the state from intervening more and more in economic matters, and the struggle between the political parties (as well as their internal divisions) tends towards the abolition of governmental control in the various branches of the country's economy. In matters concerning currency and the banks the necessity of strict control is nevertheless admitted; and despite protestations of steadily increasing vehemence against state tutelage, one rarely hears a demand for a relaxation of the restrictions imposed on banks and financial establishments.

The cornerstone of the banking organisation of the United States is the Federal Reserve System, an institution admirably adapted to American conditions. Its practical advantages and the astonishing exactness with which it meets the needs of the economy are doubtless a result of its having been created very late, 137 years after the Declaration of Independence. It was, in fact, not until 23 December 1913 that President Woodrow Wilson signed the Federal Reserve Act, establishing the Federal Reserve System. This central organisation consists of the Federal Reserve Board in Washington and of twelve regional central banks (Federal Reserve Banks) with twenty-two branches.

Each regional bank has its own Board of Directors, fixes discount rates for its own region and determines the amount of the reserves which each private member bank must deposit with the regional Federal Reserve Bank. The majority of the directors of each Federal Reserve Bank are elected by the commercial banks of the particular region, while the remainder are appointed by the Federal Reserve Board in Washington. This organisation was designed to provide all the flexibility needed in face of the varied problems which may arise in the different states of this immense country. Previously the inconsistency and insufficiency of the conflicting techniques employed in problems of currency circulation had been responsible for monetary instability of the worst kind. The federal system, with its twelve regional banks of issue in Boston, New York, Philadelphia, Cleveland, Richmond, Atlanta, Chicago, St. Louis, Minneapolis, Kansas City, Dallas and San Francisco, has entirely eliminated this disadvantage (see map, p. 130).

The principal task of the Federal Reserve Board in Washington is to ensure balanced interplay of the great financial forces and an adequate response to the demand for credit, having regard, above all, to the continuing development of the economy and to monetary stability. Other functions, equally important, are entrusted to it, such as the collection and interpretation of the information and reports which reach it dealing with all questions important to the economic and financial evolution of the country. For this purpose, a vast department of statistical analysis, especially in the field of production in all its aspects, a department which has acquired a world reputation for exact and authoritative work.

The monetary history of the United States is marked by a long period of evolution. Not until 1913 did the Federal Reserve Act lay the basis for a real monetary system. The notes issued by the twelve Federal Reserve Banks then became the most widely used form of currency, supplanting gold coins, gold certificates and the notes issued by the various national banks.

A radical change came about, however, in 1934, with the Devaluation Law; which at the same time transformed the very basis of the currency, abandoning the Gold Standard and adopting the Gold Bullion Standard. This devaluation lowered the value of the dollar by 40·94% in relation to gold. The new dollar was worth then 59·06% of the old dollar; the official price of an ounce of fine gold rose from $20·67183 to $35, a purchase price fixed by the American Treasury. This rate is still in force today.

After the numerous bank crashes following the Stock Exchange crisis of 1929, the whole private banking system of the United States was reformed by the Banking Act of 1933. A thorough reform was carried out, setting up a strict separation between deposit business and the issue of securities.

Despite the restrictions imposed, the American commercial banks have retained completely their private character. They are, however, subject to strict surveillance and control, exercised in the various sectors by the Comptroller of the Currency, the Federal Reserve Board, the Federal Deposit Insurance Corporation and the Banking Department of each state.

The same law of 1933 created the Federal Deposit Insurance

Districts of THE FEDERAL RESERVE SYSTEM

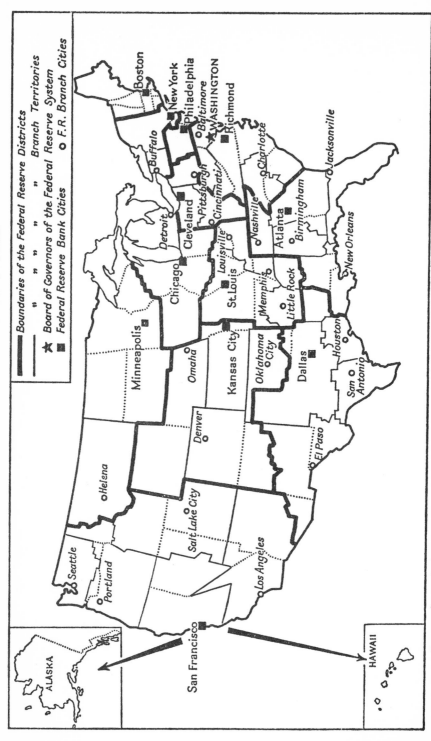

Boundaries of the Federal Reserve Districts
       "   "   "   "   "   "   Branch Territories
★ Board of Governors of the Federal Reserve System
■ Federal Reserve Bank Cities   ○ F.R. Branch Cities

For number and salaries of officers and employees of the Federal Reserve Banks 31 December 1964 see table, p. 144.

Corporation, which guarantees all bank deposits (not only savings deposits) up to a limit of $10,000. Since 98% of deposit accounts have credit balances of less than $10,000, only 2% of all deposit accounts are not covered by this insurance. The Federal Deposit Insurance Corporation believes that, by the use of other means, it can protect all depositors from possible loss, principally by exercising a strict supervision over the accounts of all banks, which have to publish a balance-sheet every three months.

As soon as the balance-sheet gives grounds for doubting the solvency of the bank, the Federal Deposit Insurance Corporation has the right to demand that the depositors' funds be transferred to other banks. This possibility excludes practically all risk for the depositor.

In the total of 14,281 banks in the 50 states of the Union on 31 December 1964, 13,820 were insured with the Federal Deposit Insurance Corporation and only 461 were not taking advantage of it (for detail see p. 147).

At the same date the deposits administered by the 14,281 banks amounted to about $358 milliard, of which $349 milliard were insured and $9 milliard not.

According to their special sphere of operation and the method of control to which they are subject, American banks may be classified as follows:

Commercial Banks, which fall into two categories; that is:

National Banks: these enjoy a concession granted by the Federal Government in Washington. They are subject to federal law but must also fulfil the legal requirements of the state in which they operate.

State Banks: these enjoy a concession granted by one or other of the 50 states in the Union: they are subject to the laws of the state in which they have their head office, but this does not dispense them from observing bank regulations published by the Federal Government.

Mutual Savings Banks, which also enjoy a concession granted by one or other of the 50 states of the Union and which are subject to the laws and regulations of the state in which they have their head office.

Each National Bank is obliged to be a member of the Federal Reserve System. For State Banks membership is optional. However, both groups of banks are obliged to deposit a portion of their reserves with the Federal Deposit Insurance Corporation in Washington.

According to the Banking Act of 1933 the Investment Banks work outside the Federal Reserve System. These banks are either limited companies, partnerships, limited partnerships or co-operative societies, and are concerned essentially with the financing of new enterprises, either on their own account or by offering securities and debentures for public subscription. In France operations of this kind are delegated essentially to commercial banks.

The United States has about 4,800 investment firms, of which about 650 have their offices in New York. Among the most important New York houses may be mentioned:

1. Bache & Co.
2. Blyth & Co. Inc.
3. Dean, Witter & Co.
4. Dillon, Read & Co. Inc.
5. Eastman Dillon, Union Securities & Co.
6. Equitable Securities Corporation
7. Fahnestok & Co.
8. The First Boston Corporation
9. Glore Forgan, Wm. R. Staats Inc.
10. Goldman, Sachs & Co.
11. Hallgarten & Co.
12. Halsey, Stuart & Co.
13. Harriman Ripley & Co. Inc.
14. Hayden, Stone & Co.
15. H. Hentz & Co.
16. Kidder, Peabody & Co. Inc.
17. Kuhn, Loeb & Co. Inc.
18. Lazard Frères & Co. (French)

19. Lehman Brothers
20. Merrill Lynch, Pierce, Fenner & Smith Inc.
21. Model, Roland & Co. Inc.
22. Morgan Stanley & Co.
23. Paine, Webber, Jackson & Co.
24. Paribas Corporation (French)
25. Shearson, Hammil & Co.
26. Smith, Barney & Co. Inc.
27. Stone & Webster Securities Corporation
28. White, Weld & Co.

Below are listed the twenty most important private commercial banks of the United States, listed in order of the total of their deposits on 30 June 1965:

Name	Head Office	Founded	Deposits
1 Bank of America N.T. and S.A.	San Francisco	1904	14,351,236,316
2 First National City Bank .	New York	1812	11,802,776,000
3 Chase Manhattan Bank. .	New York	1799	11,800,304,301
4 Manufacturers Hanover Trust Co.	New York	1831	6,370,549,089
5 Chemical Bank New York Trust Co. . . .	New York	1824	5,688,346,155
6 Morgan Guaranty Trust Co..	New York	1861	5,257,070,969
7 Security-First National Bank .	Los Angeles	1875	4,329,246,244
8 Continental Illinois National Bank & Trust Co. of Chicago	Chicago	1857	4,285,423,316
9 Bankers Trust Co. . .	New York	1903	4,257,008,000
10 First National Bank of Chicago	Chicago	1863	3,641,469,059
11 Wells Fargo Bank . .	San Francisco	1852	3,434,361,937
12 Crocker-Citizens National Bank	San Francisco	1870	3,253,912,530
13 Mellon National Bank & Trust Co. . . .	Pittsburgh	1870	2,914,231,863
14 United California Bank .	Los Angeles	1903	2,823,799,999
15 National Bank of Detroit .	Detroit	1933	2,678,560,298
16 Irving Trust Co. . . .	New York	1851	2,633,318,422
17 First National Bank of Boston	Boston	1784	2,067,818,452
18 The Cleveland Trust Co. .	Cleveland	1894	1,679,615,141
19 First Pennsylvania Banking & Trust Co. . . .	Philadelphia	1812	1,346,254,650
20 Manufacturers National Bank of Detroit . . .	Detroit	1933	1,302,332,802

At the head of the two largest New York banks are the two Rockefellers: David Rockefeller, President of the Board of Management of the Chase Manhattan Bank, and James S. Rockefeller, Chairman of the Board of Directors of the First National City Bank.

The Securities and Exchange Commission (S.E.C.) was created by an Act of Congress entitled the Securities Exchange Act of 1934. It is an independent, bipartisan, quasi-judicial agency of the United States Government.

Organised 2 July 1934, the Commission is composed of five members, not more than three of whom may be members of the same political party. They are appointed by the President, with the advice and consent of the Senate, for five-year terms, the terms being staggered so that one expires on 5 June of each year. The Chairman is designated by the President.

The Commission's staff is composed of lawyers, accountants, engineers, security analysts and examiners, together with administrative and clerical employees. The staff is divided into Divisions and Offices (including nine Regional Offices), each under charge of officials appointed by the Commission (see diagram, p. 136).

The Commission reports annually to the Congress. These reports contain a review of the Commission's administration of the several laws.

As of 30 June 1964, fourteen stock exchanges were registered under the Exchange Acts as national securities exchanges (see map, p. 137):

> American Stock Exchange
> Boston Stock Exchange
> Chicago Board of Trade
> Cincinnati Stock Exchange
> Detroit Stock Exchange
> Midwest Stock Exchange
> National Stock Exchange
> New York Stock Exchange
> Pacific Coast Stock Exchange
> Philadelphia–Baltimore–Washington Stock Exchange

    Pittsburgh Stock Exchange
    Salt Lake Stock Exchange
    San Francisco Mining Exchange
    Spokane Stock Exchange.

Four exchanges were exempted from registration by the Commission:

    Colorado Springs Stock Exchange
    Honolulu Stock Exchange
    Richmond Stock Exchange
    Wheeling Stock Exchange.

The Commission is charged with the responsibility for the oversight of the national securities exchanges. Each national securities exchange reports to the Commission disciplinary actions taken against any member, member-firm or person connected therewith, for violation of any rule of the exchange, of the Securities Exchange Act of 1934, or of any rule or regulation thereunder.

Unless a security is registered on a national securities exchange under the Securities Exchange Act or is exempt from such registration it is unlawful for a member of such exchange or any broker or dealer to effect any transaction in the security of the exchange.

The Securities Exchange Act of 1934 provides for the registration with the Commission of national securities associations and establishes standards for such associations. The Act contemplates that such associations will serve as a medium for the co-operative self-regulation of over-the-counter brokers and dealers.

The National Association of Securities Dealers Inc. (N.A.S.D.) is the only association registered under the Act (see table, p. 138).

The registration of brokers and dealers engaged in an interstate over-the-counter securities business also is an important phase of the regulatory plan of the Act. Not only must they conform their business practices to the standards prescribed in the law and the Commission's regulations thereunder for the protection of investors (as well as to the fair trade practice rules of their association); but, in addition, they may violate these regulations only at the risk of possible loss of registration with the Commission and the right to continue to conduct an inter-state

The functional organisation of the
SECURITIES AND EXCHANGE COMMISSION

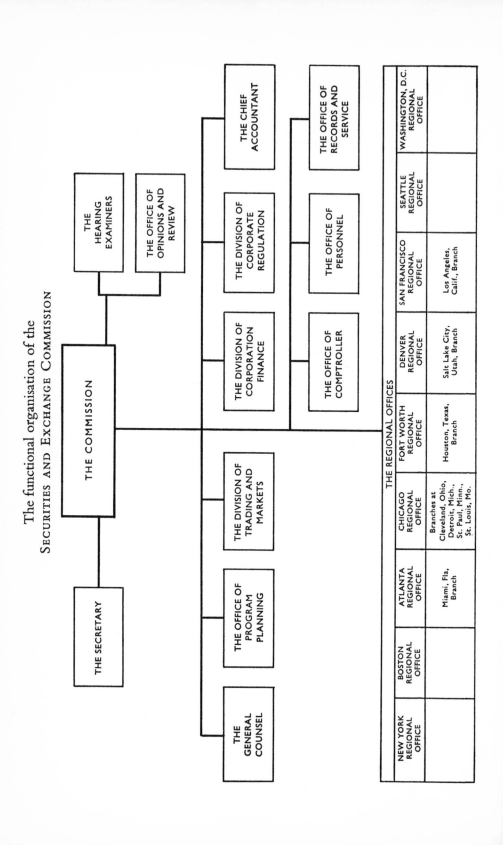

Regional Offices of the
SECURITIES AND EXCHANGE COMMISSION

Legend:
- ★ Headquarters Office
- ■ Regional Offices
- □ Branch Offices
- ● Registered Exchanges
- ○ Exempt Exchanges

Boston
New York
Philadelphia
WASHINGTON
Pittsburgh
Richmond
Cleveland
Wheeling
Detroit
Cincinnati
Atlanta
New Orleans
Chicago
St. Paul
St. Louis
Miami
Fort Worth
Houston
Denver
Colorado Springs
Salt Lake City
Spokane
Seattle
Los Angeles
San Francisco
ALASKA
HAWAII
Honolulu

Brokers and dealers registered under the Securities Exchange Act of 1934[1] — effective registrations as of 30 June 1964 classified by type of organisation and by location of principal office

Location of principal office	Number of registrants				Number of proprietors, partners, officers, etc.[2],[3]			
	Total	*Sole proprietorships*	*Partnerships*	*Corporations[4]*	*Total*	*Sole proprietorships*	*Partnerships*	*Corporations[4]*
Alabama . . .	33	9	2	22	114	9	5	100
Alaska . . .	4	4	0	0	4	4	0	0
Arizona . . .	29	6	3	20	118	6	8	104
Arkansas . . .	26	5	2	19	98	5	4	89
California . . .	419	145	79	195	1,799	145	570	1,084
Colorado . . .	78	22	6	50	286	22	22	242
Connecticut . .	44	11	11	22	197	11	51	135
Delaware . . .	19	4	6	9	83	4	28	51
District of Columbia .	97	20	12	65	433	20	56	357
Florida . . .	119	33	10	76	375	33	28	314
Georgia . . .	39	6	8	25	248	8	32	208
Hawaii . . .	36	10	3	23	166	10	8	148
Idaho . . .	16	6	0	10	50	6	0	44
Illinois . . .	187	29	52	106	915	29	264	622
Indiana . . .	59	22	4	33	200	22	8	170
Iowa . . .	39	9	5	25	165	9	14	142
Kansas . . .	31	9	5	17	133	9	15	109
Kentucky . . .	19	6	5	8	68	6	26	36
Louisiana . . .	46	19	9	18	136	19	43	74
Maine . . .	25	9	2	14	72	9	10	53
Maryland . . .	55	16	13	26	231	16	83	132
Massachusetts .	200	81	28	91	899	81	233	585
Michigan . . .	58	10	13	35	345	10	91	244
Minnesota . .	63	8	7	48	339	8	40	291
Mississippi . .	20	8	5	7	61	8	15	38
Missouri . . .	86	24	13	49	579	24	149	406
Montana . . .	13	6	1	6	32	6	2	24
Nebraska . . .	27	9	0	18	102	9	0	93
Nevada . . .	6	2	1	3	15	2	2	11
New Hampshire .	9	5	0	4	22	5	0	17
New Jersey . .	204	100	32	72	493	100	80	313
New Mexico . .	7	3	3	1	20	3	10	7
New York (excluding New York City) .	386	184	42	160	900	184	155	561
North Carolina . .	39	8	7	24	212	8	20	184
North Dakota . .	9	1	0	8	33	1	0	32
Ohio . . .	118	19	32	67	620	19	196	405
Oklahoma . . .	40	16	4	20	100	16	8	76
Oregon . . .	29	6	5	18	100	6	10	84
Pennsylvania . .	222	60	74	88	973	60	397	516
Rhode Island . .	22	3	7	12	73	3	21	49
South Carolina . .	21	4	2	15	73	4	4	65
South Dakota . .	4	2	0	2	9	2	0	7
Tennessee . .	44	9	4	31	231	9	18	204
Texas . . .	179	68	16	95	637	68	61	508
Utah . . .	40	13	6	21	117	13	14	90
Vermont . . .	4	3	0	1	6	3	0	3
Virginia . . .	49	13	12	24	210	13	72	125
Washington . .	84	42	2	40	296	42	4	250
West Virginia . .	11	5	3	3	27	5	7	15
Wisconsin . . .	50	7	2	41	246	7	27	212
Wyoming . . .	9	6	0	3	14	6	0	8
TOTAL (excluding New York City)	3,473	1,125	558	1,790	13,675	1,127	2,911	9,637
New York City . .	1,347	285	509	553	7,387	285	3,795	3,307
TOTAL . .	4,820	1,410	1,067	2,343	21,062	1,412	6,706	12,944

[1] Does not include fifty registrants whose principal offices are located in foreign countries or other territorial jurisdictions not listed.
[2] Includes directors, officers, trustees and all other persons occupying similar status or performing similar functions.
[3] Allocations made on the basis of location of principal offices of registrants, not actual location of persons. Information taken from latest reports filed prior to 30 June 1964.
[4] Includes all forms of organisations other than sole proprietorships and partnerships.

securities business, or of suspension or expulsion from the association and of the benefits of such membership. The broker–dealer registration requirement does not apply to firms engaged solely in a municipal-securities business.

As of 30 June 1964 a total of 2,467 issuers had 4,076 securities listed on registered securities exchanges, of which 2,879 were stocks and 1,197 bonds. Of these totals, 1,389 issuers had 1,611 stock issues and 1,115 bond issues listed and registered on the New York Stock Exchange. Thus, 56% of the issuers, 56% of the stock issues and 93% of the bond issues were listed on the New York Stock Exchange.

The market value on 31 December 1963 of stocks and bonds, both listed and unlisted, admitted to trading on one or more stock exchanges in the United States was approximately $561 billion.

New York is incontestably the foremost financial centre in the world, with an unrivalled money-market. When one speaks of Wall Street one thinks principally of the Stock Exchange which is to be found at the heart of the financial district. However, one often forgets that there are three stock exchanges in New York:

The New York Stock Exchange, situated in Wall Street, the oldest and most famous, founded in 1792;

The American Stock Exchange;

The National Stock Exchange (Natex), a new exchange opened in March 1962.

With its three exchanges, the New York stock-market is incontestably the most important in the world. The New York Stock Exchange in Wall Street surpasses all other exchanges in the world in the value of the stocks quoted.

In 1961, of a total of nearly 810,000 enterprises in business in the United States, only 1,150 have their shares quoted on the New York Stock Exchange: but these 1,150 firms give employment to more than 14 million workmen and employees — that is to say, about 20% of the total civil labour force of the country. The total assets of these firms exceed $270 milliard, that is to say about 30% of the total private capital invested in the economy. Their gross receipts are as high as $230 milliard. An analysis of these figures

These two tables show the importance of each Stock Exchange

Dollar volume and share volume of sales effected on securities exchanges in the calendar year 1963 and the six-month period ended 30 June 1964.

Twelve months ended 31 December 1963

(Amounts in thousands)

	Total dollar volume	Bonds		Stocks		Rights and warrants	
		Dollar volume	Principal amount	Dollar volume	Share volume	Dollar volume	Number of units
Registered exchanges	66,157,485	1,740,458	1,653,777	64,313,920	1,838,359	103,107	40,949
American	4,917,837	72,925	67,457	4,755,286	336,261	89,626	18,044
Boston	270,504	0	0	270,477	5,505	27	46
Chicago Board of Trade	0	0	0	0	0	0	0
Cincinnati	40,856	87	112	40,768	834	1	4
Detroit	334,893	0	0	334,883	8,775	10	38
Midwest	1,755,705	(1)	(1)	1,755,659	43,773	46	35
National	408	0	0	408	389	0	0
New York	56,564,379	1,667,283	1,586,041	54,886,501	1,350,885	10,595	20,923
Pacific Coast	1,542,511	68	67	1,539,647	51,293	2,796	1,844
Phila.–Balt.–Wash.	685,875	95	100	685,774	15,701	6	15
Pittsburgh	33,368	0	0	33,368	796	0	0
Salt Lake	4,766	0	0	4,766	13,802	0	0
San Francisco	256	0	0	256	4,855	0	0
Spokane	6,127	0	0	6,127	5,490	0	0
Exempted exchanges	21,055	9	10	20,080	1,208	66	282
Colorado Springs	84	0	0	84	415	5	0
Honolulu	20,207	0	10	20,132	771	66	282
Richmond	390	0	0	390	9	0	0
Wheeling	374	0	0	374	13	0	0

1 Less than 500.

Six months ended 30 June 1964

	Total dollar volume	Bonds		Stocks		Rights and warrants	
		Dollar volume	Principal amount	Dollar volume	Share volume	Dollar volume	Number of units
Registered exchanges	39,859,731	1,559,364	1,402,277	38,103,922	1,057,326	196,445	68,058
American	3,660,921	37,673	36,616	3,514,702	194,809	108,546	8,612
Boston	159,912	0	0	159,330	3,035	582	278
Chicago Board of Trade	0	0	0	0	0	0	0
Cincinnati	23,769	26	33	23,736	442	7	3
Detroit	251,524	0	0	251,423	6,141	101	49
Midwest	1,153,170	0	0	1,151,125	25,239	2,045	1,016
National	157	0	0	157	172	0	0
New York	33,223,562	1,520,900	1,364,804	31,627,600	778,094	75,062	54,183
Pacific Coast	927,472	86	86	919,754	27,206	7,632	2,764
Phila.–Balt.–Wash.	429,541	679	738	426,392	9,947	2,470	1,153
Pittsburgh	24,267	0	0	24,267	570	0	0
Salt Lake	1,589	0	0	1,589	4,298	0	0
San Francisco Mining	262	0	0	262	3,415	0	0
Spokane	3,585	0	0	3,585	3,958	0	0
Exempted exchanges	9,121	8	7	9,113	557	0	0
Colorado Springs	42	0	0	42	215	0	0
Honolulu	8,366	8	7	8,358	326	0	0
Richmond	528	0	0	528	13	0	0
Wheeling	185	0	0	185	3	0	0

NOTE.—Data on the value and volume of securities sales on the registered exchanges are reported in connection with fees paid under Section 31 of the Securities Exchange Act of 1934. Included are all securities sales, odd-lot as well as round-lot transactions, effected on exchanges except sales of bonds of the U.S. Government which are not subject to the fee. Comparable data are also supplied by the exempted exchanges. Reports of most exchanges for a given month cover transactions effected during the calendar month, but the reports may be of transactions cleared during the calendar month. Clearances generally occur on the fourth business day after that on which the trade was effected. Figures are rounded and will not necessarily add to the totals as shown.

reveals how considerable is the total wealth represented by the shares dealt in at the New York Stock Exchange.

In addition to the three official exchanges, there also exists in New York a free, unofficial market, called 'over the counter', although the many dealings on this market are directly between operators, and are usually carried out by telephone. Since this is not an organised market, no statistics are available on its turnover. The brokers who work in it usually represent important firms registered with other exchanges. Many shares are channelled into this market because they are not in demand on the official exchanges. This does not in any way mean that shares of doubtful value are in question.

The dominant situation of New York in all sectors of financial activity includes also the foreign-exchange market. Dealings in foreign exchanges play a very important role in New York and banks do important business in them. Some specialise in particular currencies, but all deal in sterling, Canadian dollars and Swiss francs, the leaders of this market.

Plans of reform for the banking system of the United States are at present being studied. In February 1962 the Comptroller of the Currency set up a committee (consisting of twenty-four bankers and legal experts), appointed principally to prepare a report on the national banks and their future. Addressed to the White House, this report defines the means to be employed to attain certain objectives which President Kennedy had himself defined in his own economic report of January 1962; these objectives, which aim at a revision of banking and financial legislation as a whole, are based on the proposals of another body, set up on private initiative: the Commission on Currency and Credit.

The White House has set up an inter-departmental working-party to examine the multiple problems posed by this project of reform and to study the changes to be made in the policy of the Federal Government, so as to give better guarantees of the soundness, efficiency and continuing growth of the financial and banking institutions of the private sector.

For his part, the Comptroller of the Currency has not been

behindhand and has instituted a detailed analysis of the obstacles offered by federal laws and regulations to the efficient functioning of the system and to the exploitation of opportunities still open to it, to meet the needs of an expanding economy. The outcome of these researches reflects the views of many qualified representatives of the banking sector and deserve to be studied with the closest attention by the inter-departmental working-party.

The Comptroller of the Currency had first of all asked those banks with which he is concerned to send him suggestions of a practical kind. About 1,500 national banks responded to this invitation. The committee was thus provided with a great quantity of information, which confirmed opinions already widely held: the federal laws and regulations contain all kinds of antiquated provisions which hamper the banks in their endeavours to serve both their clientele and the common good.

It is possible to class the different elements of present federal legislation dealing with banks and banking alone, under three main headings: the National Bank Act, the Federal Reserve Act and the legislation dealing with the Federal Deposit Insurance Corporation. Only the national banks are subject to all these laws and regulations and also to the judgments having the force of law to which they have given rise.

The national banks, which provided the necessary intelligence, were then particularly qualified to take a comprehensive and practical view of the problem. Their suggestions bear for the most part, as was to be expected, on the National Bank Act; this law is ninety-nine years old, and well-informed circles agree in considering a great many of its provisions outmoded.

The following are the most important of the recommendations made by the committee:

the proportion of the reserves which the Federal Reserve Board requires member-banks of the Federal Reserve System to retain should be fixed at between 8% and 12%;

the top limits on the interest allowed on fixed-period deposits and on savings deposits, which commercial banks have to observe, should be replaced by a more flexible regulation, which would take prevailing economic circumstances into better account;

the complementary regulation, dealing with the reserves to be retained against time deposits and savings deposits, should be cancelled (it stands at present at 5%);

the conditions to be fulfilled in the rediscounting of bills are completely out of date; they should be cancelled and Federal Reserve Banks should be authorised to make advances to member-banks at the normal rate of discount under any securities which appear to them to be adequate;

the restrictions enacted against loan transactions, investment business and the formation of trusts should be alleviated and simplified;

the regulation, control and surveillance of commercial banks should come within the competence of the Treasury, on the

Number and Salaries of Officers and Employees of Federal Reserve Banks, 31 December 1964

Federal Reserve Bank (including branches)	President Annual salary	Other officers No.	Other officers Annual salaries	Employees[1] No.	Employees[1] Annual salaries	Total No.	Total Annual salaries
	$		$		$		$
Boston . .	35,000	24	395,000	1,258	5,863,427	1,283	6,293,427
New York .	70,000	65	1,299,250	4,064	24,034,648	4,130	25,403,898
Philadelphia .	40,000	31	513,000	913	4,590,797	945	5,143,797
Cleveland . .	40,000	36	556,000	1,451	7,749,144	1,488	8,345,144
Richmond .	40,000	37	582,000	1,401	6,678,819	1,439	7,300,819
Atlanta . .	40,000	43	622,200	1,297	5,937,149	1,341	6,599,349
Chicago . .	55,000	43	704,750	2,794	13,728,381	2,838	14,488,131
St. Louis . .	35,000	35	556,500	1,127	5,239,171	1,163	5,830,671
Minneapolis .	40,000	25	363,250	633	2,992,281	659	3,395,531
Kansas City .	37,500	32	470,100	1,193	5,334,471	1,226	5,842,071
Dallas . . .	40,000	30	440,450	955	4,229,075	986	4,709,525
San Francisco .	40,000	42	613,000	1,927	9,540,320	1,970	10,193,320
TOTAL .	$512,500	443	$7,115,500	19,013	$95,917,683	19,468	$103,545,683

[1] Includes 813 part-time employees.

Total assets

The statement of condition of all Federal Reserve Banks combined, 31 December 1964, amounted to a total of (in thousands of dollars) .   62,868,178
The total gold certificate reserves   15,074,979
and the Federal Reserve Notes issued   35,342,215

Summary of United States Banks
Situation 30 June 1963
(compiled by *Polk's Bank Directory*, Nashville, Tennessee)

No.	States and territories	Total banks	Total branches	Deposits	Capital account	Total assets
				$	$	$
1	Alabama . .	241	106	2,446,318,846	248,699,483	2,738,582,382
2	Alaska . .	13	36	254,790,510	19,017,129	279,622,914
3	Arizona . .	14	230	1,688,003,124	132,937,722	1,878,989,175
4	Arkansas . .	242	62	1,596,925,959	159,443,697	1,764,219,960
5	California . .	146	2,101	30,704,301,679	2,226,975,637	34,182,594,332
6	Colorado . .	190	..	2,402,581,403	232,473,066	2,673,044,824
7	Connecticut .	136	330	5,903,233,137	579,438,505	6,648,777,127
8	Delaware . .	22	63	965,505,943	112,407,720	1,096,163,438
9	District of Columbia	13	67	1,832,027,535	146,048,203	2,011,595,778
10	Florida . .	368	..	5,753,188,821	566,828,924	6,442,642,934
11	Georgia . .	426	133	3,356,849,849	352,069,708	3,820,363,356
12	Hawaii . .	12	103	891,201,229	88,739,207	1,016,916,912
13	Idaho . .	28	105	713,648,289	61,417,495	790,660,685
14	Illinois . .	1,006	..	20,794,139,596	1,923,469,482	23,248,500,249
15	Indiana . .	444	360	5,405,485,703	503,034,259	6,018,453,194
16	Iowa . .	675	192	3,483,695,475	371,504,859	3,890,487,857
17	Kansas . .	596	..	2,818,486,068	294,471,389	3,132,322,689
18	Kentucky . .	349	181	2,582,063,493	276,905,073	2,892,408,998
19	Louisiana . .	199	202	3,231,894,358	311,807,881	3,579,141,461
20	Maine . .	78	160	1,248,378,542	140,125,545	1,410,193,089
21	Maryland . .	124	347	3,522,910,528	325,666,511	3,928,361,528
22	Massachusetts .	343	601	12,838,436,117	1,423,099,688	14,744,587,619
23	Michigan . .	367	697	10,777,233,475	866,522,278	11,874,847,868
24	Minnesota . .	701	6	5,248,657,173	484,519,482	5,858,358,904
25	Mississippi .	193	157	1,560,346,926	150,732,248	1,721,854,645
26	Missouri . .	632	..	6,784,160,584	684,898,574	7,578,517,765
27	Montana . .	125	..	901,620,637	78,507,841	995,726,535
28	Nebraska . .	427	..	1,884,588,218	201,266,313	2,132,383,956
29	Nevada . .	7	50	601,873,552	45,539,823	659,741,488
30	New Hampshire	109	3	1,177,064,643	136,175,905	1,345,870,628
31	New Jersey .	262	548	10,039,452,315	876,067,457	11,154,033,902
32	New Mexico .	61	64	827,954,999	75,718,760	911,182,374
33	New York. .	492	1,806	80,345,492,077	7,693,178,983	91,799,316,683
34	North Carolina .	160	618	3,187,763,685	349,300,849	3,684,279,349
35	North Dakota .	159	37	888,002,387	92,286,780	988,880,751
36	Ohio . .	558	764	12,771,092,296	1,232,722,216	14,324,085,016
37	Oklahoma . .	395	..	3,105,829,769	337,059,698	3,473,359,915
38	Oregon . .	51	230	2,337,538,874	196,104,055	2,583,045,972
39	Pennsylvania .	636	1,027	19,318,037,716	2,114,264,430	21,860,132,603
40	Puerto Rico .	9	102	604,365,605	80,213,847	731,408,468
41	Rhode Island .	18	133	1,644,205,869	155,388,163	1,849,580,587
42	South Carolina .	142	187	1,190,193,279	131,899,739	1,354,035,186
43	South Dakota .	173	71	859,892,103	85,560,392	954,862,365
44	Tennessee . .	295	255	3,945,582,316	370,879,704	4,383,403,846
45	Texas . .	1,081	..	14,473,660,438	1,551,565,533	16,297,770,937
46	Utah . .	50	88	1,117,377,690	95,675,302	1,244,146,031
47	Vermont . .	57	38	621,683,911	62,625,673	693,212,780
48	Virginia . .	283	384	3,797,196,206	372,597,847	4,262,520,144
49	Washington .	94	334	3,628,172,466	319,003,995	4,032,523,791
50	West Virginia .	182	..	1,477,472,372	180,856,246	1,684,981,443
51	Wisconsin. .	578	160	5,240,444,525	475,913,823	5,805,905,041
52	Wyoming . .	57	..	453,104,490	45,441,419	505,350,082
	Territories:					
	American Samoa	1	..	11,958,230	681,502	12,815,656
	Virgin Islands .	3	7	20,864,174	1,788,802	23,622,312
	Panama Canal Zone . .	n.a.	n.a.	n.a.	n.a.	n.a.
	Caroline Islands.	n.a.	n.a.	n.a.	n.a.	n.a.
	Guam, Mariana, Marshall, Midway and Wake Islands . .	..	10	..	..	..
	TOTAL .	14,023	13,155	$315,276,949,204	$30,041,538,862	$354,970,387,524

n.a. = not available

Comparative development since 30 June 1945

Period	Total banks	Total branches	Deposits	Capital account	Total assets
30 June 1945	14,725	3,886	152,319,028,000	10,455,584,000	163,313,733,000
30 June 1950	14,712	4,911	166,645,315,888	14,326,353,400	182,256,366,463
30 June 1955	14,369	6,898	211,707,183,781	18,236,773,297	233,240,543,759
30 June 1960	14,039	10,282	253,210,597,776	25,374,066,966	285,043,696,459
30 June 1962	13,965	12,104	290,018,539,038	28,332,205,739	326,582,217,931
30 June 1963	14,023	13,155	315,276,949,204	30,041,538,862	354,970,387,524

The twelve Federal Reserve Banks are not included in the above table; nor are the other state financial and banking institutions.

federal level. The Federal Reserve Board should be relieved of its responsibilities in this field, so that all its energies could be directed to the conduct of monetary policy;

the national banks should be authorised, within certain limits, to open branches even though the individual states had laws forbidding the opening of branches by the chartered banks of these states.

The recommendations in the report of the committee on the possibility of opening branch banks are among the most interesting. This question has for many years given rise to many controversies among bankers, Congressmen and the departments responsible for banking regulations. At the present moment the federal laws lay down that a national bank must conform with the laws of the state in which it conducts business. This means that in California a national bank may open branches wherever it likes within this state. On the other hand, an Illinois bank cannot even open a branch on the other side of the street. While banks can freely open such branches abroad, they are categorically forbidden to open branches in the United States beyond the borders of the state in which they conduct business.

In conclusion, the committee suggests modifying existing federal legislation in such a way that all national banks should be authorised to open branches within the borders of the state in which their principal establishment is situated, in addition to any rights which the laws of their state give them in the matter of opening branches. Should the recommendations of the committee be adopted, a first and important step would have been taken along the road which must eventually lead to uniform legislation on bank branches for all the United States. The consequences would be very sensible in Illinois, in Florida, in Texas and in the other states where the establishment of branch banks is today forbidden.

On 31 December 1964 the total number of banks in the United States was 14,281.

Total number of banks insured by the Federal Deposit
    Insurance Corporation, Washington
National Banks 4,773
State chartered banks, members of Federal Reserve
    System 1,451
State chartered banks, not members of the Federal Reserve System, but insured by the F.D.I.C. . 7,269
Mutual Savings Banks insured 327
                                    —————— 13,820
Total number of banks not insured by the F.D.I.C.
Non-insured banks of deposit 235
Non-deposit Trust Companies, not eligible for insurance 47
Non-insured Mutual Savings Banks 179
                                    —————— 461
        Total 14,281

About 800,000 people are employed in banks in the United States.

These are the nine richest states in the United States (see summary, p. 145):

	Bank deposits in milliards of dollars
New York	80·3
California	30·7
Illinois	20·8
Pennsylvania	19·3
Texas	14·5
Massachusetts . . .	12·8
Ohio	12·7
Michigan	10·8
New Jersey	10·0

United States banks had, on 31 December 1964, a total of 180 branches in forty-five foreign countries and overseas areas of the

United States; five national banks were operating 139 of these branches and six state banks were operating forty-one. The number and location of these foreign bank branches were as shown in the table:

Latin America .	.	.	77	*England* .	.	. .	17
Argentina	.	.	16				
Bahamas .	.	.	2	*Africa*	.	. .	3
Brazil	.	.	15	Liberia	.	.	1
Chile	.	.	2	Nigeria .	.	.	2
Colombia	.	.	5				
Dominican Republic.			3	*Near East*		. .	5
Ecuador .	.	.	2	Dubai	.	.	1
El Salvador	.	.	1	Lebanon .	.	.	3
Guatemala	.	.	2	Saudi Arabia	.	.	1
Jamaica .	.	.	1				
Mexico .	.	.	5	*Far East* .	.	. .	40
Nicaragua	.	.	1	Hong Kong	.	.	6
Panama .	.	.	10	India	.	.	5
Paraguay.	.	.	2	Japan	.	.	12
Peru	.	.	2	Malaysia .	.	.	7
Trinidad .	.	.	1	Okinawa	.	.	1
Uruguay.	.	.	2	Pakistan .	.	.	2
Venezuela	.	.	4	Philippines	.	.	5
Virgin Islands (British)			1	Thailand .	.	.	2
Continental Europe	.	.	15	*United States Overseas Areas*			
Belgium .	.	.	2	*and Trust Territories*		.	23
France	.	.	4	Canal Zone	.	.	2
Germany	.	.	3	Guam	.	.	1
Greece .	.	.	1	Puerto Rico	.	.	15
Italy	.	.	1	Truk Islands	.	.	1
Netherlands	.	.	3	Virgin Islands .		.	4
Switzerland	.	.	1	TOTAL	.	. .	180

The most active American banks with foreign branches are: First National City Bank, New York; The Chase Manhattan Bank, New York; the Morgan Guaranty Trust Company of New York; the Bank of America, San Francisco; the First National Bank of Boston; the Continental Illinois National Bank and Trust Company of Chicago.

New York is the last place in the world for a stranger to open a bank. It is already heavily banked — by institutions that have been on the scene a long time and know their way around. Competition is keen. People are busy. Despite high costs and

	Name	Head Office	Country
1	Midland Bank Ltd.	London	England
2	Barclays Bank D.C.O. . . .	London	England
3	Bank of London & South America Ltd.	London	England
4	The Chartered Bank	London	England
5	The Standard Bank Ltd. . . .	London	England
6	The Hongkong & Shanghai Banking Corporation	Hong Kong	Hong Kong
7	Thos. Cook & Son (Bankers) Ltd. .	London	England
8	Société Générale	Paris	France
9	The Royal Bank of Canada . .	Montreal	Canada
10	Canadian Imperial Bank of Commerce	Toronto	Canada
11	Bank of Montreal	Montreal	Canada
12	The Toronto-Dominion Bank . .	Toronto	Canada
13	The Bank of Nova Scotia . . .	Halifax, N.S.	Canada
14	The Fuji Bank Ltd.	Tokyo	Japan
15	The Mitsubishi Bank Ltd. . . .	Tokyo	Japan
16	The Sumitomo Bank Ltd. . . .	Osaka	Japan
17	The Mitsui Bank Ltd. . . .	Tokyo	Japan
18	The Nippon Kangyo Bank Ltd. .	Tokyo	Japan
19	Dai-Ichi Bank Ltd.	Tokyo	Japan
20	The Bank of Tokyo Ltd. . . .	Tokyo	Japan
21	The Tokai Bank Ltd. . . .	Nagoya	Japan
22	The Sanwa Bank Ltd. . . .	Osaka	Japan
23	The Bank of Kobe Ltd. . . .	Kobe	Japan
24	Swiss Bank Corporation . . .	Basle	Switzerland
25	Swiss Credit Bank	Zürich	Switzerland
26	Banca Nazionale del Lavoro . .	Rome	Italy
27	Banco di Napoli	Naples	Italy
28	Algemene Bank Nederland . .	Amsterdam	Netherlands
29	Israel Discount Bank	Tel Aviv	Israel
30	Bank Leumi Le-Israel . . .	Tel-Aviv	Israel
31	Banco Popular de Puerto Rico .	San Juan	Puerto Rico
32	Banco de Ponce	Ponce	Puerto Rico
33	Banco Nacional de Mexico . .	Mexico D.F.	Mexico
34	Banco da Lavoura de Minas Gerais .	Bello Horizonte	Brazil
35	Philippine National Bank . . .	Manila	Philippines
36	National Bank of Pakistan . . .	Karachi	Pakistan
37	Bank of China	Taipeh	Formosa
38	Intra Bank	Beirut	Lebanon

extreme competition, foreign banks are lured to New York because that is where the money is. Beside that, certain significant facts have decided foreign banks to open branches in the city of sky-scrapers, such as:

the fact that New York is the commercial gateway to America, the hub of the import–export business;

more corporations transacting international business have offices, if not headquarters, in New York than in any other city;

New York is the mainspring of the United States capital-market, the biggest in the world;

New York has more banks with extensive interests and con-tacts in foreign countries than any other American city.

In short, New York is where the business is. That is why it is and has been heavily banked and why, nevertheless, foreign banks have opened branches in New York at a brisk rate since 1961. So powerful is the lure of New York that the Midland Bank Ltd., for example, one of Britain's major clearing banks, has de-cided to breach its traditional policy of no banking office abroad.

The New York legislature in 1961 amended the law to allow foreign bank branches. The reason: some of the multi-billion dollar giants, particularly the First National City Bank, New York, had found that they could not get branch licences in certain foreign countries, on the grounds of lack of reciprocity in New York.

Prior to 1961, foreign banks were allowed to maintain agencies in New York — and they still are. An agency is a limited-service banking office. It may carry only those customer balances that arise from international transactions, such as remittances by American importers, or the sale of American securities for an in-vestor abroad. Checking accounts and deposits are prohibited. In as much as the branches, unlike the agencies, are free to accept deposits, it seems likely that the disparity between the two groups will continue to be narrowed.

As at 30 June 1965 there were fifteen foreign banks, operating twenty branches, and twenty-three foreign banks' agencies, mak-ing a total of thirty-eight. The table on p. 149 gives their names.

12. Banks in Canada

Canada has an area of 9,932,783 sq. kilometres and a population of only 20,000,000; it is still a young country, though doubtless a great economic future awaits it.

At present Canada has two great financial centres, both of comparatively recent date: Montreal (about 2,200,000 inhabitants, if the surrounding urban districts are counted) and Toronto (about 2,000,000 inhabitants with the surrounding districts). The financial history of these two centres does indeed go back to the colonial period, that is to say, the period before 1867, but it is only in the course of the twentieth century that financial institutions have appeared, such as banks and stock markets. The financial structure is still far from meeting the needs of the nation; nevertheless, the two financial centres are maintaining the same rhythm of development as the country as a whole.

Of course, one can hardly talk of financial centres without mentioning the political capital of the country: Ottawa, 500,000 inhabitants, seat of the Government and of the central bank of issue, the Bank of Canada. Ottawa, Montreal and Toronto form, as it were, the financial foundation of the country. Moreover, in the two latter towns the Bank of Canada maintains its principal branches, to which are appointed special representatives of its securities and foreign-exchange departments; such representatives are not appointed to the other branches set up in the principal towns of Canada.

Up till 1935, when the Bank of Canada was founded, the classic tasks of a bank of issue were undertaken by the Ministry of Finance and the private commercial banks, called chartered banks, which issued their own notes, the state reserving to itself only the issue of the small denominations of two dollars or less and of metallic currency.

It was, then, very late in her history that Canada founded a central bank of issue. To be precise, the Bank of Canada was founded on 11 March 1935. Its entire capital of $5 million (Canadian) is held by the Minister of Finance. The Bank is administered by a Board of Directors consisting of a Governor, a Deputy-Governor and twelve administrators. The Governor and Deputy-Governor are appointed for periods of seven years by the administrators with the approval of the Governor-General in council; the administrators are appointed by the Ministry of Finance with the approval of the Governor-General in council, for periods of three years each. The Deputy Minister of Finance is a member of the Board of Directors and a member of the Executive Committee, but has no vote.

The head office of the bank is in Ottawa. There are agencies in Calgary, Halifax, Montreal, Ottawa, Regina, St. John (New Brunswick), Toronto, Vancouver and Winnipeg. The agencies' principal business is to act as financial agents of the Government of Canada and to deal with the issue and recall of currency.

When the Bank of Canada began operations it undertook to honour all Canadian notes then current. These have been replaced in public circulation by bank-notes; these notes are legal tender. The bank has sole right of issue.

An interesting initiative of the Bank of Canada has been the foundation of the Industrial Development Bank, set up by a federal law which began operations on 1 November 1944. The functions of the bank are defined in the preamble to the Act: 'To favour the economic prosperity of Canada, increasing the efficacy of monetary policy by assuring a supply of credit for industrial enterprises, which may reasonably be expected to succeed if a high level of national revenue and employment are maintained, by supplementing the activity of other lenders and granting industry capital aid adapted to the problems involved in financing small enterprises.'

The President of the Industrial Development Bank is the Governor of the Bank of Canada, and its administrators are those of the Bank of Canada, and the Deputy Minister of Commerce. On 30 September 1965 the bank had thirty regional and branch offices throughout Canada. The capital is $50 million (Canadian) — $38 million subscribed and paid up on 30 September 1965 — and the bank may also mobilise funds by the issue of debentures. The acceptance of deposits is expressly forbidden.

When the Canadian dollar was adopted as the national currency in 1858, this was not because of sympathy with the American dollar but because the decimal system was familiar through the widespread use of the American dollar and also of Mexican, Spanish and Portuguese currencies. The adoption of the unfamiliar pound sterling would have caused confusion.

In contrast to the United States, Canada possesses a highly centralised banking system. The commercial banking system consists of eight federal charter banks, subject to the bank law. Five of them have agencies scattered across Canada; two carry on their business almost entirely within the Province of Quebec and other French-language districts, and the eighth has branches in the three principal towns of the country.

In addition to the eight chartered banks, which have a near monopoly of the banking business of the country, there are two other banks of fair importance: the National Trust Company in Toronto, founded in 1898, with thirteen agencies and $130 million in deposits; and the Montreal City and District Savings Bank in Montreal, founded in 1846, with forty-seven agencies in Montreal, five in other towns and $250 million in deposits.

On 31 December 1964 the eight chartered banks had 5,784 branches and agencies, of which 5,577 were in Canada and 207 in other countries. There was then one branch bank to 3,300 inhabitants, as against one to 4,000 in England and one to 7,300 in the United States.

The following table lists the eight chartered banks in order of the amount of their assets as on 3 December 1964 (in thousands of Canadian dollars).

All Canadian banks are members of the Canadian Bankers Association, whose headquarters is in Toronto. This professional liaison organisation encourages co-operation between members and also acts as a court of arbitration, settling differences which may arise between members and fixing uniform rates of commission. Banking practice in Canada is modelled much more closely on the British system than on the American — perhaps because most of the first Canadian bankers were of Scottish extraction.

Name	Head Office	Founded	Total assets 31 December 1964 in $1,000 Canadian	Number of branches	
				Canada	Abroad
1 The Royal Bank of Canada . .	Montreal	1869	5,998,896	1,047	102
2 Canadian Imperial Bank of Commerce	Toronto	1867	5,664,755	1,304	32
3 Bank of Montreal .	Montreal	1817	4,857,407	942	12
4 The Bank of Nova Scotia . . .	Halifax	1832	3,049,475	657	57
5 The Toronto-Dominion Bank . .	Toronto	1855	2,689,945	644	3
6 Banque Canadienne Nationale . .	Montreal	1874	961,252	613	1
7 The Provincial Bank of Canada . .	Montreal	1861	512,248	365	..
8 The Mercantile Bank of Canada . .	Montreal	1853	137,954	5	..
		TOTAL	23,871,932	5,577	207

In the course of the first quarter of the nineteenth century in the period following the establishment of the first banks in Canada, banking business has developed according to the varying demands of the economy. Rapid progress is still being made. The upsurge of the Canadian economy has been marked by two main characteristics: successive periods of rapid expansion in colonisation and continuing dependence of the export market on the exploitation of natural resources (grain, forests, minerals, etc.). As a result Canadian banks have had to expand constantly into freshly settled territories and to devise methods of financing new industries and products.

From the beginning the system had a strongly marked international bias. Great importance was attached to the financing of foreign trade, to foreign-exchange transactions and to co-operation with banks in other countries. In addition, as regional isolation gradually disappeared and the economy became integrated, Canadian banks, originally local businesses, began to form a national network — partly by means of amalgamations, of which there was a great number in the first quarter of the present century.

Canadian banks play a prominent role in international money-markets, especially in London and New York, where most of them have very important branches. The following foreign banks are represented in Canada:

Italy: Banca Nazionale del Lavoro (Montreal)
Switzerland: Crédit Suisse (Canada) Ltd. (Montreal)
    Banque pour le Commerce Suisse-Israëlien (Toronto: head office in Geneva)
Japan: The Bank of Tokyo Ltd. (Toronto).

Montreal has two stock exchanges: the Montreal Stock Exchange, 80 members, which is the oldest, and the Canadian Stock Exchange, 100 members. In practice the two exchanges operate as one except that mining shares are dealt with principally on the Canadian Stock Exchange. Toronto has only one exchange, the Toronto Stock Exchange, 113 members, but the volume of transactions exceeds that of the two Montreal exchanges. Canadian exchanges are not subject to an official state control. Only the Securities Exchange Commissions of the Provinces of Quebec and of Ontario function as control organisations. Stock-exchange members enjoy great liberty in the formulation and enforcement of their regulations.

If Canada were not in the immediate neighbourhood of Wall Street in New York, the two great business centres of Montreal and Toronto certainly would have become of much greater importance in the world of international finance. In view of the immense potential of Canada, it would be natural to see foreign capital flowing towards Montreal and Toronto, but consolation is found in thinking of the brilliant future which awaits Canada, predestined to become a great economic power. Indeed, Canada has long been one of the great trading nations of the world and in recent years has moved into fourth place in the value of its foreign trade, after the United States, Great Britain and Federal Germany.

13. BANKS IN JAPAN

Three important dates punctuate the history of Japan:

1868. Imperial restoration. This feudal and xenophobic state, practically unknown and totally isolated, suddenly becomes an integral part of the Asiatic world.

1895. Japan, victor over China, completes her transformation from feudal state to modern state.

1945. Japan is conquered by the Allies. The unconditional surrender is signed on 2 September 1945; Japan is compelled to reform herself and to follow a new line of development.

Today Japan with its 98 million inhabitants comes fifth in order of population, after China (700 million), India (480 million), U.S.S.R. (225 million) and the U.S.A. (195 million). Its capital, Tokyo, is the largest city in the world, with 9,700,000 inhabitants. Japan has five other towns of more than a million inhabitants: Osaka (2,700,000), Nagoya (1,500,000), Kyoto (1,300,000), Yokohama (1,200,000) and Kobe (1,100,000).

Japan is the most important country in the Far East, both in respect of population and of trade: it has achieved a very high stage of industrial civilisation. Its railways are models of their kind and it is the largest shipbuilding country in the world. For ten years the rate of industrial growth has been the fastest in the world, against a background of remarkable monetary stability, ensuring a continuous amelioration in the standard of living of the common people. Highly developed agricultural techniques ensure an increasing productivity. Success has been due to several factors: a considerable reserve of trained manpower, and of organised work-forces: the technical ability of the ambitious and dynamic men at the head of industrial and commercial enterprises: faultless financial direction and firm discipline imposed on the banks and industry by the very powerful authority of the Bank of Japan (bank of issue).

Japan is a country of contrasts, where small farmers and modest traders and contractors mingle with powerful trusts, the embodiment of modern capitalism with all that it means in terms of boldness and calculating resolution. More than ever the trusts are regarded by the Japanese public as the symbol both of Japanese power and Japanese tradition.

The three best-known and most powerful trusts are the Mitsui, Mitsubishi and the Sumitomo, called the *Zaibatsu*. They are three family trusts, having very different origins, using very different methods, but whose power is more or less equal; they occupy dominant positions in the Japanese economy, emerging like islands in an ocean of small and middling companies. Other less important family trusts exist in Japan, such as Asano, Asashi, Ayukawa, Hattori, Hitachi, Matsushita, Nomura, Okura, Yasuda, Yasvah and Yawata; hundreds of companies are grouped in these trusts.

The *Zaibatsu* are based on a parent partnership firm, the trust being organised in divisions, each pursuing its own specialised business, incorporated as separate limited companies (banks, assurance firms, shipping, manufacturing or trading firms) but all subject, in their general policy, to the parent firm. The *Zaibatsu* have their own banks, which figure among the most important

Name	Head Office	Deposits
1 Fuji Bank Ltd.	Tokyo	3,895,304,659
2 Mitsubishi Bank Ltd.	Tokyo	3,752,897,252
3 Sanwa Bank Ltd.	Osaka	3,683,729,575
4 Sumitomo Bank Ltd.	Osaka	3,639,720,261
5 Industrial Bank of Japan Ltd.	Tokyo	2,922,268,060
6 Tokai Bank Ltd.	Nagoya	2,899,062,613
7 Dai-Ichi Bank Ltd.	Tokyo	2,545,184,050
8 Mitsui Bank Ltd.	Tokyo	2,467,584,995
9 Nippon Kangyo Bank Ltd.	Tokyo	2,333,191,000
10 Long-Term Credit Bank of Japan	Tokyo	2,084,754,761
11 Kyowa Bank Ltd.	Tokyo	1,650,096,905
12 Mitsubishi Trust & Banking Corporation	Tokyo	1,586,464,640
13 Sumitomo Trust & Banking Company Ltd.	Osaka	1,560,050,634
14 Daiwa Bank Ltd.	Osaka	1,557,483,697
15 The Bank of Tokyo Ltd.	Tokyo	1,533,200,357
16 Mitsui Trust & Banking Company Ltd.	Tokyo	1,491,898,616
17 Bank of Kobe Ltd.	Kobe	1,322,618,714
18 Saitama Bank Ltd.	Urawa	1,122,649,125
19 Yasuda Trust & Banking Company Ltd.	Tokyo	1,113,719,669
20 Hokkaido Takushoku Bank Ltd.	Sapparo	973,545,764

in the world, such as the Mitsubishi Bank, which is classed as twenty-first among the great world banks, with deposits of $3,753 million on 31 December 1964 and 160 branches in Japan and abroad; the Sumitomo Bank, twenty-third, with deposits of $3,640 million and 140 branches; the Mitsui Bank, forty-third, with deposits of $2,468 million and 110 branches.

The preceding table will give a clearer idea of the importance of these three banks among the twenty largest Japanese banks (31 December 1964 (in U.S. dollars)).

In each of the principal towns of Japan there is a Bank Association and all the regional Associations are united in the National Union of Bank Associations in Tokyo, which acts as a central liaison agency linking together all Japanese banks.

The following foreign banks are established in Japan:

Name	Head office of the foreign banks	Localities where the agencies are established
1 Bank of America N.T. and S.A.	San Francisco	Tokyo, Osaka, Kobe and Yokohama
2 The American Express Company Inc.	New York	Tokyo
3 The Chase Manhattan Bank	New York	Tokyo and Osaka
4 First National City Bank	New York	Tokyo, Osaka, Kobe and Yokohama
5 Continental Illinois National Bank & Trust Company of Chicago	Chicago	Tokyo and Osaka
6 Morgan Guaranty Trust Company	New York	Tokyo, representative office
7 Wells Fargo Bank	San Francisco	Tokyo, representative office
8 The Chartered Bank	London	Tokyo, Osaka, Kobe and Yokohama
9 The Hongkong & Shanghai Banking Corporation	Hong Kong	Tokyo, Osaka, Kobe and Yokohama
10 Mercantile Bank Ltd.	London	Tokyo and Osaka
11 Banque de l'Indochine	Paris	Tokyo
12 Deutsche Bank	Frankfurt/Main	Tokyo, representative office
13 Commerzbank	Düsseldorf	Tokyo, representative office
14 Algemene Bank Nederland	Amsterdam	Tokyo, Osaka, Kobe
15 Bank of India	Bombay	Tokyo and Osaka
16 Bank of Korea	Seoul	Tokyo and Osaka
17 Bank of China	Peking	Tokyo and Osaka
18 Bangkok Bank	Bangkok	Tokyo

The spectacular resurgence of post-war Japan on the economic horizon has even eclipsed the progress, staggering though it be, of Germany. These successes were made possible by the banks, which put their powerful resources at the disposition of the respective national economies. By granting important credits the World Bank in Washington contributed towards the renaissance of Japan. On 30 June 1965 these credits amounted to a total of $661 million in thirty-one separate loans.

Japan at present possesses nine stock exchanges, situated in the following towns, listed in order of importance: Tokyo, Osaka, Nagoya, Kyoto, Kobe, Hiroshima, Fukuoka, Niigata and Sapporo. That of Tokyo, founded in 1878, is an ultra-modern stock exchange and by far the most important. Two sessions are held each day: the first from 8.50 a.m. to 11 a.m. and the second from 12.50 p.m. to 3 p.m.

It is the investment-houses which are most active on the stock exchanges. They form an impressive organisation, both because of the number of their collaborators and employees, their resplendent and impressive buildings, as well as the number and ability of their correspondents and representatives in the smallest cities of Japan.

The four principal Japanese investment-houses are:

Nomura Securities Company
Yamaichi Securities Company
Daiwa Securities Company
Nikko Securities Company.

The Nomura Securities Company alone handles 25% to 30% of all transactions on Japanese stock exchanges.

On the Tokyo Stock Exchange alone it is not uncommon for the clerks to deal with more than 10 million shares in one day. This stock exchange is a free association, under a Board of Governors composed of a President, two Vice-Presidents and seventeen members. The President is elected by the Board, though the election has to be approved by the Minister of Finance. The stock exchange has 100 full members (stockbrokers) and, in addition, there are *saitoris* members. The difference between the two groups is that the full members can operate on their own behalf or on the behalf of clients while *saitoris* members can only operate on behalf of full members.

One of the most powerful pillars of the Japanese banking system, the nerve centre of Tokyo finance, is the Bank of Japan (bank of issue; founded in 1882). Indeed, the Bank of Japan crowns the banking pyramid, a true bankers' bank. Its head office is in Tokyo, and thanks to its network of fourteen important branches distributed across Japanese territory the bank is able to keep its finger on the economic and monetary pulse and to frame its policies accordingly. Although the Bank of Japan is to be considered a state bank, it retains, nevertheless, a certain measure of independence. The Japanese Government holds 55% of the capital of the bank, and this majority holding enables it to give directives to the bank, which in turn and in concert with the Ministry of Finance can give instructions to other Japanese banks.

The Governor of the Bank of Japan is appointed by the Minister of Finance. The principal function of the bank is to act as financial counsellor to the Government, to collaborate in devising a monetary policy and to carry it out. This policy is determined by a Council of seven members, the Governor of the bank, a representative of the Ministry of Finance, a representative of the Agency for Economic Planning and four representatives of private business and financial interests. The preponderant influence of the Bank of Japan is reinforced by the fact that the bank acts as Agent of the Treasury in control of foreign exchange and is, in addition, responsible for supervising the whole Japanese banking system.

However the power to authorise the establishment of new banks as well as effective control of all Japanese banks is vested in the Ministry of Finance. It is also this Ministry which determines the limit for currency in circulation. The Bank of Japan is not content merely to be simultaneously a bank of issue and a central bank — both the bank of the Treasury and also of all credit establishments — it also dominates the whole credit system, effectively controlling the distribution of credit.

The mixed bank is the standard Japanese type; commercial

banks are at complete liberty to make both middle- and long-term investment-loans — even though their resources derive largely from deposits at call.

By the regulations dealing with exchange business, Japanese banks divide into two groups:

Class A: banks authorised to carry out all bank and stock-exchange transactions with foreign countries. They number 12: Fuji Bank, Mitsubishi Bank, Sanwa Bank, Sumitomo Bank, Industrial Bank of Japan, Tokai Bank, Mitsui Bank, Dai-Ichi Bank, Nippon Kangyo Bank, Daiwa Bank, Bank of Kobe and Bank of Tokyo.

Class B: all other banks. These are authorised only to buy and sell foreign currencies in the home market on behalf of their clients. They are permitted to maintain an internal dollar account or to deposit their funds with the Bank of Japan; they have however no right to have foreign correspondents or to deal directly with foreign countries.

The Bank of Tokyo (successor to the Yokohama Specie Bank) deserves special mention. It specialises in financing foreign-trade operations and possesses a vast network of branches abroad. This bank, which has its head office in Tokyo, maintains:

25 branches in Japan
18 branches abroad, including one in Paris (116, rue du Faubourg Saint-Honoré)
20 agencies in various countries
2 affiliated banks: Bank of Tokyo of California, head office in San Francisco (U.S.A.) and agencies in Los Angeles and Gardena; Bank of Tokyo Trust Company, head office in New York
1 associate bank: International Bank of Iran and Japan, head office in Tehran with an agency *Bazar*.

The Japanese economy is at present evolving with such rapidity that any attempt to determine its permanent characteristics is quite illusory. If this rhythm of development continues, while the Asian continent undergoes continual metamorphosis, where will the Japanese economy be in ten or fifteen years from now? Doubtless Japan will be the third industrial power in the world, coming behind only the U.S.A. and the U.S.S.R.

14. BANKS IN THE STATES OF THE COMMUNIST BLOC

The Communist bloc is composed of the following states:

Country	Capital	Population (millions)	Currency	Bank of issue
1 Albania . .	Tirana	1·7	Lek	State Bank of Albania
2 Bulgaria . .	Sofia	8·0	Lev	National Bank of Bulgaria
3 China . .	Peking	700·0	Yuan	State Bank of the People's Republic of China
4 Czecho-Slovakia	Prague	15·0	Koruna CS	State Bank of Czecho-Slovakia
5 East Germany .	Berlin-East	17·3	East Mark	Deutsche Notenbank
6 Hungary . .	Budapest	10·0	Forint	National Bank of Hungary
7 Korea (North) .	Pyongyang	10·0	Won	Central Bank of Korea
8 Mongolia . .	Ulan Bator	1·0	Tugrik	State Bank of the Mongolian People's Republic
9 Poland . .	Warsaw	32·0	Zloty	National Bank of Poland
10 Rumania . .	Bucharest	20·0	Leu	State Bank of the Rumanian People's Republic
11 U.S.S.R. . .	Moscow	225·0	Rouble	State Bank of the U.S.S.R.
12 Vietnam (North)	Hanoi	18·0	Döng	State Bank of the Democratic Republic of Vietnam

TOTAL 1,058·0 million, or about 33% of world population

In the following pages, we give a brief sketch of the banking system at present in operation in the U.S.S.R. and in the other states of the communist bloc. Balance-sheets for the various categories of bank are not published. It is therefore impossible to determine the relative importance of each institution.

(a) Banks in the U.S.S.R.

The U.S.S.R. covers about 20% of the surface of the globe (22·3 million sq. kilometres) and its influence extends over nearly a third of the world population. The U.S.S.R. is a country of contrasts, and difficult to describe. It is a vast territory which is not entirely Europe, nor is it entirely Asia. To be sure, one sees many Asiatics in the streets of a town like Moscow; for them, Moscow plays to some extent the role of a Communist Mecca, but, all things considered, the manners and customs of the Russians are closer to those of Europe than to those of China or India.

The U.S.S.R. comprises fifteen Federal Republics (Russia, Armenia, Azerbaidjan, Belorussia, Estonia, Georgia, Kazakhstan, Kirghizia, Latvia, Lithuania, Moldavia, Tadjikistan, Ukraine, Uzbekistan, Turkmenistan) which enjoy a certain measure of autonomy. The territory is inhabited by more than a hundred different nationalities, totalling about 225 million people.

Its currency, the rouble, is the money of account of all these socialist states, who fall into line with its foreign and economic policy. In addition, the U.S.S.R. is possibly the leading producer of gold in the world. Every single country from the Baltic and the Black Sea to the Sea of Okhotsk and the Sea of Japan is more or less directly subject to the same economic plans and the same directives. The instruments which put these plans into operation are the public banks of the U.S.S.R. and the public banks of the satellite countries.

The great banks of the Western World may possess a powerful and highly developed organisation, with a vast international field of action, but the financial bodies established by the Government of the U.S.S.R. can also display impressive banking institutions with a comparable field of action.

Since 1917 the U.S.S.R. has lived under a régime with a

precisely formulated economic doctrine: planning. This means that all economic achievements, tempo of production and expansion in various branches of industry, and correlation between them, are no longer the result of the blind and automatic interplay between private interests, but are the outcome of a deliberate policy determined by a single central authority. The Plan has no means of foreseeing the future but seeks to establish by active intervention the relationships and interconnections which it deems imperative to achieve in the interest of the country.

In order to put the Plan into effect, the Soviet Government passed a series of measures, with the object of ensuring a rational distribution of productive forces, the regulation of industrial and agricultural productivity, and a distribution of the products thus obtained between the various branches of the national economy. By virtue of the co-ordination of effort between the various branches of the economy, such a closely linked interrelationship is set up between them that the various elements of the national economy fuse together in a single harmoniously developing whole, an elastic spiral, charged with considerable potential energy, whose transformation into kinetic energy is manifested by rhythms of expansion hitherto unknown to man in the history of the development of productive power.

Planning has allowed the U.S.S.R. to achieve the second place among the great economic powers of the world. The Soviet banking system inevitably plays an important part in regulating this planned economic development since the flow of products between economic units is accompanied by a flow in the opposite direction of an equivalent expressed in terms of money. The object of the Soviet budget is above all to obtain the maximum output of resources and to redistribute, by means of the banking system, these resources between the various branches of the national economy.

The State Bank of the Union of Soviet Socialist Republics, founded by the decree of 12 October 1921, with capital provided by the state by means of an allocation, has the exclusive monopoly of issuing notes. It is responsible for providing, through the agency of its 6,008 branches in the principal districts of the

Union, the credits necessary to the development of industry and agriculture. The State Bank also carries out all banking operations and all Treasury business entrusted to it by the Ministry of Finance. In addition, the Ministry directs the general policy of the bank, ratifies decisions on the rates of interest and commission, sanctions the plan of operations for the year to come and the report on the past year. The State Bank is one of the most important control levers of the Soviet economy. It controls the total of currency available — the deposits of productive undertakings, of organisations and of private individuals.

The Soviet banking system is organised in accordance with a decree of the Central Executive Committee, dated 30 January 1930, and coming into operation on the following 1 April. At present the bank is responsible for settling all accounts between undertakings. In this way those economic organisations which belong to the socialised sector of the Soviet economy are deprived of the right to grant one another credit, in any form at all, against the delivery of goods. The balance-sheets of industrial undertakings no longer, therefore, contain debit and credit entries.

As soon as goods are delivered, the undertakings receive a corresponding sum through the agency of the State Bank. Since it is principally between various elements in the socialised sector that accounts have to be settled, the most important activity of the bank consists in developing to the highest degree possible its system of offsetting claims between these elements, without using cash: this is possible since each undertaking has its own current account with the bank. The State Bank concludes agreements with industrial and commercial enterprises, organising in detail the settlement of all accounts for a particular client, taking into account the special character of the different sectors of the national economy.

How, then, is credit made available to nationalised industries and co-operative societies? In a very simple way, conforming as closely as possible to the demands of the Plan. The State Bank opens a current account for each enterprise and each economic organisation. This account may have a credit balance, if the enterprise has resources available, or a debit balance if it has been

granted credit. The plan of production for any given undertaking
is the basis for its financial plan. The amount of working capital
necessary is determined by the value of the reserves of raw material
which the undertaking has in store, by the importance of the productive operations engaged in, and by the amount of the existing
finished and half-finished products. The sum of these values, less
the working capital of the undertaking, fixes the amount of short-
term credit necessary for putting the financial plan into operation.

These plans need the approval of the State Bank and of the
Supreme Economic Council.

If it is to obtain credit, an enterprise must faithfully carry out the
economic Plan. As a result the State Bank does not grant credit to
its clients until it has minutely studied their plans; it also supervises their execution. A direct result of the system is, then, that
the State Bank supervises industrial and commercial enterprises
in all matters concerning the realisation of the Five Year Plan.

Since the State Bank has such wide powers over industrial and
commercial undertakings, it has in its hands all information
necessary to draw up a balance-sheet as complete and as genuine
as possible; a balance-sheet that faithfully reflects the actual conditions of the national economy under its control. In this way the
bank forms an excellent information service, permitting the
Government to form a precise assessment of the financial and
economic situation of the country.

As all enterprises are obliged by law to deposit their cash assets
with the State Bank, the latter has at its disposal the necessary resources to supply the various organisations with the funds they
need. If resources are insufficient to establish a satisfactory balance,
additional funds are provided for the bank by the national budget.
In this way an increase in the volume of money in circulation is
always a result of an increase in productivity; and so a close link
is set up between public finance and banking operations, between
the budget and currency. The impossibility of the granting of
excessive credit and a balanced budget constitute the essential
guarantees for the suppression of inflation. This close link between budget and bank is all the more indispensable in that the
latter, because of its very wide powers, plays a most important

role in the framework of Soviet economy. The budget of the Soviet state is of a national-economic character, and is closely linked with all branches of the national economy. The budgetary revenue is formed principally in the sphere of material production. Budgetary funds are used for financing capital construction and other requirements of the state.

Figures show vividly the tremendous importance of the state budget and the scale of its revenue and expenditure. We shall quote the main indices of the state budget of the U.S.S.R. for 1962: the revenue is set at 81,918,641,000 roubles and the expenditure at 80,369,904,000 roubles, the revenue thus exceeding the expenditure by 1,548,737,000 roubles.

Like the entire life of the Soviet Union, the budget system is based on principles of democratic centralism. The organs of state power, beginning with the Supreme Soviet of the U.S.S.R. and ending with the town and rural Soviet of Working People's Deputies, have their own independent budgets. All the local Soviets are endowed with complete budgetary rights and have the corresponding financial resources at their disposal. The independence of each organ of state power as regards its own budget is combined with the unity of the state budgetary system, with its centralisation: the state budget of the U.S.S.R. as a whole is annually approved as a Law by the Supreme Soviet of the U.S.S.R. This shows the organic community of interests and end-purposes of the entire Soviet state.

The terms 'finance' and 'credit' are, of course, current not only in socialist economy; they denote certain categories in capitalist economy as well. However, behind these outwardly similar terms there are absolutely dissimilar concepts, with a different nature and a different economic, social and political content, which reflect the disparity between the two economic, social and political systems — capitalism and socialism — and the fundamental difference between socialist production relations and capitalist production relations.

In a socialist economy the use of credit is very important and is one of the state's principal means of creating the material and technical basis of Communism.

Credit and the banks extending credit are a state monopoly in the U.S.S.R. Under socialism, banks play a very important role. V. I. Lenin, founder of the Soviet state, wrote: 'Socialism would have been impossible without big banks.' As the example of the Soviet Union shows, banks are more than simply an apparatus for the mobilisation of temporarily free monetary means and the granting of credits against mobilised resources. Under socialism, banks play an important role in organising a nation-wide accounting of production and distribution of products, and in controlling by the rouble the fulfilment of production, trade and purchasing plans, and the progress of capital construction.

In the U.S.S.R. the credit system has changed many times to conform with the development of the country's economy and with the changes in the relations between branches, organisations and enterprises of the national economy which have taken place at particular stages of this development.

At present, the Soviet banking system is constructed of the following principal banks with head offices in Moscow:

State Bank of the U.S.S.R. . . .	Gosbank
All-Union Bank for Financing Capital Investments	Stroibank
Bank for Foreign Trade of the U.S.S.R. .	Vneshtorgbank[1]

The figures concerning the above-mentioned banks are not published.

The State Bank of the U.S.S.R. has a monopoly of issue of notes of the State Bank and also of treasury notes and metal coins in the territory of the U.S.S.R.

---

[1] On 17 June 1966 a Soviet bank called Wozchod Commercial Bank Ltd. was established in Zürich and registered as a Swiss company. Its capital of 10 million Swiss francs is held by the following Soviet banking institutions:

55% by the State Bank of the U.S.S.R.
45% by the Bank of Foreign Trade of the U.S.S.R.
5% by the State Savings Banks of the U.S.S.R.

The bank is subject to the Swiss federal banking law and notably it has to observe the traditional banking secrecy. A percentage of its personnel must be of Swiss nationality.

There are three kinds of money in circulation: notes of the State Bank of the U.S.S.R. in 100-, 50-, 25- and 10-rouble denominations; treasury notes of 5, 3 and 1 rouble; and coins from 1 rouble to 1 kopek (1 rouble equals 100 kopeks).

State Bank notes are secured by gold, precious metals and other assets of the State Bank of the U.S.S.R. It must be noted that these 'other assets' include short-term credit granted against the security of commodity values, whose total value is considerably higher than the entire sum of the notes in circulation.

Treasury notes are secured by all the property of the U.S.S.R. and their economic nature is identical with that of the State Bank notes. No special form of security (gold or other bank assets) has been established for treasury notes, but this does not deprive them of stability or of their importance as one of the sources of short-term bank credit, since they are secured by the whole mass of state property.

Figures about the State Bank notes' circulation are not published.

The Soviet Government decided that as from 1 January 1961 the Soviet rouble would be equal to 0·987412 gramme of fine gold, and the rate of exchange of one U.S. dollar would be 90 kopeks. In accordance with this decision, the State Bank of the U.S.S.R. has recalculated the rate of exchange of the rouble with regard to foreign currencies.

On 1 January 1960 the network of the State Bank's local branches consisted of 6,008 offices, branches and agencies. The sum of short-term credit extended by the State Bank increases with the development of production and the turnover of goods. For example, the credit investments of the State Bank on 1 January 1962 amounted to 48,400 million roubles, as against 44,200 million roubles on 1 January 1961. In this period the credit investments in industry increased by 8%, in agriculture by 14·3% and in trade by 11·7%. Towards the close of the Seven-Year Plan of Economic Development for 1959–65 the credit investments of the State Bank in the national economy have increased by approximately 50% to 55%.

The State Bank of the U.S.S.R. is the centre of short-term credit for all branches of the country's national economy. In the U.S.S.R. credit is founded on production and commodity circulation and is a necessary condition for the formation of working funds at all stages of socialist production, from the procurement of raw materials to the sale of finished products. In the U.S.S.R. all enterprises are the property of the state or of collective farms and co-operatives. All are judicial entities and are run on a self-supporting (*khozraschet*) basis. State enterprises have their own working funds, on the scale necessary for their normal economic and financial activity.

The State Bank's short- and long-term credit plans are set up territorially for each economic administrative region. The branches of the bank are actively engaged in this work. Estimates of credits to be extended to most branches of the national economy are drawn up on the basis of planned data of the Economic Councils, the administration of the local industry, the republican, regional and territorial chains of the trading system, and the collective farms.

The regional, territorial and republican (autonomous republic) offices of the State Bank send the drafts of credit plans to the State Bank's offices in the Union Republics. After thoroughly checking the data and summing up the plan for a Union Republic, the office concerned sends the draft on to the Head Office of the State Bank of the U.S.S.R. in Moscow.

The immense capital investments being made in the U.S.S.R. have required, and continue to require, large domestic financial resources. They require also the development and implementation of a system of allocating funds and controlling the economical utilisation of these funds, to facilitate the measures aimed at rapidly increasing productive capacity and the country's basic wealth as envisaged in the economic development plans.

The system of financing and crediting capital investments, and also the organisation of the banks providing the necessary funds, are being developed and improved side by side with the development of Soviet economy and the improvement of the methods of its planning.

At present, the financing by means of long-term credits of the main body of capital investments in production projects as well as in cultural, everyday public service and housing projects in the towns are handled by the All-Union Bank for Financing Capital Investments (known as the Stroibank of the U.S.S.R.).

Like the State Bank of the U.S.S.R., the Stroibank is directly under the jurisdiction of the Council of Ministers of the U.S.S.R. The Stroibank is a special banking institution which exercises state financial control over capital investments. It carries out all its operations through a network of offices, branches and authorised agents at the State Bank's branches. The State Bank, which is the only note-issuing and cash-providing centre of the U.S.S.R., acts as cashier to the clientele of the Stroibank.

In addition, the State Bank and the Stroibank extend credit to workers, engineers, technicians, office employees, teachers, doctors and, in a number of cases, to collective farmers and other groups of working people, for individual housing construction, for purchase of household articles, and so on.

The Stroibank's resources for financing capital investments are, in the main, budgetary allocations and reserve funds accumulated through depreciation allowances and deductions from the profits of enterprises. In its sphere of activity the Stroibank controls the observance of plans and the planned cost of building, secures the mobilisation of the resources for building projects, and so forth.

As a rule, the capital investments of state enterprises and organisations are financed on a non-repayable basis. The possibility of financing state capital investments on a non-repayable basis is due to public ownership of the basic funds created through capital investments, and in the monetary accumulations that are received in the process of utilising these basic funds.

Foreign trade is an important organic part of the national economy of the U.S.S.R. At all stages of the history of the U.S.S.R. foreign trade has been and continues to be conducted on the basis of state monopoly (Article 14 of the Constitution of the U.S.S.R.).

All foreign-exchange resources are concentrated in the hands of the state, and all international settlements are made solely through the banks. In 1961 the volume of Soviet foreign trade reached the level planned for 1965 and amounted to 10,600 million roubles.

The Soviet Union is today a mighty industrial power and Soviet economists have estimated that during the next twenty years the volume of Soviet foreign trade can increase five times and more, and this will immeasurably heighten the role of the U.S.S.R. in international trade.

The Bank of Foreign Trade of the U.S.S.R. specialises in the transactions of foreign trade and foreign-exchange business (a function performed until 1961 by the State Bank of the U.S.S.R.). It effects collections, issues, letters of credit and carries on other operations in respect of settlements with foreign banks, handles the clearing accounts of these banks for the trade turnover and non-commercial payments, and also handles currency-exchange transactions for tourists arriving in or leaving the U.S.S.R.

The Bank for Foreign Trade of the U.S.S.R. effects foreign-exchange transactions with more than 1,300 foreign banking institutions in more than ninety countries of the world and she has two important affiliations in foreign countries, the Banque Commerciale pour l'Europe du Nord in Paris, and the Moscow Narodny Bank Limited in London with a branch in Beirut (Lebanon).

A few words must be said about the savings banks. The functions of the state savings banks are the receipt and payment of deposits; the sale and purchase of state loan bonds; and money transfers, by order of depositors, for payments in respect of communal services. The balance of deposits by the population in savings banks on 1 January 1948 came to 1,260 million roubles (in new roubles), and by 1 January 1962 this balance had increased to 11,660 million roubles.

The level that has been attained by the money incomes of the population has facilitated the rise of the material and cultural well-being of the Soviet people.

Soviet scientific achievements and industrial growth rates have encouraged the assumption that things are going relatively well in the Soviet economy. The Russians, however, express grave misgivings when talking among themselves. For years, the Soviet press has been filled with innumerable complaints of poor quality, misdirected investment, shortages of desired items, excessive inventories of unwanted goods and dissatisfaction among workers and peasants. Russian industry operates on the basis of detailed output plans handed down from above. Plants are spurred to fulfil production goals by means of complex bonus-incentive plans based on a variety of quantitative and qualitative indicators. These plans inevitably go awry, and Soviet planners have found it impossible to juggle these indicators to bring forth the right assortment and quality of goods. People are kept busy, but, for want of a market economy, they lack power to determine what shall be produced.

The shortcomings of the system have made it abundantly clear that drastic changes are needed. Economists have been in the forefront in criticising the present system and in suggesting changes. Increasingly, they take the capitalist system as a guide for reform.

In their observation of the market economies of the West, the Russians have become increasingly impressed with the neat way in which the competitive profit-and-loss system works to increase production — by the most efficient producers — of things that are in demand, and to reduce production — by the least efficient producers — of things that are not in demand. In many of the reform plans advanced by the Soviet economists, expansion of the role of profits has been highlighted.

The ironies in this situation are endless and require no particular emphasis. The crowning irony, of course, is the fact that Russian economists, who forty-eight years ago launched a revolution to destroy capitalism and all its works, now find that they must imitate its most characteristic institution — the system of profit and loss. The Russians of the present day are beginning to see the light.

From harsh, practical experience the Russians have learned that the free-market economy has undeniable advantages. We should learn from their experience; not to imitate them in state planning and suppressions of freedoms, but to strengthen our system of profit and loss and individual enterprise.

(b) *Banks in the People's Republic of China*

The Chinese Government, in deliberate imitation of the banking system of the U.S.S.R., has set up in Communist China the People's Bank of China, which has at present about 38,000 agencies distributed throughout the country which may be found even in the most distant localities of this immense territory. The People's Bank of China is responsible for the issue of currency and for all currency transactions made necessary by the Plan. It holds on an average 99% of the capital of all undertakings; transactions between undertakings are handled by the bank as transfers. The bank alone is authorised to extend credit to industrial and commercial undertakings and ensure the existence of a sound proportional relationship between goods produced and money in circulation.

There is also the Bank of China, specialising in international commercial transactions and owning branches in many foreign countries (not to be confused with the bank of the same name whose head office is in Taipeh on the island of Formosa, Nationalist China), the Bank for Construction, the Bank for Communications, the Kincheng Banking Corporation, the National Industrial Bank of China, the National Commercial Bank of Shanghai and the Shanghai Commercial and Savings Bank. All these banks operate on behalf of and under the control of the People's Bank of China.

(c) *The Banks of ten other Communist states*

The banking system in operation in Albania, Hungary, East Germany, Bulgaria, North Korea, Mongolia, Poland, Rumania, Czecho-Slovakia and North Vietnam is modelled on that of the U.S.S.R. The various banks of issue distribute credit and control the national economy as a whole.

(d) *The International Bank for Economic Co-operation*

At the ninth meeting of the Executive Committee of the Council for Mutual Economic Assistance in Warsaw, a statute for a joint bank of member-states was formally adopted on 22 October 1963. The new bank was scheduled to begin its operations on 1 January 1964 — the date envisaged for replacing the current clearing arrangements in Eastern-bloc trade by a clearing mechanism based on transferable roubles.

The establishment of such a bank has long been called for by Eastern-bloc countries, and was given official sanction at the third meeting of the Executive Committee in Bucharest (16–20 December 1962). This move, in its turn, followed a basic policy decision by the First Secretaries of Party Committees and the Prime Ministers of Council for Mutual Economic Assistance (COMECON) countries in the summer of 1962 aimed at introducing new measures and organisational improvements to increase the effectiveness of the COMECON.

The eight member-states of the bank are: Bulgaria, Czecho-Slovakia, East Germany, Hungary, Mongolia, Poland, Rumania and the U.S.S.R. (but not Albania).

The head office of the bank was established in Moscow.

Discussions as to the various forms that such a centralised economic policy could take and, particularly, resistance by some Eastern-bloc countries against centralised planning have held up even such a relatively minor decision as that of establishing a joint bank for over one year. The authority now to be given to the newly constituted 'International Bank for Economic Co-operation' offers less scope for activity than had been expected when the project was first announced.

While it had been assumed that the bank would assist in the granting of joint credits to development countries, participate in financing Eastern-bloc capital projects and help to establish commercial relations — as yet undefined — with Western countries, recent statements by the Chairman of the Executive Committee of the COMECON have made it clear that in the near future the bank will be concerned primarily with extending short-term credit under the present intra-bloc clearing arrangements. Of course, this does not rule out a future expansion of its activity. It now looks as if the bank will not — at least in its first business years — achieve the objective set out in its statute: to stimulate trade between COMECON countries. To fulfil its purpose the bank obviously requires certain prerequisites in the field of trade policy which do not yet exist. Consequently, the bank is itself expected to replace the present bilateral clearing mechanism by a multilateral payments system, and to extend short-term loans in the form of so-called 'transferable roubles' with a view to facilitating the compensation of mutual claims at the year-end settlement of clearing surpluses or deficits.

In the past the settlement of outstanding trade claims has been effected by means of overdrafts — arising from the fluctuations in East–West clearing — which have to be repaid in the following clearing period through merchandise deliveries. The principle of settling outstanding claims annually is far more strictly adhered to in intra-bloc trade than in East–West clearing arrangements, which allow debit or credit balances, of considerable size, to persist for years. Sometimes, it is true, it has proved necessary to convert these balances into long-term credits.

The Eastern-bloc Payments Union differs from the present European Monetary Agreement (EMA) in that all payment transactions within the Eastern-bloc area are subject to clearing arrangements, whereas under the European Monetary Agreement the clearing mechanism is limited to those countries whose currencies still need some kind of support. At present this applies to only two currencies. The European Monetary Agreement is therefore in a position to delegate this authority to another bank — the Bank for International Settlements, Basle — as trustee, without having to establish a separate bank for the purpose.

The International Bank for Economic Co-operation (I.B.E.C.) — which was obviously named after Western models — is endowed with a capital stock of merely 300 million roubles ($330 million U.S.) since its lending activity will be on a moderate scale and loans will have to be repaid within a year's time. The capital quotas of individual countries are fixed in accordance with their trade volume:[1]

The European Monetary Agreement, by contrast, has been

[1] The member quotas are as follows: U.S.S.R. 116 million roubles, East Germany 55 million, Czecho-Slovakia 45 million, Poland 27 million, Hungary 21 million, Bulgaria 17 million, Rumania 16 million, Mongolia 3 million.

endowed with a fund of $607 million U.S., or double the capital of the Eastern-bloc bank.

The new bank is designed primarily to foster clearing transactions in intra-bloc trade. It has been authorised to deny its credit facilities to or impose penal interest on any member-country which infringes upon the established regulations for international payment transactions. The foundation of the new bank is not likely to have any impact on East–West payments traffic although it may facilitate East–West multilateral clearing settlements. It should always be kept in mind that the bank's foreign-exchange roubles do not represent a convertible currency in the Western sense of the term, but are, in fact, limited to intra-bloc settlement of outstanding trade claims. Besides, the fundamental question remains unanswered: whether international trade among planned economies can be reorganised in such a way as to put the new multilateral clearing mechanism to practical use.

(e) COMECON — Council for Mutual Economic Assistance
The COMECON was set up on 25 January 1949 at a meeting in Moscow of the Ministers of Economic Affairs of the states of the Communist bloc with the purpose of counteracting the effects of the Marshall Plan then in operation.

Today the member-states of the COMECON are: Albania, Bulgaria, Czecho-Slovakia, East Germany, Hungary, Mongolia, Poland, Rumania and the U.S.S.R.

China, North Korea, North Vietnam and Yugoslavia are not members of this organisation. These states are represented only by observers. The headquarters of the institution is in Moscow.

Since 1962 the activity of the COMECON showed some remarkable new trends which are certain to affect the Western World and its trade with the Eastern bloc before long. First, there was a change in Council membership in 1962. Albania has — at least for the time being — practically withdrawn from the work of the Council, although it has not formally left or been excluded by the Council. The Mongolian People's Republic, on the other hand, was admitted as a new member at the sixteenth Council meeting in Moscow (6–7 June 1962). While this admission makes no practical difference either in trade between member-countries or in East–West trade — Mongolia being able to transact only a very limited volume of foreign commerce — it must be considered a rather important political gesture in that the Council for the first time extended its activity to an Asian people's republic which hitherto had been specifically excluded from membership. This move is the more significant since it occurred in a period of mounting strains between the Soviet Union and China. According to the previous statute of the COMECON, European countries only were eligible for Council membership.

Still more important than the admission of a new member-state was a change in the organisation of the COMECON itself, which was likewise decided upon at the Moscow meeting. Thus it was resolved to establish an Executive Committee composed of the Deputy Prime Ministers of member-states who are at the same time the heads of economic planning in their respective countries. The foundation of the Executive Committee obviously follows a pattern already realised in the Western World by the High Authority of the European Coal and Steel Community and by the European Economic Community Commission — the institution of a supranational authority.

Also, there were established new Permanent Committees for the Co-ordination of Scientific and Technical Research, for Statistics and for Standardisation. In addition, a separate Institute for the Promotion of Standardisation was set up by the COMECON. By establishing such an institute, the COMECON for the first time possesses a joint agency for carrying out specific functions — in addition to the already existing conventional organs of an international organisation. Whereas the COMECON has so far been content with issuing recommendations and proposals and has not — either in principle or under the terms of its statute — actively interfered in the economic activity of its members, this new institute now provides a platform for a more autonomous policy of the COMECON as distinct from the economic policies of member-states.

There are clear indications — although as yet not openly admitted by Eastern-bloc economists — that the successful develop-

ment of the European Economic Community has made a profound impact on the organisers of Eastern economic planning.

The activities of the COMECON — like other Eastern-bloc
efforts at integration — have hitherto been obstructed by such
obstacles as excessive red-tape, overstressing of national sovereignty
and the dualism of party and government.

The progress in Western economic integration and the pooling
by Western countries of all resources enabling a more efficient
use of mass-production methods have convinced Eastern-bloc
countries that their co-operation must be placed on a new footing
and intensified if the COMECON is to compete successfully
with the European Economic Community. For this reason greater
stress is now being laid on the principle of international socialist
division of labour, a doctrine enunciated in a longwinded
document issued in Moscow in June 1962.

The co-operation between the socialist states is allowing each
of them to make the fullest and most rational use of its resources
and develop its productive forces. A new type of international
division of labour is taking shape in the process of economic,
scientific and technical co-operation among the socialist countries,
in the process of co-ordinating their plans of economic development.

Through a policy of selective capital investment on plant and
equipment as well as by adjusting and specialising production
programmes, it is hoped to achieve a twofold specialisation in
industry: some lines of industry are to be concentrated in certain
countries, and mass-production techniques are to be introduced
wherever possible. This process of concentrating production in
certain countries and, within these countries, in certain large
manufacturing units and their subcontractors has only just started.
In this connection great importance is being attached to questions
of standardisation as witnessed by the establishment of the
Institute for the Promotion of Standardisation.

A considerable obstacle in the way of international division of
labour in Eastern-bloc countries is provided by the price structure
in these countries — there being almost no means of calculating
comparable indices due to the lack of comparable prices. For this

reason it was decided in 1962 to revise the present system of price formation and to introduce multilateral clearing in Eastern-bloc international trade. To this end, the establishment of a Permanent Commission for Monetary and Financial Matters was approved at the seventeenth meeting of the COMECON in Bucharest (14–20 December 1962). At the subsequent gathering of the Executive Committee a recommendation was adopted, proposing the revision of current prices in intra-bloc trade by adjusting them to the average prices on world markets in the 1957–61 period. The Executive Committee further recommended the introduction of multilateral clearing and the establishment of the 'International Bank for Economic Co-operation'.

There can be no doubt that the working out of a new price system and the introduction of multilateral clearing — which had existed hitherto as well, but could not be used to any great extent — constitutes a tough problem which cannot be solved easily. A number of recent economic studies undertaken by Eastern-bloc theoreticians show that the COMECON has been seriously discussing these problems in the past two years. As a result of this fundamental research, its Economic Committee has considerably gained in importance and prestige over this period. Simple or complex methods of calculating the effectiveness of capital investment and the profit ratios of foreign trade are by now being used in several Eastern-bloc countries with widely differing results since the underlying factors vary greatly according to the general level of economic advancement in the individual countries.

While differences of opinion have never been absent from the activities of the COMECON, resistance to the COMECON programme in member-states is increasing as more serious efforts are made to achieve an advanced state of international division of labour. Such a division of labour necessitates not only a departure from the autarchic way of thinking in member-countries, but also the renunciation of many traditional national industries. Consequently, it leads to economic interdependence and reliance upon other countries — a process rejected by member-countries not only for selfish reasons but also because of recurring difficulties in intra-bloc supplies. Surprisingly, the governments of Eastern-bloc countries thus find themselves compelled to leave the decision on the new form of international division of labour to their national executives. The reason for this attitude is that the co-ordination of long-term plans agreed upon in June 1962 interferes with national economic planning.

These fundamental decisions on the new style of international division of labour were, significantly, not made by the governments of member-countries or by a COMECON meeting but by a conference of Party chiefs in June 1962. Such gatherings of supreme Party chiefs are, moreover, henceforth to lay down the fundamental policy of COMECON activity and consequently the agenda of COMECON meetings. The dualism of Party and Government which is a characteristic feature of the Soviet state is thus being introduced into the international co-operation between Communist countries. This is a new development in international relations and a basic distinction from Eastern ways of integration.

Expected development in Eastern-bloc countries of some important economic indicators:

	1960		*1980*	
	Soviet Union	*Other COMECON countries*	*Soviet Union*	*Other COMECON countries*
Population (million people).	212	98	300	120
Fuel (on a hard-coal basis) (million tons) . . .	700	270	2,900	500
Electricity (million kWh) .	293	114	2,850	650
Steel (million tons) . .	65	21	250	80

3

THE SEVEN INTERNATIONAL BANKING AND FINANCIAL INSTITUTIONS OF WASHINGTON

WASHINGTON is not only the federal capital of the United States; it is also the headquarters of state capitalism, orientated towards the financing of economic development on a world or a hemisphere plane. It is in Washington that one finds the headquarters of those gigantic banking and financial institutions which dispense to other state organisms, to foreign states and to private enterprises the millions necessary to ensure the realisation of world-scale development plans.

Thirty years ago, when an American farmer needed money to improve his farm, or when a manufacturer needed a few million dollars to buy machinery or extend his factory, they would normally turn to Wall Street businessmen. Today they go to Washington and are sure to obtain from some government agency all the money they need. Wall Street can offer no effective resistance to this formidable overwhelming competition from the state.

In addition, federal laws subject all banks, without distinction, to rigorous inspection by various government organisations. The time is long past when the great magnates of finance exercised a despotic power over the country's trade, industry, credit and finances and amassed immense fortunes in the period of a few decades. However, one must not assume that the financial power and influence of Wall Street have totally vanished. Its gigantic organisation is still there, functioning as a barometer of world economy. It still plays a role of the first importance in great international financial transactions. On the surface nothing appears to have changed. In reality the power of Wall Street is broken since it lacks the essential: political influence. The kings of finance have surrendered their sceptre to a more powerful monarch: the state.

In Wall Street it is not only money which spells power. The great lawyers also play an important role and are at times as powerful as the bankers. Famous lawyers exercise an enormous influence in Wall Street. It is in chambers that the great companies are formed, that trusts are established and prices fixed which are to destroy a competitor; here documents are drawn up which stretch legality to breaking-point; here contracts are drawn up for supplies on a gigantic scale to the various states of the world.

Wall Street is the place where great personalities spend their formative years before being summoned to public office. Many men whose names will be remembered in United States history have made the journey from New York to Washington.

Edward E. Stettinius Jr., Secretary of State for Foreign Affairs under President Roosevelt (1944), was a partner of the bank J. P. Morgan & Co., which on 24 April 1959 amalgamated with the Guaranty Trust Company to form the Morgan Guaranty Trust Company of New York.

Averell W. Harriman, Secretary of State for Commerce under President Truman (1946), was a partner of the bank Brown Brothers, Harriman & Co. Mr. Harriman is still the Ambassador-at-Large of President Johnson.

James Forrestal, Secretary of State for War under President Truman (1946), was a partner in the bank Dillon, Read & Co.

Douglas C. Dillon, Secretary of State for the Treasury under President Kennedy (1961), was a partner of the bank Dillon, Read & Co.

Washington houses the head offices of the seven great international banking and financial institutions, namely:

1. The International Bank for Reconstruction and Development (World Bank).

2. The International Finance Corporation.
3. The International Development Association.
4. The International Monetary Fund.
5. The Inter-American Development Bank.
6. The Export–Import Bank of Washington.
7. The Agency for International Development.

Very few experts can claim to know all the complex mechanisms of these seven institutions, even though five of them have an international character and only two are purely American: the Export–Import Bank of Washington, and the Agency for International Development, which gives American exporters the well-known guarantee, A.I.D.

In the following pages we give a brief sketch of the structure and activity of each of the above-mentioned institutions.

1. The International Bank for Reconstruction and Development (The World Bank)

The bank commenced operations on 25 June 1946.

Objects: to assist the economic development of member-states, principally by encouraging increased productivity.

Resources: subscriptions from member-states and loan issues.

Loans: to member-governments or to public or private organisations guaranteed by their governments.

Relationship with other credit sources: cannot take action, if funds can be obtained under reasonable terms from private sources.

Duration of loans: generally fifteen to twenty-five years.

Rate of interest: from 5% to 6%, including commission of 1%.

Very early in the course of the Second World War the economic and financial experts of the Allied Powers began to consider the means which would have to be devised to face the economic problems of the peace. They agreed that, if the peace was to be won, it would be necessary to plan not merely for immediate aid and for the physical reconstruction of economies destroyed by the war, but also, by appropriate international and internal measures, for the expansion of production and of employment as well as of trade and of consumption of those goods which form the material foundation of liberty and well-being of all peoples.

Various recommendations, framed with the economic objectives which the Allies had determined, were examined. In 1941 various monetary and financial plans for the post-war period were already being studied. In the course of the next three years discussion of these plans was to give birth to the outline plan of two complementary financial institutions.

Balance-sheet 30 June 1965 (run from 1 July to 30 June each year)
Capital stock authorised: 220,000 shares of
  $100·000 par value each. Subscribed:

216,694 shares by 102 member-states	$21,669,400,000	
Less Uncalled portion of subscriptions	19,501,410,000	
		2,167,990,000
Reserves		894,542,370
Funded debt		2,723,989,353
Effective loans held by Bank		5,480,681,755
(including undisbursed balance of $1,662,573,606)		
TOTAL of the balance-sheet of the Bank		7,721,212,569

The first, which was to become the International Monetary Fund, was intended to ensure international currency stability by helping to finance temporary deficits in member-states' balance of payments and by taking steps to bring about the progressive elimination of restrictions on exchange; it was also to enforce respect of the rules governing international financial relations.

The second institution — which was to become the International Bank for Reconstruction and Development (generally known as the World Bank — was, as its name shows, intended to help in financing reconstruction and development in its member-states.

In spring of the year 1944, after prolonged and searching discussions between representatives of the American Treasury and of the British Treasury, and consultations with representatives of other countries, plans for these two institutions had reached an advanced stage. As a result it was resolved to hold a Monetary and Financial Conference of the United Nations. After preliminary meetings held in Atlantic City, representatives of forty-four

nations met in Bretton Woods in New Hampshire on 1 July
1944: three weeks later, they completed the definitive draft of
the articles of association of both the Fund and the Bank, so
that they might be submitted to the various participating governments. The articles of association of the bank were officially
accepted by the majority of the participants on 27 December
1945. Six months later, on 25 June 1946, the bank began its
operations and appealed for capital.

Official relations between the bank and the United Nations
are governed by an agreement, approved by the Board of
Governors of the bank in September 1947 and by the General
Assembly of the United Nations in November of the same year.

The bank is a specialised agency as defined in Article 57 of
the Charter of the United Nations. The agreement concluded
between the bank and the United Nations recognises explicitly
that, in view of its international responsibilities and of the terms
of its articles of association, the bank is an independent international organisation and must function as such. The agreement
contains provision for such matters as reciprocal representation,
consultation and exchange of information other than confidential
matters. The agreement provides that no official recommendation
shall be made by either organisation to the other, unless normal
consultations shall have been held beforehand.

The agreements negotiated later on between the United
Nations and the bank's two subsidiaries, the International
Finance Corporation and the International Development Association, are conditioned by the terms of the agreement between the
bank and the United Nations.

Liaison between the bank and the United Nations is maintained
by a committee, consisting of the Secretary-General, the Director-
General of the Special Fund of the United Nations, the Executive
Director of the Council for Technical Assistance of the United
Nations, the Presidents of the Bank and of the International
Development Association. The committee meets at least four
times a year, and the members exchange information and discuss
both current programmes and projects in spheres where common
interests and concern are present.

The representatives of the bank are also present at the meetings of the various organisations of the United Nations when matters which interest them are under discussion; in particular, meetings of the General Assembly, of the Economic and Social Council and of the Regional Economic Commissions. The bank also shares in the work of the Special Fund of the United Nations, the President being a member of the triumvirate which forms the Consultative Committee of the Fund.

The bank is represented by an observer at the annual meeting of the Bank for International Settlements in Basle. It is in contact with the Organisation of American States, the Organisation for Economic Co-operation and Development in Paris, the Consultative Committee of the Colombo Plan and the Inter-American Development Bank in Washington.

The articles of association of the bank contain provisions which grant it, within the territory of its members, legal competency as well as certain privileges and immunities. Each member-state must take within its own territory all necessary steps to put these provisions into effect within the framework of its own laws. The archives of the bank are inviolable. The possessions of the bank have immunity against seizure, attachment or distraint, until a final judgment has been given against it. The bank, its possessions and revenues, as well as its authorised operations and transactions, are exempt from all tax and all duties. It is also exempt from obligation to collect or pay any tax or duty.

No tax may be levied upon emoluments paid by the bank to those executive directors, their deputies and officials who are not nationals of the country where they are employed. No tax may be levied upon a security issued by the bank, if such a tax were to be a form of discrimination against the security, imposed merely because it had been issued by the bank: nor can such a tax be levied if its only basis in law is the place of issue, currency of issue, the currency subscribed or paid for the security or the existence of a branch of the bank in the country.

The bank is organised as follows:

(*a*) a Board of Governors, to which each member-state appoints a Governor and an Alternate.

(*b*) Executive Directors and Alternates, of which there are at present twenty; of whom five are appointed by the largest shareholders and the fifteen others elected by the other member-states.

(*c*) an international personnel, controlled by the President. The President is chosen by the Executive Directors.

In the discharge of their duties, the President, the directors and the personnel of the bank owe allegiance only to the bank and to no other organisation. Each member-country has pledged itself to respect the international character of this allegiance and not to attempt to influence any member of the staff of the bank in the discharge of his official responsibilities.

The functional organisation of the bank is made clear in the diagram opposite, which also includes the names of higher executives.

Insufficiencies in the mechanism of planning and of administration form one of the greatest obstacles to the economic development of a country. To provide aid in this sphere, the bank has created, with the assistance of the Ford and Rockefeller Foundations, an Institute of Economic Development, with headquarters in Washington. The Institute's first course commenced on 1 January 1956. The courses last six months. The Institute is a college, reserved for important functionaries of the member-states, responsible for dealing with questions of economic development.

The object of the courses is to give young nationals of the member-countries the opportunity of becoming familiar with the activities of the bank, and with the methods adopted in handling problems of economic development. All those participating in the study-sessions hold important positions in Ministries, State Banks, planning agencies and other organisations responsible for economic development. The organisation which employs them grants them leave of absence, so that they may attend the courses of the Institute, and pays a registration fee of $1,500 for each student. Supplementary costs are borne by the Bank.

The Institute has perfected a range of grouped and interconnected studies, in which all students participate. The programme is designed to give a general survey of problems involved in economic development, treated from a point of view of particular interest to functionaries, who direct organisations handling such problems.

In general, the subjects studied are as follows: techniques necessary in the drawing up of a development plan, historical aspects of development, structural relationships between public finance, general economy, currency and the banks, agricultural development, international exchange and payments, studies of certain branches of industry, criteria to be used in assessing the value of programmes and projects.

The Director of the Institute has eminent economists and university teachers as his collaborators. In addition, the Institute calls upon lecturers, highly qualified in their own field, who come from various governmental services, the United Nations, the universities and other organisations. An important part of the programme is formed by visits to public institutions and to industrial, commercial, agricultural and financial establishments, either in the United States or in other member-countries.

Thanks to the close liaison between the Institute and the operational departments of the bank, empiric data, essential to a practical study of problems of development, are made available to the students. The students also devote some time to the study of standard projects of the bank. They thus come directly into contact with the functionaries responsible for these projects and as they follow the resolution of practical problems can observe how the operational procedures of the bank are applied.

In the field of development aid, the World Bank plays a predominant role. Along with its affiliated organisations, the International Finance Corporation and the International Development Association, it places annually important capital sums at the disposal of underdeveloped countries, to be used in financing the expansion of their economies. Since it began business on 25 June 1946, up to 30 June 1965 (nineteen years), the World Bank has granted credits for an amount of $8,935 million, to fifty-eight countries.

The statement of loans 30 June 1965 was $5,480,681,755.

The financial resources which enable the bank to grant such important credits are derived principally from the capital paid up by its members ($2,168 million), from borrowing on the international money-markets ($2,724 million) and also from the profits resulting from its operations ($895 million). One must also mention the repayment of loans and the sale of the bonds of the lenders to the bank.

On 30 June 1965 the funded debt of the bank, expressed in United States currency, amounted to $2,723,989,353, issued in the following states:

	U.S. dollars
United States of America . .	1,996,068,000
Germany (Federal Republic) .	382,437,500
Switzerland	187,538,879
Great Britain	46,804,016
Canada	40,626,041
Holland	36,514,917
Italy	24,000,000
Belgium	10,000,000
TOTAL	2,723,989,353

The bank's credit is firmly based on the fact that 90% of the capital authorised, that is to say, $19,501 million, serve as reserve and guarantee.

The proportion of subscriptions not yet called up, although it is not at the disposal of the bank for making loans, constitutes in fact a guarantee by its members of the bank's obligations, because the risks inseparable from the loan operations of the bank are shared proportionally between its members, and thus each member supports with its own credit the obligations of the bank *pro rata* to the portion of its subscription not yet called up. This capital structure has shown itself efficacious and has enabled the bank to borrow considerable sums in the principal financial centres of the world. Indeed the bank depends, in great measure, on international financial centres to finance its activities: it borrows as much as it lends.

On 30 June 1965 the permanent staff of the bank and of the International Development Association numbered 1,094 employees from sixty-five countries.

2. The International Finance Corporation

Affiliated to the World Bank.

Commenced operations in July 1956.

Objects: to contribute to economic development by encouraging private investment in productive enterprises in member countries, especially in underdeveloped countries.

Resources: contributions from member-countries and profits from the cession of *droits de souscription.*

Loans: partial financing of productive enterprises (not guaranteed by the member-government) by means of loans, by direct investment or by guaranteeing issues.

Relationship with other credit sources: cannot take action if funds can be obtained from private sources under reasonable terms.

Duration of loans: ten years.

Rate of interest: current rate 7%, plus participation in profits.

Balance-sheet 30 June 1965 (run from 1 July to 30 June each year)

Capital stock authorised: 110,000 shares of $1,000		$110,000,000
Subscribed: 99,047 shares by 78 member-states		99,047,000
Reserves against losses		23,140,812
Loans	$41,635,635	
Equity (at cost)	21,069,684	
		62,705,319
Total of the balance-sheet of the Corporation		$130,170,618

The International Finance Corporation, created under the auspices of the World Bank, is a finance institution, planned to supplement the operations of the bank by encouraging the development of private enterprise in underdeveloped countries. Under the terms of the Charter of the Corporation the Directors of the World Bank, appointed or elected by the member-countries, are also Directors of the Corporation. The President of the World Bank, in virtue of his office, presides over the Board of Directors of the International Finance Corporation and acts as Director-General.

The financial operations of the Corporation may take various forms: taking up shares, straightforward loans, loans associated with the provision of capital, or combinations of these various methods of financing. The Corporation may place investments only in member-countries or in territories associated with them. It has adopted the rule of not investing in the most highly developed countries. As a general rule, the Corporation is principally interested in private investment projects, based essentially on some form of industry.

The projects or enterprises which benefit from the Corporation's investments must have a sound financial structure, be under capable and experienced management and offer the prospect of profitable activity. Any enterprise which benefits from the financial participation of the Corporation must be so planned as to contribute effectively to the economic development of the country in which it is situated. These criteria apply in principle to all the Corporation's operations, whether direct participation is involved or merely the guaranteeing of issues.

The Corporation does not invest in undertakings belonging to the state or administered by the state (this field is reserved for the World Bank). It does not participate in operations whose essential object is the repayment or extension of credits, or the direct financing of exports or imports (a field reserved for the Export-Import Bank of Washington). Nor does it participate in projects concerning public services, land development or the sale of land.

In making an investment the Corporation does not prescribe how it is to be expended, nor does it require that funds placed at the disposal of an enterprise be spent in a particular country.

The Corporation transfers its investments, in whole or in part, whenever a favourable opportunity offers. In this way, coffers are replenished and other investments in productive enterprises are made possible. The Corporation is very different from the related organisation, the World Bank. While the bank, which has milliards of dollars available for loans, undertakes great development projects, the object of the Corporation is very different: to help in industrial development in the private sector alone, utilising much smaller resources.

On 30 June 1965 the capital of the Corporation, subscribed by seventy-eight member-countries, amounted to $99,047,000. Such a sum alone could hardly make any significant contribution to economic development. But the Corporation, by encouraging private sources of capital to participate in its investments, has ensured that for every dollar it invests three or four dollars originating in the private sector are invested in its enterprises. In certain special cases a relatively small investment by the Corporation has ensured very important investments of private capital.

An amendment to its articles of association, authorising investment in private enterprises, passed by the Board of Governors in September 1961, gave a new flexibility to its operations. Direct investment by the Corporation in national undertakings allows the latter to avoid the exchange risks involved in international loans; moreover, the simpler investment techniques which the Corporation can now employ — direct loans and providing part of the capital of an enterprise for example — have the double advantage of being familiar to business heads and more acceptable to them. That the Corporation is now able to acquire a share in the capital of undertakings also allows it to contribute to the expansion of the money-markets of underdeveloped countries.

The Corporation can now underwrite new share issues, support local underwriting syndicates and undertake to cover, if need be, a proportion of an issue, and this facilitates the operations of investment-houses and local underwriting syndicates. For this reason the Corporation, above all international institutions, is exceptionally well placed to support local markets and to stimulate the initiative of business heads and encourage private investment.

The Corporation also paves the way for an increase in the number of joint ventures, by playing, as it were, the role of guardian angel to private investors. It transfers its investments to new holders as opportunity offers and, in countries where the practice of industrial investment is not yet firmly established, it reserves a proportion of the shares held for possible purchasers from the country itself, who may appear as soon as the new enterprises begin to show tangible results.

Within the World Bank group — composed of the bank, the International Development Association and the International Finance Corporation itself — the Corporation has, since the beginning of 1962, taken the lead in the study of proposals which may result in the creation of new financing companies in which private interests predominate or in the provision of technical and financial assistance to companies already in existence. During the financial year 1962-3 the World Bank and the International Finance Corporation undertook their first joint ventures in this sphere.

The bank has granted loans to development companies in Morocco, Pakistan and the Philippines, while the Corporation has subscribed capital. In a fourth case, in Spain, the Corporation has agreed to invest capital, without the bank's co-operation, in a recently created institution. Studies have also been made in considerable detail of other proposals for investment in new or already existing institutions in Finland, Malaysia, Nigeria, Thailand, Turkey and Venezuela.

Governmental and business circles alike recognise more and more the need for institutions of this type which have been making a growing contribution to economic development since the Second World War. Soundly constituted and efficiently run, they can encourage the expansion of private industrial enterprises, mobilise national capital and stimulate a steady flow of investment. In many countries these development companies are the only private institutions which can grant middle- and long-term credit. They also provide an advisory service in technical and administrative matters and newly established industries in under-developed countries can, through their agency, have access to foreign private capital and keep in touch with the latest technical advances.

The object of the Corporation, as a member of the World Bank group, is to help in establishing or in reorganising industrial financing companies, belonging as far as possible to the private sector, and to ensure that such companies be financially viable and administered in complete independence. It provides the capital they lack and which they need to finance their borrowings and to take shares in particular undertakings. In addition, the Corporation gives them active help in finding foreign investors.

The Corporation is equally concerned that the various financing companies should retain their national character: it believes that shares should be as widely distributed among native stockholders as the resources of the national business circles allow. It is prepared, if need be, to treat its own holding in a company as a national portfolio and to undertake to sell its shares only to nationals of the country in which the investment is made, in order to prevent foreigners from obtaining control of these institutions and to safeguard the autonomy of national interests.

3. THE INTERNATIONAL DEVELOPMENT ASSOCIATION

Affiliated to the World Bank.

Commenced operations on 8 November 1960.

Objects: to facilitate the economic development of the member-countries by granting loans on more flexible conditions than those of the World Bank.

Resources: contributions from member-countries.

Loans: development credits to member-countries, to public and private institutions within their boundaries.

Relationship with other credit sources: cannot take action if funds can be obtained from normal sources or from the World Bank.

Duration of loans: fifty years' maximum, with a period of ten years' grace, and repayment in stages.

Rate of interest: no interest. Commission of 0·75% per annum, payable on the amounts drawn and not reimbursed.

Since the war nations have practised economic aid and multilateral financial co-operation on an unprecedented scale.

The International Development Association is one of the most recent international organisations, specially created as an instrument of this co-operation. According to its articles of association,

the object of the Association is to encourage economic development, to increase productivity and consequently to raise the standard of living in the more backward quarters of the globe. The
organisation is allied to the World Bank, but the financial resources of the two institutions are quite distinct. Like the World
Bank, the Association helps to finance carefully selected and
elaborated development projects; but it provides capital on more
liberal repayment terms and can participate in the financing of a
more varied range of projects than the bank.

Balance-sheet 30 June 1965 (run from 1 July to 30 June each year)
Subscriptions: Amounts subscribed by 94 member-states $995,695,000
    of which by 18 member-states of the first
    group $751,345,000
    and 76 member-states of the second group .   244,350,000

Transfer from International Bank for Reconstruction and
    Development   50,000,000
Supplementary resources   740,745,000
Effective development credits held by the Association (granted
    to 25 member-states — including undisbursed balance of
    $580,584,145)   995,272,825
      TOTAL of the balance-sheet of the Association   .   . $1,639,950,603

$50 million of the World Bank's net income for the fiscal year 1963–4 were
    transferred to the Association in the form of a grant.

     The creation of the International Development Association
took place after long discussions on the advisability of accelerating
economic growth in underdeveloped regions by the influx of
international funds, repayable under conditions other than those
traditional.
     The articles of the Association laid down that only members
of the World Bank could become members of the Association
and prescribed initial subscriptions to the capital amounting to
$1 milliard, if all members of the bank became founder members
of the Association. A member's initial subscription was proportional to its subscription to the capital of the bank.
     On 24 September 1960 a sufficient number of members of the

bank had accepted affiliation to the Association for the articles of association to be applied.

By the terms of these articles the members of the Association are divided into two groups: those which appear in the first group, that is to say,

Australia	Finland	Kuwait	Sweden
Austria	France	Luxembourg	United Kingdom
Belgium	Germany	Netherlands	United States
Canada	Italy	Norway	
Denmark	Japan	South Africa	

are the eighteen most highly developed and most highly industrialised countries of the free world; those in the second group are less highly developed countries.

Subscriptions are paid differently by the two groups. Initial subscriptions from the countries in the first group must be paid entirely in freely convertible currency such as the Association can use in granting development credits. Countries in the second group pay only 10% of their initial contribution in convertible currency; the remainder is paid in the country's own currency and may not be utilised by the Association without the consent of the particular member-country. It is evidently the eighteen countries of the first group who really finance the Association, although it is true that the Association may grant credits for projects situated in territories dependent on or associated with those countries.

All countries in the second group may receive credits from the Association; certain assisted countries may simultaneously receive loans from the World Bank and credits from the Association; other countries, the circumstances being different, may receive credits from the Association alone.

During the post-war period of economic growth and political change the demand for development capital increased considerably. In an increasing number of underdeveloped countries, nevertheless, the need for foreign capital and opportunities for making efficient use of it increased more rapidly than opportunities to raise loans on traditional conditions. Factors resultant on many countries' having become independent complicate the problem: these countries can no longer rely to the same extent on the financial support of the powers on which they were formerly dependent, for example, in guaranteeing loans contracted abroad; on the other hand, they do not yet command the confidence which would permit them to borrow as much as they would like.

The International Development Association has no preconceived policy in allocating its funds. It is, however, careful to ensure a wide geographical distribution of its development credits and to grant proper priority to the poorer countries.

Although the Association is a separate entity, with its own financial resources, it is closely allied to the World Bank. Member-states are represented by the same person, both in the bank and in the Association; these have common personnel. This joint administration not only saves money, it also ensures efficient co-ordination of policy and method between the two institutions.

All credits have hitherto been granted for a period of fifty years. No interest is payable but a commission of 0·75% per annum is charged on amounts drawn and not yet repaid.

Obviously the Association cannot hope to see its resources reconstituted in the near future by the repayment of the credits which it has granted. It will therefore be able to continue to make loans only if it receives, when the time comes, fresh contributions from member-states.

In the course of the annual assembly held in September 1962 the Board of Governors asked the Executive Directors to study the future financial needs of the Association and to prepare a report on the subject. The Directors informed the Governors in their report that on a basis of projects, the study of which was well advanced, that portion of the initial resources of the Association which was in freely convertible currency and which had — in June 1963 — not yet been committed, would permit new commitments for a period of only six to nine months. The Directors concluded that it was desirable to provide the Association with fresh resources, so that it might continue its operations and that an increase in total resources at its disposal was amply justified.

On the other hand, their report shows that member-states of

These are the twenty-five countries in receipt of development credits, expressed in U.S. dollars (statement 30 June 1965).

Members in whose territories loans have been made	Disbursed portion	Undisbursed portion	Total
Bolivia	2,149,584	12,850,416	15,000,000
Chile	5,359,658	13,640,342	19,000,000
China (Formosa)	12,412,985	919,985	13,332,970
Colombia	9,281,507	10,218,493	19,500,000
Costa Rica	2,138,871	3,361,129	5,500,000
Ecuador	..	8,000,000	8,000,000
Ethiopia	3,839,111	9,660,889	13,500,000
Haiti	349,855	..	349,855
Honduras	5,404,897	3,595,103	9,000,000
India	287,923,691	197,076,309	485,000,000
Jordan	2,954,034	5,545,966	8,500,000
Kenya	82,054	7,217,946	7,300,000
Korea	13,939,845	60,155	14,000,000
Mauritania	..	6,700,000	6,700,000
Nicaragua	2,364,914	635,086	3,000,000
Pakistan	35,122,163	207,667,837	242,790,000
Paraguay	1,425,157	8,174,843	9,600,000
Syrian Arab Republic	..	8,500,000	8,500,000
Salvador, El	2,375,352	5,624,648	8,000,000
Sudan	7,680,603	5,319,397	13,000,000
Tanzania	2,274,574	16,325,426	18,600,000
Tunisia	2,941,477	2,058,523	5,000,000
Turkey	11,698,760	44,001,240	55,700,000
United Kingdom			
for Bechuanaland	169,588	3,430,412	3,600,000
for Swaziland	2,800,000	..	2,800,000
TOTAL	414,688,680	580,584,145	995,272,825

the first group are ready to place at the disposal of the Association fresh resources in freely convertible currency.

The table on p. 200 indicates the amount to be provided by each Government of the eighteen member-states of the first group.

Statement of subscriptions, voting power and supplementary resources

Member	Subscriptions		Voting power		Supplementary resources		Total subscriptions and supplementary resources
	Total	Percent of total	Number of votes	Percent of total	Amounts paid in	Amounts not yet due	
	$				$	$	$
Australia	20,180,000	2·03	4,536	1·84	...	19,800,000	39,980,000
Austria	5,040,000	0·51	1,508	0·61	...	5,040,000	10,080,000
Belgium	8,250,000	0·83	2,150	0·87	...	8,250,000	16,500,000
Canada	37,830,000	3·80	8,066	3·28	...	41,700,000	79,530,000
Denmark	8,740,000	0·88	2,248	0·91	...	7,500,000	16,240,000
Finland	3,830,000	0·38	1,266	0·52	...	2,298,000	6,128,000
France	52,960,000	5·32	11,092	4·51	...	61,872,000	114,832,000
Germany	52,960,000	5·32	11,092	4·51	...	72,600,000	125,560,000
Italy	18,160,000	1·82	4,132	1·68	...	30,000,000	48,160,000
Japan	33,590,000	3·37	7,218	2·93	...	41,250,000	74,840,000
Kuwait	3,360,000	0·34	1,172	0·48	...	3,360,000	6,720,000
Luxembourg	375,000	0·04	575	0·23	...	375,000	750,000
Netherlands	27,740,000	2·79	6,048	2·46	...	16,500,000	44,240,000
Norway	6,720,000	0·67	1,844	0·75	...	6,600,000	13,320,000
South Africa	10,090,000	1·01	2,518	1·02	...	...	10,090,000
Sweden	10,090,000	1·01	2,518	1·02	15,135,000	15,000,000	40,225,000
United Kingdom	131,140,000	13·17	26,728	10·86	...	96,600,000	227,740,000
United States	320,290,000	32·17	64,558	26·23	...	312,000,000	632,290,000
TOTAL	$751,345,000	75·46	159,269	64·71	$15,135,000	$740,745,000	$1,507,225,000

The United Nations have classified the countries of the world as either 'developed' or, in contrast, 'underdeveloped' or in process of development. According to this classification the world contains, out of 128 independent states, only twenty-seven 'developed' states.

These twenty-seven nations are:

Australia	Germany (West)	New Zealand
Austria	Great Britain	Norway
Belgium	Hungary	Poland
Canada	Iceland	Rumania
Czechoslovakia	Ireland	South Africa
Denmark	Italy	Sweden
Finland	Japan	Switzerland
France	Luxembourg	U.S.S.R.
Germany (East)	Netherlands	United States of America

Albania, Bulgaria, Spain, Greece, Portugal, Yugoslavia and the whole of Africa (with the exception of South Africa) are considered underdeveloped countries, as are Latin America and the whole of Asia (with the exception of Japan).

4. THE INTERNATIONAL MONETARY FUND

Commenced operations 6 May 1946.

Objects: to facilitate international co-operation in monetary matters and to resolve short-term balance-of-payments difficulties by the granting of credits or by any other appropriate means.

Resources: contributions from member-countries in gold and in their own currency.

Loans: loans are granted by putting hard currency at the disposal of the borrower-country in exchange for the deposit with the International Monetary Fund of an equivalent amount in the currency of the borrower-country.

Duration of loans: three to five years.

Interest rates: 0·5% to cover costs, plus interest on purchases of currency above quota, at a rate which increases with the duration and amount of the overdraft. The minimum rate is 2% per annum.

Balance-sheet 30 April 1965 (runs from 1 May to 30 April each year)
Total contributions from the 102 member-states $15,993,083,333
Reserves $290,085,915
    TOTAL of the balance-sheet of the Fund $16,692,262,236
The financial year runs from 1 May to 30 April.

The articles of association of the International Monetary Fund were written during the monetary and financial Conference of the Allied Governments, held at Bretton Woods (New Hampshire) between 1 and 22 July 1944. The Fund came into existence on 27 December 1945, when twenty-nine governments responsible for 80% of the contributions had signed the articles in Washington. The Fund is an institution constituted by the association of a certain number of states who have undertaken to adhere to its articles of association and to favour international monetary co-operation and to encourage the expansion of world trade.

The Fund realises its objectives by three principal methods:

1. The meetings of its twenty Executive Directors and Alternates form a monetary conference in permanent session, permitting a thorough exchange of views on monetary questions and exchange problems.

2. On request it provides its members with experts who will advise on and assist in the resolution of their financial and monetary difficulties.

3. Against appropriate guarantees its currency reserves are at the disposal of its members to enable them to resolve short-term current payments difficulties.

In the pursuit of these objectives, the Fund endeavours to help its members to find a concrete solution to their foreign payments problems, in conformity with the principles of co-operation embodied in its articles of association.

By signing the articles the member-states agreed to conform

to certain rules of conduct in the sphere of finance and foreign exchange. Member-states consult the Fund in order to ensure that their exchange policy and their monetary measures are in harmony with their obligations under the articles. Among matters on which consultations have been held, one may mention official parities of the currencies of member-states, multiple-rate systems and discriminatory and restrictive measures in foreign-exchange matters.

The Fund is obliged, by the terms of its articles, to keep itself well informed on the financial and monetary situation of its members. Conversely, each member-state is obliged to provide the Fund with detailed information on its financial and monetary situation. By this means member-states are kept continually abreast of developments in the financial situation throughout the world. Whatever may be their geographical importance or the level of their technical progress, all benefit from authoritative advice based on the experience which the Fund has gained in the solution of its many problems.

The Fund carries on a vast programme of technical assistance in the monetary sphere; missions are sent to all parts of the world; studies, reports and publications dealing with international finance are produced. It has advised certain countries on alterations in parity or exchange rates, on modifications in multiple-rate systems, on exchange control and on questions of monetary and financial policy which play an important role in international payments. Its experts have helped certain countries to establish or to adapt to their special needs such instruments as central banks and exchange systems.

The Fund sells currencies from its holdings to member-states. These sales are subject to certain conditions; an important condition laid down is that as a general rule sales occurring in any period of twelve months may not exceed 25% of the quota of the member-state interested. In exceptional circumstances the Fund can lift this embargo and authorise larger sales. A member-state buying currency from the Fund must pay in its national currency. The articles of the Fund impose conditions for the repurchase by member-states of their national currency against gold or convertible currencies. These provisions are designed to ensure that the Fund holds reserves in the currencies of all member-states, sufficient at any moment to meet their need for foreign currency.

After the declaration of February 1952 in which the Fund defined its policy on currency transactions, it was decided that any purchase of currency by a member-state should be repayable within a period of three to five years or be partially redeemed by the purchase of the currency of the member-state in question by another member-state. It was also decided that members could take advantage of a system of 'lines of credit', allowing them to draw on the resources of the Fund within well-defined limits and for a maximum period of one year.

The sale of currency is subject to a commission of $\frac{1}{2}\%$, payable either in gold, or partly in gold and partly in national currency. In addition, member-states must pay a higher interest on the amount by which the Fund's holding in their national currency exceeds their quota.

The articles of the Fund oblige it to collaborate closely with other international institutions. As a result there are frequent contacts with specialised institutions dealing with problems of great importance to the Fund. An agreement reached with the United Nations dealing with such collaboration lays down the main lines of a programme of mutual assistance between the United Nations and the Fund, considered as an independent international organisation. The World Bank and the Fund work in close co-operation. Certain Executive Directors and deputy Directors of the Fund are also Directors of the Bank and this is also true of some of the Governors.

Supreme authority within the Fund is vested in a Board of Governors, to which each member-state appoints a Governor and a deputy. Normally the Board of Governors holds an annual meeting at which Ministers and Treasury officials of the member-states meet. The Board of Governors has delegated many of its powers to the Executive Board. Nevertheless, the conditions of admission for new members, the revision of quotas, the election of Executive Directors and certain other important powers remain the prerogative of the Board of Governors. The Executive

Board is composed of five Executive Directors, appointed by the five member-states whose quotas are the highest, and of fifteen Executive Directors elected by all the other member-states through the intermediate of their representatives on the Board of Governors. The Managing Director exercises the functions both of Chairman of the Executive Board and head of the administrative staff of the Fund. On 30 April 1965 the Fund staff numbered 674 persons. Nationals of sixty-four countries are now in the staff.

On 21 June 1961 the Executive Board unanimously elected Pierre-Paul Schweitzer, Managing Director and Chairman of the Executive Board of the International Monetary Fund. His term of office began on 1 September 1963 and will last five years. A Frenchman with an international reputation, he gained the votes of Americans and Europeans.

At the Annual Meeting in September 1964, a large number of Governors spoke in favour of an increase in quotas. There was unanimous approval of the resolution 'that the Executive Directors proceed to consider the question of adjusting the quotas of members of the Fund and at an early date submit an appropriate proposal to the Board of Governors'.

On 26 February 1965 the Executive Directors adopted a report entitled *Increase in Quotas of Fund Members*, to be submitted to the Board of Governors.

The report includes two resolutions, the first proposing a general increase of 25%, appropriately rounded off, of all quotas, and the second proposing special quota increases for sixteen members. The first resolution had to be voted on as a whole, but, for the second resolution, votes could be cast on all or each of the special quota increases. By 31 March 1965 both resolutions had been adopted by the Governors by more than the required majority of four-fifths of the total voting power.

The revised quotas are shown in the tables on pp. 206–7.

The International Monetary Fund Institute was established in May 1964 to expand and diversify the Fund's training activities.

One of the first tasks undertaken by the new Institute was to acquaint the French-speaking member-states which had recently

Proposed increase quotas (first resolution)

Member	Present quota (Million U.S. dollars)	Increased quota under first resolution (Million U.S. dollars)	Member	Present quota (Million U.S. dollars)	Increased quota under first resolution (Million U.S. dollars)
1 Afghanistan	22·50	29	52 Korea	18·75	24
2 Algeria	60·00	75	53 Kuwait	50·00	63
3 Argentina	280·00	350	54 Laos	7·50	10
4 Australia	400·00	500	55 Lebanon	6·75	9
5 Austria	75·00	94	56 Liberia	11·25	15
6 Belgium	337·50	422	57 Libya	15·00	19
7 Bolivia	22·50	29	58 Luxembourg	15·00	19
8 Brazil	280·00	350	59 Malagasy Republic	15·00	19
9 Burma	30·00	38			
10 Burundi	11·25	15	60 Malaysia	100·00	125
11 Cameroons	15·00	19	61 Mali	13·00	17
12 Canada	550·00	690	62 Mauritania	7·50	10
13 Central African Republic	7·50	10	63 Mexico	180·00	225
14 Ceylon	62·00	78	64 Morocco	52·50	66
15 Chad	7·50	10	65 Nepal	7·50	10
16 Chile	100·00	125	66 Netherlands	412·50	520
17 China	550·00	690	67 New Zealand	125·00	157
18 Colombia	100·00	125	68 Nicaragua	11·25	15
19 Congo (Brazzaville)	7·50	10	69 Niger	7·50	10
20 Congo, Democratic Republic of	45·00	57	70 Nigeria	50·00	63
			71 Norway	100·00	125
21 Costa Rica	20·00	25	72 Pakistan	150·00	188
22 Cyprus	11·25	15	73 Panama	11·25	15
23 Dahomey	7·50	10	74 Paraguay	11·25	15
24 Denmark	130·00	163	75 Peru	37·50	47
25 Dominican Republic	25·00	32	76 Philippines	75·00	94
			77 Portugal	60·00	75
26 Ecuador	20·00	25	78 Rwanda	11·25	15
27 El Salvador	20·00	25	79 Saudi Arabia	72·00	90
28 Ethiopia	15·00	19	80 Senegal	25·00	32
29 Finland	57·00	72	81 Sierra Leone	11·25	15
30 France	787·50	985	82 Somalia	11·25	15
31 Gabon	7·50	10	83 South Africa	150·00	188
32 Germany, Federal Republic of	787·50	985	84 Spain	150·00	188
			85 Sudan	45·00	57
33 Ghana	55·00	69	86 Sweden	150·00	188
34 Greece	60·00	75	87 Syrian Arab Republic	30·00	38
35 Guatemala	20·00	25			
36 Guinea	15·00	19	88 Tanzania	25·00	32
37 Haiti	11·25	15	89 Thailand	76 00	95
38 Honduras	15·00	19	90 Togo	11·25	15
39 Iceland	11·25	15	91 Trinidad and Tobago	20·00	25
40 India	600·00	750			
41 Indonesia	165·00	207	92 Tunisia	22·50	29
42 Iran	70·00	88	93 Turkey	86·00	108
43 Iraq	55·00	69	94 Uganda	25·00	32
44 Ireland	45·00	57	95 United Arab Republic	120·00	150
45 Israel	50·00	63			
46 Italy	500·00	625	96 United Kingdom	1,950·00	2,440
47 Ivory Coast	15·00	19	97 United States	4,125·00	5,160
48 Jamaica	20·00	25	98 Upper Volta	7·50	10
49 Japan	500·00	625	99 Uruguay	30·00	38
50 Jordan	11·25	15	100 Venezuela	150·00	188
51 Kenya	25·00	32	101 Vietnam	22·50	29
			102 Yugoslavia	120·00	150

Proposed increases in quotas for sixteen members (second resolution)

Member	Quota on 26 February 1965	New quota under first resolution	New quota under first and second resolutions
Austria	75	94	175
Canada	550	690	740
Finland	57	72	125
Germany	787·5	985	1,200
Greece	60	75	100
Iran	70	88	125
Ireland	45	57	80
Israel	50	63	90
Japan	500	625	725
Mexico	180	225	270
Norway	100	125	150
Philippines	75	94	110
South Africa . . .	150	188	200
Spain	150	188	250
Sweden	150	188	225
Venezuela	150	188	250

joined the Fund with the general nature of the Fund, its policy objectives and financial resources, and the potential benefits of Fund training. For this purpose the Institute organised, between July and December, two six-week seminars conducted in French for high officials from those countries. Each government in the French-speaking areas of Africa and one government in Asia was invited to designate a senior financial official to attend one of the seminars. Seventeen countries were able to take advantage of the invitation.

In March 1965 the Institute began the first of its regular twenty-week courses on Financial Policy and Analysis conducted in English. Twenty participants, broadly representative of all areas of the world, attended this course. Of these, thirteen are employed in the central banks of their countries and seven in Finance Ministries or Treasuries.

The emphasis of the course is on monetary and fiscal policy, with attention focused on, but not confined to, the problems of developing countries. It draws extensively on the experience that the Fund has gained in its contacts with member-countries. The course has been formulated with the objective of enhancing the usefulness of the participants to their employing agencies. At the same time it is hoped that the first-hand acquaintance which participants will gain with the Fund's objectives, operations and procedures will contribute to a closer understanding and to smoother working relations between the Fund and its members.

In view of the nature of the regular course, participants have been selected with particular attention to their policy responsibilities. The Fund recognises that governments in the developing countries may equally wish to send more junior staff members to Washington for studies which emphasise the technical aspects of financial and economic analysis. The I.M.F. Institute is therefore planning to present over the years a variety of courses, dealing with subjects at different levels and addressed to officials of Central Banks, Ministries of Finance and comparable government agencies in Fund member-countries. The present professional staff of the I.M.F. Institute consists of six economists, and it is intended to augment this number. During 1966 the Institute will move into new quarters where its technical accommodation will make it possible to handle several groups of participants at the same time.

The programme for 1965–6 comprised five different courses: two on Balance-of-Payments Methodology, one conducted in English from 30 August 1965 to 8 October 1965, and the other in French from 21 February 1966 to 1 April 1966; these two courses were designed to help member-countries to improve their balance-of-payments statistics and their presentation for purposes of economic analysis. Two courses were given on Financial Policy and Analysis, the first conducted in French from 14 October 1965 to 22 December 1965, and the second in English from 14 March 1966 to 29 July 1966. One special course, conducted in English from 4 January 1966 to 11 February 1966, followed the general lines of the special courses given in French during July–August and October–December 1964.

5. THE INTER-AMERICAN DEVELOPMENT BANK

Its legal existence dates from 30 December 1959 (1 October 1960 bank officially commenced operations).

Objects: the bank is a regional hemispheric agency created by twenty American nations — nineteen Latin American countries and the United States — to accelerate the economic development of the member-countries, individually and collectively. The bank provides the capital and the technical assistance needed to back the efforts of Latin American states to ameliorate social conditions and to achieve a balanced economic growth.

Resources: the ordinary capital resources are currently authorised at $2,150,000,000; fund for special operations, $900,000,000; Social Progress Trust Fund (Alliance for Progress), $525,000,000; other financial resources by borrowing on the international money-markets.

Loans: loans are made to member-states principally to finance specific projects. The bank, however, also makes loans to development institutions or similar agencies in order that they, in turn, may relend the proceeds to finance specific development projects whose requirements are not large enough to warrant a direct loan from the bank. In making loans to a private enterprise the bank need not require a guarantee of repayment by the government of the country where the investment is made, although it can do so when circumstances warrant.

Relationship with other credit sources: the bank co-operates with other credit institutions. Before making a loan, the bank satisfies itself that the prospective borrower cannot obtain financial aid from private sources on terms which, in its opinion, are reasonable. The bank also satisfies itself that the borrower and his guarantor, if any, are able to meet their obligations.

Duration of loans: from the bank, ordinary loans, eight to twelve years, but they can range up to twenty years for special projects; from the Fund for special operations, fifteen to twenty years; from Social Progress Trust Fund (Alliance for Progress) up to twenty years or more.

Interest rates: ordinary loans from the bank, $5\frac{3}{4}\%$; fund for special operations, 4% to $5\frac{3}{4}\%$; Social Progress Trust Fund (Alliance for Progress), $1\frac{10}{4}\%$ to $2\frac{3}{4}\%$.

Proposed items of the balance-sheet 31 December 1964
(1 January–31 December annually)

(a) Bank — Ordinary Capital

Capital stock authorised: 215,000 shares of $10,000 par
value each $2,150,000,000

128,498½ shares subscribed by twenty member-states .	1,284,985,000
Less Callable portion	903,405,000
Paid-up capital	381,580,000
General reserve	11,919,839
Special reserve	1,921,590
Funded debt	272,593,548
Investments	310,768,005
Loans outstanding held by bank	180,886,559

Ordinary loans extended from the bank's ordinary capital resources are repayable in the currency or currencies in which they are made. The bank may extend lines of credit from its ordinary capital to finance exports of capital goods among the Latin American member-countries. These operations must be carried out through national agencies in the member-states, designated specifically for this purpose.

(b) Fund for special operations

Contribution quotas paid by the twenty member-states .	$218,921,000
General reserve	1,430,509
Funds held in trust	26,937,000
Investments	63,539,245
Loans outstanding held by bank	48,800,530
Non-negotiable, non-interest-bearing demand-notes denominated in members' currencies	88,392,831

The resources of the Fund for special operations enable the bank to make loans on terms and conditions appropriate for dealing with special circumstances which may arise in specific countries or with regard to specific projects. The bank's agreement requires that the resources of the Fund shall be held, used, obligated, invested or otherwise disposed of in a manner completely separate from ordinary capital resources. Loans of such nature are repayable on terms and conditions which are more flexible than those applying to ordinary capital resources.

(c) *Social Progress Trust Fund*

Fund established by the United States Government on
19 June 1961 with an amount of $394,000,000, increased,
on 17 February 1964, with an additional amount of
$131,000,000, total $525,000,000

As of 31 December 1964 $162,000,000 has been received
by the bank from the United States. The remainder,
$363,000,000, is to be made available to the bank by the
United States from time to time as needed to meet commitments of the Trust Fund.

Total loans approved . . $450,035,000
Undisbursed balance . . 294,544,844
                              ——————— 155,490,156
Less Repayments . . . 4,648,047

Loans outstanding $150,842,109

The Social Progress Trust Fund, which the bank has administered since
19 June 1961, under an agreement with the United States Government, was
established to promote social development in Latin America as part of the
Alliance for Progress programme. The bank uses the resources of the Trust
Fund to finance projects and programmes in four social development fields.
They are settlement and improved land use, housing for low-income groups,
community water supply and sanitation facilities, and higher education and
advanced training. In addition the bank uses the Trust Fund to provide
technical assistance for purposes connected with projects in the above fields
and for the mobilisation of domestic financial resources and the strengthening
of financial institutions. Loans from the Fund are extended at lower interest
rates and repayment terms are longer than those extended from the ordinary
capital resources of the Fund for special operations.

In 1964 the bank obtained a substantial volume of financial
resources in the private capital markets of the world. Results of
the bank's efforts to mobilise additional public resources for Latin
America's development from non-member capital-exporting
countries should also be mentioned. During the year 1964 talks
were held with the Governments of the United Kingdom, the
Netherlands and Spain, regarding arrangements under which
funds from these countries for the development of Latin America
might be channelled through the bank. These events show the
receptivity that exists in certain capital-exporting countries to

the idea of using the bank's knowledge and experience in channel-
ling funds for the development of Latin America.

On 31 December 1964 the funded debt of the bank, expressed
in United States currency, amounted to $272,593,548, issued in
the following states:

United States of America	$225,000,000
Italy	24,193,548
Germany	15,000,000
United Kingdom	8,400,000

The accelerated lending rate maintained by the bank since it
began operations has resulted in the commitment of a substantial

Country	Paid in	Callable (subscribed by 31 December 1964)	Callable (subscribed or to be subscribed in 1965)	Total
Argentina	51,570,000	112,240,000	60,670,000	224,480,000
Bolivia	4,140,000	9,010,000	4,870,000	18,020,000
Brazil	51,570,000	112,240,000	60,670,000	224,480,000
Chile	14,160,000	30,820,000	16,660,000	61,640,000
Colombia	14,150,000	30,795,000	16,645,000	61,590,000
Costa Rica	2,070,000	4,505,000	2,435,000	9,010,000
Dominican Republic	2,760,000	6,010,000	3,250,000	12,020,000
Ecuador	2,760,000	6,010,000	3,250,000	12,020,000
El Salvador	2,070,000	4,505,000	2,435,000	9,010,000
Guatemala	2,760,000	6,010,000	3,250,000	12,020,000
Haiti	2,070,000	4,505,000	2,435,000	9,010,000
Honduras	2,070,000	4,505,000	2,435,000	9,010,000
Mexico	33,150,000	72,150,000	39,000,000	144,300,000
Nicaragua	2,070,000	4,505,000	2,435,000	9,010,000
Panama	2,070,000	4,505,000	2,435,000	9,010,000
Paraguay	2,070,000	4,505,000	2,435,000	9,010,000
Peru	6,910,000	15,040,000	8,130,000	30,080,000
United States	150,000,000	405,880,000	205,880,000	761,760,000
Uruguay	5,530,000	5,530,000	13,010,000	24,070,000
Venezuela	27,630,000	60,135,000	32,505,000	120,270,000
TOTAL	381,580,000	903,405,000	484,835,000	1,769,820,000

portion of its ordinary capital resources. This has made it imperative for the bank to take measures designed to increase its callable capital in order to obtain additional backing to continue borrowing funds in the capital markets of the United States and Europe.

In view of this, the Board of Governors on 8 April 1963 approved resolutions calling on member-countries to adopt measures to increase the capital of the bank and the resources of the Fund for Special Operations. During the course of the year 1963 most member-nations had taken the necessary measures, and on 28 January 1964 they entered into effect.

Total subscriptions to the ordinary capital resources on a country-by-country basis are shown in the table on p. 212 (expressed in U.S. dollars).

Along with the action taken to augment its ordinary capital resources, the bank took steps looking towards a much greater increase in the resources of the Fund for Special Operations. In view of the need for providing additional resources to expand the activities of the Fund, the Board of Governors at its fifth annual meeting in Panama City in April 1964 approved a resolution recommending that the member-nations take such action as might be necessary to increase the resources of the Fund by the equivalent of $900 million through additional contributions by the member-countries, as indicated in the table on p. 214 (expressed in U.S. dollars).

In carrying out its objectives the bank is authorised to provide technical assistance to its member governments, their official or autonomous agencies, or private firms within their countries. The bank has no special forms for technical assistance applications. As in the case of loans, it does welcome preliminary inquiries, either in person or by mail, from prospective applicants. This enables the bank to determine whether a formal application should be presented or whether the applicant should seek assistance from other sources.

The basic authority of the bank is vested in the Board of Governors, composed of one Governor and one Alternate appointed by each member-country for a five-year term. The Board

Proposed additional contribution by member-countries

Country	Contributions paid up	Proposed contributions
Argentina . . .	15,471,000	33,402,000
Bolivia . . .	1,242,000	2,682,000
Brazil	15,471,000	33,402,000
Chile	4,248,000	9,171,000
Colombia . . .	4,245,000	9,165,000
Costa Rica . . .	621,000	1,341,000
Dominican Republic .	828,000	1,788,000
Ecuador . . .	828,000	1,788,000
El Salvador . . .	621,000	1,341,000
Guatemala . . .	828,000	1,788,000
Haiti	621,000	1,341,000
Honduras . . .	621,000	1,341,000
Mexico . . .	9,945,000	21,474,000
Nicaragua . . .	621,000	1,341,000
Panama . . .	621,000	1,341,000
Paraguay . . .	621,000	1,341,000
Peru	2,073,000	4,473,000
United States . .	150,000,000	750,000,000
Uruguay . . .	1,106,000	3,582,000
Venezuela . . .	8,289,000	17,898,000
TOTAL . . .	218,921,100	900,000,000

meets once a year, rotating the site of its meeting among its member-states. The direction of the bank's operation is entrusted to the Board of Executive Directors; the President, who is elected by the Board of Governors; and the Executive Vice-President, elected by the Board of Executive Directors.

The Board of Executive Directors functions continuously at the bank's headquarters in Washington, D.C. It is composed of seven members who represent the member-states and serve for three-year terms. Six are elected by groups of Latin American countries and one is appointed by the United States. Directors appoint their Alternates, who are empowered to act in the absence of the titular director.

The President of the bank is Mr. Felipe Herrera and the Executive Vice-President Mr. T. Graydon Upton.

The work of the bank has served to bring into realistic focus problems of institutional reform, development programming, economic integration, foreign trade financing, external creditworthiness, domestic resources mobilisation and training of human resources, which Latin America is facing.

Basic data of Latin America:

Area of all twenty republics	7,725,097 sq. miles
Total population end 1962	208 million
Estimated population by 1970	256 million
Gross domestic *per capita* product (1961) . . .	U.S.$400
Percentage of tax burden to gross domestic *per capita* product (1960–1) not including Bolivia, Cuba and Uruguay	11·3%
Density of rural population in proportion to cultivated land and pasture land (1962) (inhabitants per 1,000 acres) .	96
Infant mortality rate (1960–1) per 1,000 live births . .	85·4

The ultimate objective of the Inter-American Development Bank is to help raise the standard of living of the peoples of the Latin American countries.

For this fundamental task the field of activity is immense.

6. THE EXPORT–IMPORT BANK OF WASHINGTON (EXIMBANK)

The bank is a wholly government owned corporation.

Commenced operations 12 February 1934.

Object: the objects and purposes of the bank are to aid in financing and to facilitate exports and imports and the exchange of commodities between the United States or any of its territories or insular possessions and any foreign country or the agencies or nationals thereof.

Resources: the bank has a capital of $1 billion, may borrow from the U.S. Treasury up to $6 billion, and is permitted to have outstanding at any one time not more than $9 billion in loans, guarantees and insurance.

Loans: the bank does not compete with private capital and does not, therefore, extend credit when private credit is available in adequate amounts on reasonable terms. It does not engage in financing where adequate facilities are available on customary commercial terms through commercial banks or finance companies dealing in foreign drafts. The bank extends loans and guarantees for the primary purpose of promoting the export and import trade of the United States. It generally makes loans only for specific purposes. The bank extends credit only to finance purchases of materials and equipment produced or manufactured in the United States. The bank supplements and encourages the utilisation of private capital in export and import trade and in overseas investment generally.

Duration of loans: generally up to seven years in the case of credits to the export trade but they can range up to twenty years for economic infra-structural projects.

Rates of interest: normally $5\frac{1}{2}\%$ for development loans. Export credits at higher rates.

Report of operations: the bank is obliged to transmit to the Congress semi-annually a complete and detailed report of its operations. The report should be as of the close of business on 30 June and 31 December of each year.

Balance-sheet 30 June 1965 (run from 1 July to 30 June each year)

	Thousands of dollars
Capital stock held by the U.S. Treasury	1,000,000
Reserves (earnings retained for use in the business) . .	943,930
Participation certificates payable	1,022,263
Loans receivable	3,511,880
Total of the balance-sheet of the bank	3,565,366

For the fiscal year 1965/6 authorisations, including loans, guarantees and insurance underwritten, totalled $1,859·0 million. Of this sum, $435·2 million were long-term capital loans; $359·2 million, exporter and commodity guarantees and credits; $721·5 million, export credit insurance underwritten; and $340·0 million, emergency foreign trade credits. A small amount of consignment insurance rounds off the total.

Gross income of the bank during the past fiscal year was

$177·8 million. Operating and administrative expenses were $3·7 million; interest paid and other charges were $60·4 million, leaving a net income of $113·7 million. A dividend of $50·0 million was declared in the fiscal year 1965 and paid to the Treasury on 1 July. As a result, $63·7 million was added to retained income reserve, which totalled $943·9 million at the end of the fiscal year 30 June 1965.

The bank's long-term loans to buyers overseas helped finance $435·2 million purchases of U.S. equipment and services for projects on five continents. These loans embraced such diverse developments as thermal power in Japan, paper in Chile, a hotel in Ethiopia, mining equipment in Peru, an aluminium plant in India and an undersea telephone cable connecting the Philippines with Hawaii. The proceeds of these loans, spent in dollars in the United States, benefited the American producer and the recipient country as well, for it is a criterion of the bank's loans that the project be economically viable and contribute to the economy of the borrowing country.

In February 1964 President Johnson determined that it was in the national interest for the bank to issue guarantees on the sale of U.S. agricultural products to the Soviet Union, Bulgaria, Czecho-Slovakia, Hungary, Poland and Rumania. At the same time, he laid it down that the bank similarly could assist in the export of other goods and services to Yugoslavia; and in June 1964 he determined that short- and medium-term credits to Rumania were also eligible for these guarantees. The bank, in accordance with these Presidential decrees, authorised $24·2 million of such guarantees in the fiscal year, of which $4·6 million was to assist the export of agricultural commodities and $19·6 million was industrial equipment.

On 6 February 1961 President Kennedy issued a directive to the bank to provide facilities to insure American exporters where the extension of credit is warranted. The bank then invited private insurance companies to take part in a broad programme for providing foreign credit insurance.

The Foreign Credit Insurance Association (F.C.I.A.) was formed in response to that invitation. Membership of the

Association is open to any insurance company which may qualify. The bank and the F.C.I.A. are proceeding in this undertaking in accordance with Federal Law which authorised the bank to establish this programme.

The Foreign Credit Insurance Association, at the direction of the bank, is to administer the details of the programme. The bank will assume 100% responsibility with respect to political risks. The bank and the F.C.I.A.'s member-companies will share the policy obligations with regard to commercial credit risks.

The Foreign Credit Insurance Association's purpose is to offer private insurance facilities in partnership with the Export–Import Bank in order to assist United States exporters to become more competitive in foreign trade through a sound foreign credit insurance programme.

The F.C.I.A. is, today, an unincorporated group of over seventy private insurance companies and it sells credit insurance to United States exporters to protect them against risks inherent in overseas sales. Two types of risks normally are covered: (1) commercial risks; (2) political risks.

Commercial credit risks include:

1. Insolvency of the buyer,
2. Failure to pay within six months after due date.

Political risks may result from the following situations which are not experienced in normal domestic commercial credit, but which are inherent in otherwise sound and desirable export transactions:

1. Inconvertibility of buyer's currency to dollars,
2. Cancellation of import licence or imposition of other import restrictions,
3. Cancellation of export licence or imposition of other export restrictions,
4. War, civil commotion and revolution,
5. Expropriation of the buyer's business, or intervention in it by a foreign governmental authority,
6. Imposition of any law, decree or regulation which prevents

the buyer from depositing his local currency in an attempt to meet his payment obligation,

7. Transport or insurance charges occasioned by interruption or diversion of voyage outside the United States due to political causes.

The Export–Import Bank Act of 1945, as amended, vests the management of the bank in a Board of Directors consisting of the President of the bank, who serves as Chairman, the First Vice-President, who serves as Vice-Chairman, and three additional Directors, all appointed by the President of the United States by and with the advice and consent of the Senate. Of the five members of the Board not more than three shall be members of any one political party. All decisions in connection with the authorisation of loans by the bank are made by the Board of Directors.

The Act also provides for an Advisory Committee of nine members, appointed by the Board of Directors on the recommendation of the President of the bank, who shall be broadly representative of industry, commerce, finance, agriculture and labour. The Advisory Committee meets one or more times each year, on the call of the President, to consult the Directors on the policies and operations of the bank.

The Export–Import Bank is, in a sense, two institutions. In its insurance and guarantee activities, it is comparable to other foreign governmental institutions which provide guarantees and insurance to aid their exporters and safeguard them from undue risk on overseas sales. The impact of this phase of bank activities is obvious and easily comprehended. The insurance and guarantees against loss, and the credit which is thus brought into being, promote the exports of the United States.

In the other phase of its activities — its long-term capital loans — the bank's operation is analogous to that of an investment banker in the foreign field and parallels the activities of the multi-national lending institutions. Because of this role, the bank has pointed, quite appropriately, to the contribution which its long-term capital loans have made to the economies and thus the development of the recipient countries, which literally encircle the globe. However, the impact which the investment banking loans have on the exports of the United States needs emphasis as well.

Every dollar of long-term capital loans or project loans represents a dollar of United States exports. Thus it is that all the activities of the bank have a common character, for the funds which it brings into being, in one way or another, must be spent in the United States by the foreign buyer for the purchase of United States goods and services.

During its thirty-two years of life, the bank's net authorisations for loans, guarantees and insurance have aggregated $14·9 billion and disbursements on its loans alone, $10·2 billion. These figures indicate not only the support which the bank's operations have lent to the country's export drive but also the support which these exports have brought to the country's economy and to its balance of payments. The amounts are not unimpressive.

The bank has avoided competing with private capital and has sought the participation of American private enterprise where possible. For this reason, the $14·9 billion of net authorisations does not measure the impact of the bank's operations on the American economy. To this sum, large as it is, should be added substantial private equity investment and debt financing by commercial banks and exporters which the bank's long-term capital loans, insurance programmes and other activities have called forth.

7. The Agency for International Development (A.I.D.)

A state organisation, headquartered in the Department of State in Washington.

Commenced operations on 4 November 1961.

Objects: to promote the economic development of under-developed countries principally by means of long-term programmes designed to develop economic resources and to increase productive capacity. Aid to be granted under the Act for International Development is divided into four principal categories:

(1) support of relatively urgent strategic and political requirement (Supporting Assistance — used primarily for financing commodity imports),

(2) contributions to long-range economic and social development (Development Loans — mainly for capital projects; Development Grants — mainly for aid for education, technical assistance and in some case for roads, harbours, communications systems; and Development Research),

(3) support of International Organisation,

(4) funds to meet unforeseen events and emergencies (Contingency Fund), expenditures from which may fall under any of the above three headings.

The Agency guarantees also complete or partial reimbursement, up to $1 million, of private American investments in the event of expropriation, inconvertibility, of war-damage and of certain political risks, and offers a similar partial guarantee of up to $100 million against all risks in certain circumstances.

Resources: credits voted annually by Congress. Up to 25% of profits resulting from sale of agricultural surpluses.

Relationship with other credit sources: must have regard to the possibility for the recipient of obtaining funds from other sources in the free world on reasonable conditions.

Duration of loans: usually up to forty years with a supplementary period of grace of ten years.

Rate of interest: 0·75% to 5·75%.

The Agency for International Development was created by an Act of Congress of 4 September 1961 and began operations on 4 November of the same year.

The new aid Agency encompassed the functions previously carried on by:

(*a*) the International Co-operation Administration,

(*b*) the Development Loan Fund,

(*c*) the Food-for-Peace programme, and

(*d*) the local currency lending activities of the Export–Import Bank of Washington.

Two basic concepts underlie the new organisation:

(1) that the starting-point of United States assistance is the formulation by each country of a national development plan of priorities, and
(2) that all the tools of aid must be used in a co-ordinated fashion to facilitate the carrying out of that national plan.

The changing character of United States assistance programmes requires a continuing analysis of the Agency's administrative operations to ensure their effectiveness — at a minimum expenditure of funds to the Government.

During the past fiscal year, the Agency has intensified its efforts to improve overall administrative services, while conserving or reducing administrative costs. In addition, it has made a major effort to upgrade the quality of men and women in Washington and in the field — who are administering the programme. The search for qualified personnel continues. In addition to internal transfers of personnel to head A.I.D. missions, thirty-two new directors or deputy directors have been recruited from outside the Agency. On 31 December 1962 the Agency was employing 16,374 people, of whom 2,850 worked in Washington and 13,254 abroad. Continued use is being made of the worldwide facilities of the State Department and the skilled personnel of other Federal agencies.

Since its creation in November 1961 A.I.D. has knit the separate parties of the United States foreign assistance effort into a single organisation and staff. The country programming process has been revised and improved to make it more responsive to United States policy and strategic needs. Every effort is being made — within legal and practical bounds — to delegate more authority and responsibility to those in the field, and thereby eliminate costly reviews and duplication in Washington.

In the field, streamlining efforts are also being undertaken. Reorganisation of a number of A.I.D. missions has led to reductions in the overall numbers of United States employees overseas.

The Agency is organised along geographical lines. Authority is centred in strong regional bureaux in Washington, with appropriate delegations to competently staffed country missions, to assure that the aid will be effectively and efficiently geared to the priority needs of recipient nations. A clear demarcation line between authority, vested in geographically based bureaux, and the staff facilities required to shape policy and provide effective administrative support, will fix responsibility for all phases of programme activity at one point in the structure — the Regional Bureaux — thereby reducing delays in programme prosecution resulting from widely diffused responsibilities.

The head of the Agency for International Development has the title of Administrator. He has the status of Under-Secretary of State and he reports directly to the Secretary of State and the President. Mr. David E. Bell is Administrator of the A.I.D.

Central direction and responsibility for the economic assistance programme is fixed in the Administrator. He is responsible for the formulation and execution of the programme. He establishes procedures for maintaining continuing contact between the Regional Bureaux and country desks of A.I.D. and those of the Department of State, and between all elements of the A.I.D. and other appropriate sections and bureaux of the Department.

In the immediate office of the Administrator there are three staffs:

(*a*) A Programme Review and Co-ordination Staff, to help the Administrator review proposed programmes, allocate funds among them and establish guide-lines for their implementation.

(*b*) An Information and Congressional Liaison Staff, to provide information on the aid programme to Congress and to the public.

(*c*) An International Development Organisations Staff, whose principal responsibility is in connection with the Agency's relations with the work of the international development agencies.

The Agency, organised along geographic lines, has four regional Assistant Administrators, one each for the four major areas of the underdeveloped world: (1) Latin America, (2) Africa and Europe, (3) the Near East and South Asia and (4) the Far East.

The functions of the four Regional Bureaux are:

The formulation of aid programmes for the respective countries.

The implementation of those programmes through country missions.

The providing of expert advice on country and regional development.

The providing of certain administrative and support services.

In the field, country missions reporting to the Ambassador have operational responsibility, vested in Mission Directors.

In addition to these Regional Bureaux, the Administrator is assisted by three programme offices and four management staff offices.

The three programme offices assisting the Administrator are:

1. The Office of Development Financing, responsible for advising the Administrator on the providing of capital assistance. This includes technical and engineering review of capital projects.

2. The Office of Development Research and Assistance, which formulates research requirements and arranges for the conduct of research projects.

3. The Office of Commodity Assistance, which is responsible for formulating the policies for the distribution of commodities, both project and non-project, both agricultural and non-agricultural. It is also charged with seeing that small business enterprises participate equitably in furnishing commodities and services, and it is the focal point for the Agency's responsibilities in connection with the Food-for-Peace programme.

The four management staff offices are:

1. The General Counsel, the legal adviser.
2. The Controller, the principal fiscal officer.
3. The Office of Personnel Administration.
4. The Office of Management Services, responsible for such things as systems procedures, statistical reports, headquarters contracting and so forth.

The functional organisation of the
AGENCY FOR INTERNATIONAL DEVELOPMENT

PROGRAM CO-ORDINATION STAFF

INTERNATIONAL DEVELOPMENT ORGANISATIONS STAFF

INFORMATION STAFF

CONGRESSIONAL LIAISON STAFF

OFFICE OF CONTROLLER

OFFICE OF PROGRAM SUPPORT

OFFICE OF MANAGEMENT PLANNING

OFFICE OF PERSONNEL ADMINISTRATION

OFFICE OF SECURITY

ADMINISTRATOR

DEPUTY ADMINISTRATOR FOR OPERATIONS

DEPUTY ADMINISTRATOR FOR ADMINISTRATION

EXECUTIVE SECRETARIAT

GENERAL COUNSEL

MANAGEMENT INSPECTION STAFF

DEVELOPMENT LOAN COMMITTEE

ADVISORY COMMITTEE ON VOLUNTARY FOREIGN AID

ASSISTANT ADMINISTRATOR
BUREAU FOR AFRICA AND EUROPE

U.S. CO-ORDINATOR ALLIANCE FOR PROGRESS
BUREAU FOR LATIN AMERICA

ASSISTANT ADMINISTRATOR
BUREAU FOR NEAR EAST AND SOUTH ASIA

ASSISTANT ADMINISTRATOR
BUREAU FOR FAR EAST

COUNTRY LEVEL U.S. ESTABLISHMENTS
AMBASSADOR MISSION DIRECTOR

OFFICE OF DEVELOPMENT FINANCE AND PRIVATE ENTERPRISE

OFFICE OF MATERIAL RESOURCES

OFFICE OF ENGINEERING

OFFICE OF HUMAN RESOURCES AND SOCIAL DEVELOPMENT

OFFICE OF PUBLIC SAFETY

The functional organisation of the Agency is made clear in the diagram on p. 225.

EVOLUTION OF UNITED STATES ECONOMIC AID PROGRAMMES

Programme	Period	Objective
THE WAR YEARS Lend-Lease	1941–5	Aid to the Allies in the common struggle
POST-WAR RELIEF UNRRA, civilian supplies, British Loan, etc.	1946–8	Emergency food, shelter, clothing; first recovery steps
MARSHALL PLAN European Recovery Programme	1948–51	Restoration of industrial and agricultural production in Europe
'POINT IV' Technical assistance	1950–61	Transfer of technical skills and knowledge to underdeveloped countries
DEFENCE SUPPORT Korean War, Indo-China, the global Cold War	1952–61	Assistance to countries with heavy defence burdens, or to those making specific contributions to the common defence
START OF DEVELOPMENT LOANS Development Loan Fund	1958–61	Loans for projects in the less-developed economies
THE DECADE OF DEVELOPMENT	1962–	Support to country social and economic development efforts

The several economic and military programmes authorised by the Foreign Assistance Act are directed towards a single goal: to assist other countries which seek to maintain their independence and to develop into self-supporting nations.

This Act reflects the conviction of the President and Congress, that it is in the national interest of the United States to help these countries achieve economic progress and political stability under increasingly free and democratic institutions.

The objective is jeopardised not only by the direct threats and pressure directed against underdeveloped nations on the periphery of the Communist bloc, but equally by intensive Communist efforts to exploit conditions of economic and social misery in Latin America, Africa, the Middle East and Asia.

The security of the United States is clearly diminished when other countries fall under Communist domination, as did China in 1949, North Vietnam and the northern provinces of Laos in 1954 or Cuba in 1960.

The programme of economic and military assistance conducted by the United States, in co-operation with other free nations, are intended to make less likely the occurrence of such events in other countries. The greater part of foreign assistance has gone and goes today to countries directly menaced by Communist aggression, external or internal.

Foreign assistance, where it operates in the areas menaced by direct Communist aggression, is a straightforward extension of the national defence programme.

Even where there is no immediate danger of Communist aggression, it is clearly in the interest of the United States and the free world to assist, within their means, other countries seeking to achieve economic progress and political independence. The continued survival of free institutions depends upon the gradual development of a world community of stable, self-supporting. free nations.

United States efforts to achieve a free and secure world flow not merely from the national interest, but from a proud humanitarian tradition. A willingness to share the abundance of the United States and the talents of the American people, combined with a sense of national self-interest, has led to bipartisan support for these programmes through three administrations.

Measures employed under the Foreign Assistance Act range from providing modern military equipment to countries joined in mutual defence arrangements to supplying doctors and teachers to countries striving to improve the health and education of their people. Whether the tools are weapons or humanitarian services — or any of the other technical and capital resources provided through foreign aid — the intent is the same: to help countries striving for freedom, security and economic and social progress.

Great changes have occurred in the United States' programme of foreign assistance during the past seventeen years. A number of countries — those in Western Europe and Japan — have, with the help of substantial resources from the United States, achieved economic self-support. Others, such as Greece, Israel and Formosa, are rapidly approaching the end of their need for economic assistance. Substantial progress has been made in a number of other countries.

It would be a mistake, however, to think that the problem remaining can be solved easily or rapidly. There are formidable barriers to the achievement of economic progress and political stability in many of the less developed countries. There are obstacles of hunger, ignorance and disease, obstacles of archaic and restrictive political and social institutions, obstacles of ancient tribal or national rivalries. These can be overcome only slowly. Outside help from the United States or other free world sources can assist in overcoming them, but local leadership, energy and resources must play the major role. In many cases definite progress can and will be made. But it is certain that for the foreseeable future, the international Communist movement will continue to oppose the progress of these countries in freedom — will continue to strive to subvert the forces of change in Asia, Africa and Latin America, and to turn the countries of those continents into satellites of Moscow or Peking.

It is against this background that the United States' foreign-aid programmes should be seen — as a principal way in which the United States joins with others in the defence and the advancement of the interests of freedom.

The magnitude of the development assistance task is so great that it clearly cannot be undertaken by the United States alone. The importance of stimulating maximum effort on the part of the other industrialised nations of the free world and of co-ordinating free world aid is growing.

This co-ordination must be thought of in terms of both the recipient and the donor nations. It requires firm decision-making on the part of the recipients, so that the donor nations know what external assistance must be provided and planned for.

The co-ordination task is made the more difficult by (a) the increased number of donor nations, and (b) the increased number and geographic spread of the recipient nations.

The definition of what constitutes aid is a matter not yet entirely resolved. But it is clear that, in order to be effective, any aid granted must be on terms (length of repayment and interest rate) that do not vitiate efforts to help the recipient country.

Where interest charges are high and repayment obligations are severe, particularly in the early years, the benefits of aid can be slowed down.

There has been a marked expansion of the effort of the other industrialised nations of the free world. Progress has also been made, through the Development Assistance Group of the industrial nations, to expand the aggregate volume of their aid to less-developed countries and to recognise the need for 'soft-term' loans and credits.

This Group, which is to become the Development Assistance Committee (D.A.C.) of the new Organisation for Economic Co-operation and Development (O.E.C.D.), will continue to try to (a) expand the aggregate aid effort of the member-nations, and (b) foster greater agreement on the conditions of internal self-help required for the granting of aid.

It is recognised by all that there is no simple formula for allocating the aid burden equitably.

In addition to the work of the Development Assistance Committee (D.A.C.), aid co-ordination has been achieved through 'consortia' of nations, primarily under the aegis of the World

United States aid dispensed during the period 1 July 1945 to 30 June 1962

	(In millions of dollars)		
	Economic aid	Military aid	Total
Europe	28,873	15,940	44,813
Far East	13,743	8,417	22,160
Middle East and S.E. Asia .	12,578	5,266	17,844
Latin America . . .	6,195	616	6,811
Africa	1,665	112	1,777
Other countries . . .	3,561	708	4,269
TOTAL	66,615	31,059	97,674

Bank, which have combined to give co-ordinated aid to countries such as India.

During the period 1 July 1945 to 20 June 1962 the United
States has dispensed to foreign countries $66,615 million in the
form of economic aid and $31,059 million in the form of
military aid, distributed as in the table shown on p. 229.

These are the ten countries which have principally benefited
since the war:

	(In millions of dollars)		
	Economic aid	*Military aid*	*Total*
France	5,175·6	4,262·4	9,438·0
Great Britain . . .	7,668·2	1,045·0	8,713·2
Italy	3,463·3	2,292·5	5,755·8
Korea	3,431·4	2,002·2	5,433·6
Federal Germany . . .	4,047·6	951·9	4,999·4
Nationalist China (Formosa) .	2,051·6	2,376·7	4,428·3
India	3,952·0	..	3,952·0
Turkey	1,581·3	2,288·0	3,869·3
Japan	2,260·7	1,033·1	3,693·8
Greece	1,784·8	1,602·8	3,387·6

This is the order in which, from 1945 to 1962, ten nations
shared among themselves the largest part of American aid.
Between the lines one can read: restoration of national economies,
reconstruction of armed forces, re-equipment for defence.

In the above-mentioned figures the Marshall Plan, special
programmes for Greece and Turkey, support for the nations of
South-East Asia and of the Near East, loans and gifts of all
kinds are indiscriminately lumped together, but we felt it was
important to give the figures, because a comparison between
what was done during these seventeen years and what is being
done today is extremely illuminating.

In 1962 the countries that were the ten principal beneficiaries
of American aid were, in the order of magnitude of the amount,
as follows: India, Pakistan, Turkey, Korea, South Vietnam,
Brazil, Chile, and United Arab Republic, Nationalist China
(Formosa) and Japan. The names of only five of the nations which

figured on the first list are still to be found. The four great countries of Western Europe (France, Great Britain, Italy and Federal Germany) which were the most richly endowed in the post-war years no longer appear. On the other hand, two Asiatic nations, Pakistan and South Vietnam; two Latin American Republics, Brazil and Chile; and one African state, the United Arab Republic, have appeared. This fact alone is sufficient to illustrate how importantly American policy has been reorientated in recent years. It also means that this immense sum of money was not spent in vain. Thanks to American aid, Western Europe — the second greatest and second richest industrial complex existing in the world today — has become a vital centre of power in the free world and itself now contributes to the expansion and strength of less highly developed countries.

The continuance of some programmes, the development of fresh objectives and the consequent revisions of policy: this is not the whole story. In 1964 the whole structure of the foreign-aid programme is to be reformed. A preliminary stage in this reform has been the presentation to the White House of a precise plan, accompanied by recommendations for action, prepared by General Lucius D. Clay, the former President of the World Bank, Eugene B. Black, the former Under-Secretary of State, Robert A. Lovett, and their expert advisers. What are these recommendations? To begin with, they deal with the general concept of aid and its overall objectives, and then its future total volume and the principles governing its distribution. A second part of the report reviews, continent by continent, and at times country by country, particular situations not only with respect to the amount of credit to be granted, but also with respect to what others among the Western allies are prepared to do for the rest of the world.

'The United States is trying to do too much for too many countries,' writes General Clay, and goes on to explain: 'We cannot believe that we are serving the national interest by maintaining our present commitments indefinitely at the present rates of interest, with respect to ninety-five countries and territories which are at present receiving either military and economic assistance or merely military assistance. We should reduce substantially the number of our objectives and define them more precisely, in the light of our national interests and on the basis of a realistic appraisal of our past experience, of present needs and probable future developments. We are convinced that it is advisable to embark on reductions in present programmes.'

To effect these reductions, the Clay Commission recommended a progressive plan, scaled over three years. For the financial year 1 July 1963 to 30 June 1964, the White House had intended initially to present to Congress an aid budget of $4,900 million. Acting on the advice of the Clay Commission, the Administration decided to reduce the project to $4,525 million.

The details of the budgetary credits requested of Congress are as follows:

Request for Appropriations for Fiscal Year 1963/4 Foreign Assistance Programme

Development loans		$1,060,000,000
Development grants and technical co-operation.		257,000,000
The Alliance for Progress		
Loans	$550,000,000	
Grants	100,000,000	
		650,000,000
Social Progress Trust Fund		200,000,000
Supporting assistance		435,000,000
Contingency fund .		300,000,000
Contributions to international organisations		136,050,000
Administrative expenses, A.I.D.		57,250,000
Administrative and other expenses, Department of State		3,025,000
American schools and hospitals abroad		20,000,000
American hospitals abroad — local currency		2,000,000
TOTAL economic assistance		3,120,325,000
Military assistance .		1,405,000,000
TOTAL military and economic assistance		$4,525,325,000

After several amendments and reductions, the total for foreign aid for the financial year 1 July 1963 to 30 June 1964 finally adopted by Congress was $3,400 million. The budgetary credits proposed by the Administration had then been reduced by $1,125 million. Even though cut down, the foreign-aid budget reached a higher total than that of the previous year, which amounted to $2,600 million.

A certain number of reductions could easily be justified by the poor use to which American funds have been put, as well as by dangerous international policies pursued by certain countries. A relevant example is cited in the Clay Report: since 1945, Indonesia has received from the United States $671 million. This is enough, or even too much if we agree with General Clay's warning: 'We do not think that foreign aid can be granted to this State by the nations of the free world unless it puts its own house in order, deals fairly with foreign creditors and abstains from all international adventures.'

The Clay Report, although in general it avoids naming the countries involved, examines the situation continent by continent and formulates a certain number of recommendations:

1. In Asia, it recommends that a distinction be drawn between those countries which are allies of the United States and those which practise neutralism. The substantial efforts made in South Vietnam and Laos should be continued: these countries are in the front line of the fight against Communism. On the other hand, certain nations in South-East and Western Asia, in addition to Indonesia, should be refused military aid, since their foreign policy does not justify it: most of these allocations should therefore be suppressed.

The armed forces of Nationalist China and of South Korea are too large merely for the defence of these territories, not large enough to undertake offensive action. They should be gradually reduced.

Even if military aid to India and Pakistan is worth maintaining, the United States cannot continue to finance economic plans which compete with private industry or serve only to absorb credits without achieving any concrete result.

2. As for Africa, the United States has entered into agreements with three countries: Tanganyika, Nigeria and Tunisia: these agreements should be honoured, but after their fulfilment the United States will be able to content herself with participating along with the nations of Western Europe in multilateral programmes.

In several countries in North and North-East Africa, American bases have been installed. Aid granted in exchange should be continued but, in future, in two forms: the supplying of agricultural surpluses and the financing of specific development projects.

Generally speaking, the report recommends reducing the high cost of aid offered in exchange for the cession of military bases. This advice is intended to apply not only to Asian and African countries but also to European countries: the greatest efforts should be made, says the text, to reduce the aid granted in such cases, particularly as far as Spain and Portugal are concerned, who receive fair compensation.

The case of the Congo (Kinshasa) is examined at length and the conclusion of this study is in these terms: 'The United States should obtain maximum participation by other nations and the American contribution should not exceed half the total economic aid granted during the next two years. After which it will be proper to terminate economic assistance, except by normal methods, to this potentially rich country.'

3. Latin America is the subject of a long section of the report and President Kennedy devoted a large portion of his address to Congress to this subject as well. Both adhered to the policy embodied in the Alliance for Progress and recommended that aid be concentrated in support of those countries which are undertaking large-scale positive reforms in the field of taxation, agriculture, finance, education, etc., cited in the Charter of Punta del Este, signed in 1961.

4. Finally, in Europe, only two nations still need support from the United States: Greece and Turkey. They will continue to receive both military and economic aid for as long as they fulfil their present obligations.

But Europe does not figure in the Clay Report and in President Kennedy's message merely as a recipient of aid: in both a strong emphasis is laid upon the extent to which responsibility for an increasing proportion of the burden of aid is being assumed by Western European countries, along with Canada and Japan.

A particular tribute is paid to France. France alone, writes

General Clay, is ready to grant terms as favourable as those granted by the United States. Indeed, aid granted by France to underdeveloped countries amounted in 1962 to 6,922 million francs, or about $1,384 million. France tops the list of industrial nations. Each tax-paying French citizen has given 360 francs or 2·2% of his gross output to help underdeveloped countries.

Aid from other countries of the free world includes a substantial proportion of loans, on less liberal terms, earmarked to finance exports from the lender country.

Taking the wealthy countries together, a milliard dollars were devoted to aid in 1956; in 1961 this figure had been doubled; it has increased and will increase further from year to year. In the Clay Report special recommendations are made about each of these countries: it is said to be desirable that Italy, despite her own problems, should allocate budgetry credits for foreign aid, on generous terms; that Canada should increase her contribution; that the United Kingdom should lower its rate of interest and increase the volume of aid granted to independent countries; that Germany should increase its contribution and make it more readily available; that Japan should impose less-inflexible conditions.

Such have been the decisions. American aid is now concentrated on those countries which justify the hope that they will one day become economically self-sufficient, or whose geographical position makes them strategic outposts of the free world. It is now more selective than it was, and leaves greater scope for private investment and for loans from allies of America. However important and radical this reform may seem to be, it does not constitute a revolution, since foreign aid, although it has been considerably modified both in spirit and in direction in the course of time, remains one of the cornerstones of American foreign policy. It is, however, still true that a new era is beginning on a key front in the battle for liberty.

American aid to foreign countries is both a reality and a legend. The reality is that aid is becoming more and more an integral part of the foreign policy of the United States. The two are by now so intertwined that to terminate foreign aid would provoke a national disaster. The legend consists in believing that the foreign-aid programme is dictated entirely by altruism, that it is a sacrifice, bringing no profit to the United States. More than one American imagines that aid affects the stability of the dollar and that it is the principle cause of the drain of gold away from the United States.

The reality is, however, quite different. Most dollars paid out as foreign aid do not leave the United States. Foreign countries use them to buy American products, principally agricultural surpluses. The United States produces too much corn, too much maize, too much cotton, etc. The Federal Government buys these surpluses, in order to prevent a slump in prices. But this leaves it in an embarrassing position. They cannot be offered free to hospitals or to the poor without provoking protests from the farmers. They must be either exported or destroyed. But customers who can pay are not to be found; and so credits are granted to poor countries which permit them to buy American surpluses.

In the year 1960-1 these purchases of food products or textile fibres amounted to $1,770 million; in addition, an almost identical sum was spent on industrial products, which, again, were often in excess of internal requirements. In general, one can reckon that only about 20% of foreign aid represents an outflow of capital; this is in accordance with the figures given recently by the American Secretary of the Treasury: 80% of the dollars voted by Congress as foreign aid does not leave the United States.

With regard to the 20% which represents an outflow of dollars, what advantages does the Government of the United States derive from them? Above all, the Russians have been kept out. An official pamphlet says: 'Not one single country, in receipt of substantial American aid, has, in the course of the last fifteen years, fallen into the hands of the Communists.'

Its economic efficacy cannot be denied. By now the purchase and subsequent selling off of surpluses by the Agency for International Development form an integral part of the mechanisms regulating the American economy, and only foreign aid makes it possible to find a market for home products. Foreign aid is a prop indispensable to their international prosperity but, more than that, it is essential to the maintenance of America's international position. This aid is, it cannot be denied, generous; but America is compelled to be generous to safeguard her own position.

In the ideological war, two super-powers confront one another: the United States and Soviet Russia. The Communist bloc launched its assault against the American strongholds in 1954, and since that date the Soviet bloc has spent $7,374 million in foreign aid ($4,874 in economic and $2,500 in military aid).

The comparative table below shows the various countries of the world which have received economic aid from both the opposing blocs during the period 1 January 1954 to 1 January 1963.

Economic aid from the U.S.A. (in millions of dollars)	Country	Economic aid from the U.S.S.R. (in millions of dollars)
178	Afghanistan	515
490	Argentine	104
1,182	Brazil	74
252	Cambodia	65
79	Ceylon	69
29	Cuba	470
113	Ethiopia	114
157	Ghana	200
15	Guinea	127
36	Iceland	5
3,573	India	982
395	Indonesia	640
18	Iraq	218
5	Mali	100
49	Nepal	55
1,741	Pakistan	33
29	Somalia	63
65	Sudan	25
95	Syria	193
293	Tunisia	46
1,311	Turkey	17
617	U.A.R. (Egypt)	715
25	Yemen	44
TOTAL 10,747		4,874

To the global sum of $4,874 million the Soviet Union contributed 70% ($3,411·8 million), the European satellites 22% ($1,072·28 million) and Communist China 8% ($389·92 million). Communist aid is granted on very easy conditions. Repayment is required usually after twelve years; however, in certain cases, a period of fifty years is allowed.

On 31 December 1962 about 10,000 Communist technical experts were working in thirty non-Communist countries (this does not include Communist personnel in Cuba). Although both blocs give technical assistance of the same kind, their objectives are very different. Aid from the United States and from other allied nations of the free world is granted so that nations may defend their liberty and independence and thus become economically strong; and so that they can, if need be, increase their defence potential and thus resist possible Communist incursions. In contrast, the objective of the Communist bloc is to weaken the ties of these countries with the Western World, to weaken their defence and increase their dependence on the Communist bloc. For the latter the ultimate objective is to bring into the Communist camp the 1,400 million people who live at present in the less-developed countries of the world.

With this purpose the Soviet Union has put into operation a vigorous programme of foreign aid and one must assume that, in the years to come, its effects will be felt throughout the world. In the years between 1954 and 1964, foreign aid has enabled the Communist bloc to get a footing in many countries, even in Latin America (Argentina and Brazil).

Despite the milliards of dollars supplied as aid by the two super-powers (the U.S.A. and the U.S.S.R.) to underdeveloped countries, the rate of economic growth in the latter has only slightly increased. Up to the present there has really not been sufficient progress to justify hopes for the future. The average production per person in underdeveloped countries does not exceed $140 a year. Total production has increased at a normal annual rate of about 2% in recent years. But if one takes into account the increase in population — 200 children are born every minute in the world as a whole and of this total 3 are in

France, 25 in the other industrialised countries, 70 in the Communist bloc and more than 100 in the underdeveloped countries of the free world — production per person has increased by barely $\frac{1}{2}\%$. With so slow a rate of progress, it will be A.D. 2000 before annual revenue per person rises from $140 to $170.

These figures are a warning — and also a challenge. Unless progress is made, the disparity between the standard of living of the industrialised nations and that of the less-developed countries will continue to grow steadily larger.

The 500 million people who inhabit the industrialised countries enjoy an average annual income higher than $1,500 — eleven times as great as the average income in the underdeveloped countries. Any increase in this disparity could dangerously exacerbate the feelings of frustration and the already serious tensions which exist in underdeveloped countries. The peoples of these countries wish for more rapid progress and they are determined to achieve it in the near future. They have heard the Soviet leaders boasting of the advantages of Communism, and of its ability to transform an underdeveloped country into an industrial stronghold in the space of one generation and they are waiting for a reply from the free nations.

The countries of the Western World and the underdeveloped countries share a common objective — economic progress — and a common conviction that man shapes his own economic destiny and a common commitment to raise the standard of living throughout the world. The place of the free nations in the annals of history will probably be determined largely by the degree of success achieved in their efforts to aid all nations to realise these common objectives.

Future generations will remember the twentieth century not principally as an era of political conflict and technical invention, but as an age in which the human race dared to consider the welfare of humanity at large as a practical objective.

Communism boasts of opening the surest road towards equality, material well-being and technological and economic success. It claims to have built a bridge into the future for societies at grips with the dilemma of social revolution. But it is important to remember that the terms 'revolution' and 'Communism' are not synonymous. In the eighteenth century France experienced a revolution, fruitful in ideas and principles infinitely more revolutionary than the dogmas of Marxism.

The free Western World can offer as examples prosperous nations, socially conscious, functioning on the basis of a mixed system in which both free enterprise and government control play a part. The task which the free nations must not shirk is to help less-favoured people to accomplish their revolution peacefully and democratically. If the free nations have the strength, the imagination and the initiative needed to seize the opportunities afforded by this daring undertaking, they will bring a new, a brighter, an unhoped-for splendour to the horizon of the under-developed countries and thus make an immense contribution to the peace, security, prosperity and liberty of the human race.

4

THE BANKS AND EUROPEAN INTEGRATION

1. THE ROLE OF THE BANKS IN EUROPEAN INTEGRATION

IN the course of history bankers have always played an important role in the development of commercial and financial relationships, first between regions and then between nations. At a period when national sentiment had not yet been formed, certain Lombard and Florentine banking-houses were already operating on a European scale and the most important among them already had offices and agents in the principal European commercial centres. It was no accident that the great banking-houses quickly extended their operations beyond the frontiers of those countries in which they had their headquarters. By the very nature of their business, banks are in continuous relationship with foreign countries, since they deal with payments when goods are bought and sold, with foreign exchange, with capital investment, etc.

These constant contacts have caused bankers to follow closely the economic and political situation in countries where they do business and where their business occasions their taking risks. Bankers have thus become accustomed, earlier than manufacturers and more widely than most businessmen, to extending their interests beyond the home market.

The bankers' sense of belonging to an international profession has been further strengthened by the great contemporary movement towards European unity. As soon as the European idea was born, banks gave warm support to the groups formed to promote and defend the idea of setting up vast integrated economic regions and they have collaborated closely in their work.

But the banks have also contributed to the making of Europe by their strictly professional activities. As the restrictions on the transfer of capital have been reduced, they have extended their credit operations to foreign countries, participated in introducing leading European shares on the home market and created investment trusts interested in the stocks of neighbouring countries — stages on the road to the financial integration of the European continent.

The banks have also been active in promoting the interpenetration of the markets of the European Economic Community by the business interests of the six member-countries, by multiplying contacts between industrialists of the various countries. They have in this way anticipated the suppression of economic frontiers.

With respect to population, the six countries of the European Economic Community, with their 185 million inhabitants (West Germany, including Berlin, 60 million, Italy 53 million, France 50 million, Holland 12 million, Belgium 10 million and Luxembourg 0·330 million), roughly equivalent to 6% of the world population (3,300 million) has an importance comparable to the U.S.A. (195 million) or the U.S.S.R. (225 million).

Why must Europe be united? Because it is its last chance of survival between the two great powers, which threaten to overwhelm it: the Russian colossus, an Asiatic power, and the American colossus, western but not European, who have taken the lead in technical progress and aspire to the economic and political leadership of the world.

Europe will either unite or sink into insignificance. She must adapt or die. No other choice is open. After the era of medieval princedoms, after the era of national states, the age of continents is beginning.

The last war completely transformed the balance of world power. Alongside the U.S.A. and the U.S.S.R., the old European nations are of little moment. European disunity is a source of weakness for all of them. In contrast, political and economic unity would permit the creation of a third super-power, within which nations would subsist and preserve their own character, but would accept the sacrifice of part of their national sovereignty for the sake of an economic and political structure which would be of weight in world affairs.

The Europe of 'the Six' represents 20% of the industrial production of the world; it is the world's leading trading power. Indeed, the Six, in addition to their internal trade, represent 26% of the world commercial turnover; the United States' share is 16%, Great Britain's 10% and that of the U.S.S.R. is practically non-existent.

Banking and industrial interests have had a decisive influence in the orientation of European unity. Before the last war the French and German metallurgists had set up close relations, despite the increasing hostility publicly expressed in both countries. Since the end of the war the movement has spread, and one can affirm that economic Europe has become conscious of its strength and that it will surely be capable of bringing the brutal decadence of the continent to a halt.

The great bankers and industrialists of the Rhine and of the Hamburg–Genoa–Le Havre triangle are preparing to dominate the game; their unanimity on the policy to be pursued will enhance the role they will play. Agreements to act in co-operation have been signed between groups of important French and German banks within the framework of the Common Market: for example, between the Deutsche Bank, the most important of the group of German banks, and the Banque de Paris et des Pays-Bas, the most important of the group of French banks: between the Dresdner Bank and the Crédit Lyonnais: between popular French and German banks: with a view to concerted action, aiming at giving future exchange movements the necessary coherence and efficacy.

By the terms of these agreements the two parties put at the disposal of their respective clientele the professional advice and the facilities needed to carry out their projects within the framework of the Common Market. These problems are handled by Franco-German committees, working in close liaison with the contracting parties.

In addition, on 28 October 1960 the articles of the Banking Federation of the European Economic Community were officially signed in Paris. They had already been initialled on 10 June 1960 in Rome by representatives of the six Common-Market countries.

The following professional associations are members of the Federation:

The Belgian Banking Association.
The Association of Banks and Bankers (Luxembourg).
The Professional Association of Banks (France).
The Italian Banking Association.
The Federal Association of Private Banks (Germany).
The Netherlands Banking Association.

The Federation has a President, a Council, a Central Committee and a Secretariat. Its headquarters is in Brussels. The object of the Federation is to ensure joint action by professional associations of bankers, in achieving within the field of banking the European objectives embodied in the Treaty of Rome. The Federation wishes to put at the disposal of the authorities of the European Economic Community the experience of banking circles and their technical assistance, principally by representation on consultative bodies. The Council has also taken the necessary practical steps to ensure that the Federation can develop its contacts with the banking associations of countries not in the Common Market.

The immediate task of the new Federation is principally to encourage the study of problems of common interest to the private banks of the six countries, to ensure that they are re-presented *vis-à-vis* the official institutions of the European Economic Community, and to work out a common banking policy within the framework of the Common Market. Indeed, as the tempo of development within the European Economic Community increases each member-country will be faced by new problems, for which the optimum solution will have to be found quickly, most especially in the domain of credit.

In the years to come the Common Market will cause sweeping changes in the organisational structure of business enterprises, on the one hand, to meet the ruthless competition to be expected, and, on the other, to facilitate the centralisation of production, so that production costs may be cut to a minimum without sacrifice of quality. It is in this work of adaptation and preparation for future opportunities, that the banks of each country have a very important task to fulfil. Business undertakings, whether industrial or agricultural or commercial, will need their services more frequently than ever, not only in order to obtain a larger measure of credit to finance their operations and their investment programmes, but, in the immediate future, to obtain sound practical advice and information on the opportunities offered by the Common Market.

As soon as the Treaty of Rome was drawn up the banks set up 'Common Market' departments in their head offices, responsible for studying the situation in each of the Six, and for compiling statistics showing the comparative opportunities open to the various branches of the profession and the European competition to be expected.

As one stage in the building up of the European Economic Community follows on another, the share of the banks in the common task will grow larger and more complex. Within the Community itself, they will have to apportion credit in such a way that production and commerce are adapted to new contingencies smoothly and without interruption. Credit will have to become more selective, since demand will inevitably increase in pace with the increasing need for investment, caused by the pursuit of maximum productivity. The progressive integration of the constituent elements of the European Economic Community will doubtless imply a co-ordinated credit policy in the member-states.

It is clear that a genuine revision, a thorough remodelling, of European economic structures, will be accomplished in the years to come, foreshadowed in some measure by the centralisation observable in all sectors of the national economy of the six Common Market countries.

This brief sketch will have made plain the importance of the new tasks which face banks, great and small, and for which they have carefully prepared themselves.

2. THE UNIFICATION OF CURRENCIES AND CAPITAL MARKETS IN THE EUROPEAN ECONOMIC COMMUNITY

The right to issue currency is an essential part of national sovereignty. If a member-state of the European Economic Community were to transfer its power to issue currency to a central authority, it would find difficulty in pursuing any independent policy, not only in economic affairs, but also in defence and foreign affairs.

It is easy to understand that a complete surrender of financial rights to a central authority is essentially of much greater importance to a member-state than the surrender of other economical rights. For this reason, the establishment of a unified currency within the Community would only become possible if political integration were already an accomplished fact. It is therefore indispensable that the member-states should not relax their efforts to achieve monetary unification by promoting the co-ordination of the various currencies.

Because of the diversity of the budgetary, fiscal, parafiscal and, indeed, social systems in the member-states, identical objectives can at times be achieved only by means of policies superficially very different. In addition, as long as each country retains its autonomy in matters of such importance, monetary authorities will remain the prisoners of their national responsibilities.

Moreover, the very concept of a unified currency system raises constitutional problems, such that it would be illusory to envisage currency integration, unless a single central political authority had been already set up.

The Treaty of Rome did not establish a monetary community embracing the six countries of the Common Market. Article 104 merely states that each member-state pursues the economic policy necessary to ensure the balance of payments and to maintain confidence in its own currency. Beyond this there is only mention, in fairly vague terms, of recommendations and consultations between banks of issue.

It would certainly be difficult to persuade the man in the street that a common market could function without a common currency. One must, however, point out that bringing monetary policies into harmony and embodying this harmony in the form of a common currency presupposes the adoption of common financial and economic policies, which still remains a remote prospect. Indeed, monetary disharmony is always plainly evident in the Europe of the Six. However, the question of the gold standard and of convertibility is fundamental to European unity.

Although the architects of the Treaty of Rome prudently ignored everything to do with currency and the movement of capital, the monetary problem is the key problem for the European Economic Community. A sound and single currency is needed as a visible sign of the prosperity of the nations forming the Community. A European currency is needed to safeguard savings. The European Common Market compels a common currency. Only a strong currency will enable a financially independent Community to be the master of its own future.

The solidarity of the six European countries will have to be demonstrated by the creation of a monetary standard, and by the replacement of monetary particularism among the six states by monetary collaboration.

The new currency of the European Economic Community, which might be called the 'Euro' (plural 'Euros') would then have greater standing *vis-à-vis* the pound sterling and the dollar, both currencies of dominant nations, enjoying the support of the dominant financial centres of London and New York.

The present system of international payments is based on gold — the dollar and the pound. Why are dollars and pounds given this pre-eminence above all other currencies? Because until the immediate post-war period, Great Britain and America were the two greatest economic powers of the West. Sterling and the dollar became key currencies, because of the essential role played by Great Britain and the United States in the development of world trade.

But should not the countries of the Common Market play a more important role in the future? Because of its high rate of economic growth, the volume of its foreign trade, the investment capital available, the amount of its reserves in gold and currency, the European Economic Community can at present meet all the conditions necessary to the creation of a common currency. The quality of this currency would be immediately recognised on the exchange-market; but no common currency is possible, unless each of the member-states accepts the same economic and financial discipline in its dealings with foreign countries, and unless stable prices and a steady expansion of the economy are guaranteed within the Community.

Obviously the establishment of a common European currency would have to be preceded by the establishment of financial institutions responsible for its maintenance. A European system of federal banks would come into being, closely modelled on the Federal Reserve System of the United States, though not necessarily an exact replica of it. The European Federal Bank could co-ordinate the monetary policies of the member-states of the European Economic Community and impose an adequate degree of unity on the existing currencies — French and Belgian francs, German marks, Italian lire and Dutch florins.

Not only in the economic but also on the political plane Europe would be strong enough to influence the destiny of the world and to prevent European countries being at the mercy of one or the other of the two super-giants, both of whom tend to consider European nations as mere pawns at their disposal on a chess-board, where each of them plays for his own advantage.

At present many factors militate in favour of a unification of the money-markets of the six Common Market countries. The Banking Federation of the European Economic Community is constantly canvassing the need for a freer flow of capital. On 11 May 1960 a resolution was adopted by the Commission of the European Economic Community, intended to ensure ample freedom of movement for capital and for the interest it has earned.

Nevertheless administrative regulations, differences in taxation, customs declarations and licences to import and export, continue seriously to impede this free circulation of capital within the

Common Market. It is, however, evident that the European Economic Community is based on large productive units which require enormous capital. But at times economic barriers make it impossible to transfer savings to the place where investment would be most secure and most profitable. As long as there is no single money-market and as long as it is impossible for an industrialist to invite capital from other Common-Market countries on the same conditions as from his own, it will remain a possibility that some demands for investment capital will not be met.

At the present moment another pressing demand upon the money-market comes from the developing countries. Whether we like the idea or not, we know that the financial equilibrium of the Atlantic Community demands that it should participate as a whole in meeting this demand, that is, not only the United States, but also the countries of Western Europe. As a result it will be essential to have a unified money-market, if the necessary capital is to be directed not only to those industrial undertakings already operating in these countries, but also to those which will result from future technological developments.

If the common effort were to be crowned by the establishment of a single money-market, though not of a single currency, one problem would still remain: that of stability of exchange rates. If the public does not become accustomed again to the concept of a stable rate of exchange, there will be no genuinely unified money-market for the Common Market as a whole.

In this respect, a recent report of the European Economic Commission brings us a heartening message. It seems that it is proposed to entrust the defence of monetary stability in part to the Monetary Committee of the Commission, and in part to an informal association of the Governors of the Central Banks.

The fundamental problem is not only to foster public confidence in the stability of the exchange rate but also to ensure that the technical means necessary to realise stability exist and that administrative and governmental authorities are genuinely determined to use them. The establishment of a unified money-market for the whole European Economic Community would be a first step towards the solution of a fascinating problem — the creation of a European currency.

3. The Bank for International Settlements

This central super-bank which came into existence in May 1930, does not have its head office in a member-state of the Common Market; nevertheless it plays such an important role in European finance that this chapter must give some account of its operations.

At the Paris Conference, in the spring of 1929, it was decided to establish a Bank for International Settlements; its object would be to facilitate international movements of capital and to contribute to the establishment of friendly international financial relations.

The bank has international status. Its head office is in Basle; however, in virtue of a special charter granted by the Swiss Government, it is not subject to Swiss law. Its resources cannot be subject to seizure or requisition; Swiss courts of law are not competent to adjudicate in any dispute which may arise between the bank and the Swiss Government, and it is exempt from any Swiss tax, now and in the future. Its capital, fixed at 500 million Swiss gold francs, was subscribed by the central banks and also by the commercial banks of those countries interested in German reparations, or which were on the gold standard or the gold exchange standard.

Each year the Board of Governors submits the bank's balance-sheet to a general meeting of the shareholders. This meeting is composed, then, of representatives of those central banks which subscribed capital; if a central bank does not wish to exercise its rights its place may be taken by a bank of high standing from the same country, selected by the Governors of the Bank for International Settlements and against which the central bank in question has raised no objection.

The immediate objective of the bankers who planned the bank and drew up its articles of association was to facilitate the transfer of German reparation payments and to mobilise debts, owed by

Germany to certain states. The bank was, in fact, to function as trustee for those powers to whom Germany owed money, and who wished to recover their debts, and also for holders of debentures in the Young $5\frac{1}{2}\%$ Loan. Germany paid into the bank the annual amounts laid down by the Young Plan, consisting in part of a fixed sum which Germany was obliged to pay whatever her financial position, and of a further sum, whose payment might be delayed or even temporarily suspended.

But the bank's operations soon extended beyond this, as became clear after July 1931. The Hoover moratorium, and the consequent suspension of German payments, confirmed to some extent by the Lausanne Declaration of 16 June 1932, should have caused the bank's withdrawal from active business, if not its total liquidation; but it had already widened its field of operations and become an important international credit institution.

In order to encourage central banks to co-operate with the bank, it had been authorised to provide supplementary facilities for international financial operations. So the bank added borrowed resources to its own. It canvassed deposits not only from central banks but also from individuals and from institutions; it allowed credit interest and even granted a share in the profits of the surplus dividend to those central banks, which had made deposits for a fixed period of five years.

Its articles lay down that the bank must rigorously safeguard the liquidity of its assets, and retain sufficient immediately realisable assets, to meet its obligations as they mature. Its investment programmes are therefore dominated by the need to avoid immobilising its assets. Nevertheless, the bank has frequently intervened to co-ordinate the attempts of the central banks to achieve a better distribution of capital in Europe.

In the following pages is given a brief abstract of the main activities of the Bank for International Settlements (B.I.S.).

The first serious signs of financial disintegration in Europe appeared in Austria, and in 1930 the Austrian Government, in order to maintain its balance of payments and defend the currency, arranged a $62 million loan for which the B.I.S. acted as trustee. This proved of little avail, and in March 1931 came the

run on the Austrian Creditanstalt. Once more the B.I.S. stepped
into the breach with a loan of 100 million schillings, equivalent
to $14 million, of which 40 million schillings were subscribed
by eleven central banks, including all those linked by the B.I.S.

The crisis then spread to Germany. In order to plug the vast
holes in the German external reserves caused by the withdrawal of
foreign credit, help was mobilised under the auspices of the B.I.S.
by a group of central banks headed by the Federal Reserve Bank
of New York, the Bank of England and the Bank of France. In
the circumstances this proved entirely inadequate; and in June
1931 President Hoover proposed a moratorium for European
debts to America and also for German debts on reparation
account.

It was the B.I.S. which in May and July 1931 obtained the
collective support of the central banks for the Austrian National
Bank and the Reichsbank, both threatened by collapse of the
Austrian and German banking systems. It was the B.I.S. which
ensured the successful launching of the debenture loans of the
Compagnie Centrale des Prêts Fonciers and the Crédit Foncier
International, both international credit institutions, established
in 1930 and 1931. It was, again, the B.I.S. which, by discounting,
rediscounting or purchasing bills of exchange and treasury
bonds, met the international demand for short-term credit. In
addition, merely because the central banks had accounts, the
B.I.S. tended to become the international transfer and arbitrage
office, a world currency clearing-house.

The Second World War placed the B.I.S. in an unusually
difficult situation. It was an institution in which the two sides
of the enemy camps were represented and where therefore they
could not meet. In the very early days of the war the B.I.S. was
able to render a marked service to some of its member-countries
by removing to New York and other centres a substantial part
of their gold reserves. Also during the war, the B.I.S. continued
to provide for its members such facilities as could be extended
without involving any of them in the forbidden grounds of
trading with the enemy. During the war the B.I.S., because of its
primary function and the fact that most of its assets were German

claims, necessarily kept close connection with the German financial situation, and at the Bretton Woods conference in 1944 a resolution was adopted recommending liquidation of the B.I.S. in view of the organisation of the International Monetary Fund and the International Bank for Reconstruction and Development. Liquidation, however, was avoided.

After the end of the Second World War, the B.I.S. began to play its role in the vast task of economic and financial reconstruction of Europe. The first of these tasks was the operation of the multilateral monetary agreement between France, Italy and the Benelux countries, which was arranged in November 1947. This was the first move towards the intra-European payments agreements and later the European Payments Union, which evolved as an integral part of Europe's response to the Marshall Plan through the Organisation for European Economic Co-operation.

When Marshall Aid was first mooted it was quickly realised that the main handicap to economic reconstruction in Europe was the absence of effective payments machinery, which had inevitably been wrecked both during and immediately after the war and which had in the first place been substituted by strictly bilateral payments arrangements between these countries. It was, therefore, decided that the first task and responsibility of the Organisation for European Economic Co-operation would be to restore some semblance of a multilateral payments system.

This was done through the establishment of the European Payments Union through which the net balances due to and from the various members of the Union were settled, partly in gold, partly in credit. All information relating to payments was transmitted to the B.I.S., whose representative travelled to Paris each month to supervise the settlements.

During the lifetime of the European Payments Union (1950-8) there proved to be quite large swings in the balances between the member-countries, so that the credit margins allowed in the monthly settlements clearly served in an important degree to facilitate the reduction of trade barriers. Some large balances of lending and borrowing did, however, tend to accumulate, and

some were outstanding when the scheme came to its natural end
with the generalisation of convertibility of European currencies
at the end of 1958.

The European Payments Union was terminated and made
way for the European Monetary Agreement (E.M.A.). The
B.I.S. continues to act as Agent for the execution of the financial
operations of the E.M.A. within the framework of the Organisation for Economic Co-operation and Development (O.E.C.D.),
the successor of the Organisation for European Economic Co-
operation (O.E.E.C.).

Under the terms of this agreement the bulk of intra-European
payments has been cleared through the open market — a logical
and virtually inevitable result of the external convertibility of the
European currencies. The agreement provides for the establishment of a multilateral system for settlement by which payments
are to be settled 100% in gold or dollars, in contrast to the E.P.U.
procedure, whereby 25% of each balance to be settled was
entitled automatically to credit. Under the E.M.A. the multilateral system of settlements has therefore declined in importance,
but a European Fund has been established and has granted credits
to the one member, Turkey, which has been in continual need
of assistance not available through other channels.

The European Fund, with a capital of $600 million, of which
part was to come from the assets of the former European Payments Union, is controlled by a Board of Management under
the authority of the O.E.D.C. Council.

Among the most interesting and useful tasks entrusted to the
B.I.S. in recent years has been the collection and publication of
the available statistics in the Euro-currency market. This market
has become a major factor in international monetary transactions; its development has created considerable problems of
credit control, since the care with which large commercial and
industrial institutions have been able to gain access to the facilities
of this market has, in certain instances, veiled from the bankers
of such institutions the extent to which they were securing
credit.

A lack of information about this market was a considerable

gap in the knowledge available to central banks and governments concerning their countries' balance of payments. The B.I.S., by collecting all the available information from its member-countries, has made a notable and valuable attempt to present the facts about this market.

The B.I.S. did find a few smaller tasks which it carried through unobtrusively: the liquidation of the financial liabilities from the transfer of the Saar Territory to Germany was one such task.

The B.I.S. holds gold which on 31 March 1965 represented 43·3% of its total assets. In the event, the bank has become a major factor in the international gold-market, not merely in easing the transfer of gold between central banks, but in acting as intermediary for the disposal of supplies arriving from unusual quarters.

Thus some of the gold recently sold by the Soviet Union in order to pay for imports of grain is reported to have reached the international 'Gold Pool' through the B.I.S.

The B.I.S. has not only provided the meeting-place where the latest international arrangements for the support of sterling were elaborated; it has also taken a direct participation in them.

The power of central banks, when they act together and quickly through the B.I.S., was demonstrated in March 1961 when exchange-markets were upset by the revaluation of the German and Dutch currencies. With the central banks' governors' meeting in Basle, only an hour or so was necessary to mobilise massive support (some £250–300 million) in support of sterling.

At the head office of the bank in Basle there was established a body of genuinely international experts, making a continuous study of the problems of international monetary relationship. Among these men, Per Jacobsson was appointed in 1931 and served as the bank's economic adviser until he left it in 1956 to become Managing Director and Chairman of the International Monetary Fund in Washington.

The bank's annual reports, though very much his personal product, were but one facet of his work in Basle: even more important, he built up for himself a unique position as the confidant and informal adviser of the central bankers who went to the Board meetings.

On 31 March 1965 the bank published its thirty-fifth annual report. The publication of these reports, world-famous for the precise and detailed information they contain, is always awaited with lively interest by financial and economic circles the world over. The bank's experts are accustomed to rising above national perspectives and to viewing the world situation as a whole. These annual reports of the highest quality provide a running commentary on economic trends and policies during the previous year; the fullest available information is provided on credit development, world trade and payments and on the changes in gold reserves and events in the foreign-exchange market.

The Bank for International Settlements plays a valuable role in international monetary affairs: a token of the vision of the men who set it up thirty-six years ago and to the constructive adaptation which has been encouraged by all those who have been associated with its affairs during this eventful period.

Banking is often an exercise in discretion and, in consequence, the role of the B.I.S. tends to be overlooked, or at least underestimated, by those who are deceived by the seclusion in which these discussions take place. This is to do less than justice to an institution whose evolution has provided an admirable example of adaptation to changing conditions, of constant service to the cause of international monetary co-operation and of doing good by stealth.

Since in the events which have recently focused attention on international monetary affairs, the Bank for International Settlements has played a leading part, albeit a discreet one, we believe it is interesting to give some information about the 'Gold Pool' and the so-called 'Paris Club of Ten'.

When the London gold-market was reopened in March 1954, it was intended to introduce a greater degree of stability into international dealings and to moderate fluctuations in the price of gold; and the Bank of England sought to exert a moderating influence on the market in order to avoid violent and unnecessary movements in the price and thus to assist the market in the carrying on of its business. In general these aims were achieved until, in the autumn of 1960, it became evident that the market was vulnerable to special pressures unless supplies were assured when needed. At that time the market had come under severe strain, following speculation as to a possible change in the dollar price of gold, and on the London market the price rose for a brief period to the equivalent of over $40 per fine ounce. This led to new arrangements designed to assist orderly marketing.

It was these arrangements that later became known as the 'Gold Pool', inaugurated in October 1961.

The participating members are the Federal Reserve Bank of New York and the central banks of Belgium, France, Germany, Italy, the Netherlands, Switzerland and the United Kingdom.

In operations on the market the Bank of England acts as agent for the member-countries and for its purposes is able to draw upon gold supplies which the European central banks have undertaken to make available according to agreed quotas.

The United States has undertaken to match the combined contributions of the other participants, thus taking a 50% share in the consortium, or gold pool. When supplies are in excess of demand, purchase may be made and distributed among member-countries following the same pattern.

Over the five years of operation of the pool, the price of gold on the London market has moved comfortably within the authorised trading margins of U.S. dollars 35·35–34·65.

The so-called 'Paris Club of Ten' consists of ten of the twenty-one member-states of the Organisation for Economic Co-operation and Development in Paris. These are Belgium, Canada, France, Germany, Holland, Italy, Japan, United Kingdom, United States, Sweden.

This group has already committed itself to the provision of $6,000 million of international credits to be drawn on the case of need.

During the year 1965 the B.I.S. assumed the functions referred to in the Ministerial Statement of the Group of Ten. In conformity with the statement, which dates back to 1 August 1964, the members of the Group provide the B.I.S. with statistical data bearing on the means utilised to finance surpluses or deficits on their external account. These statistical data are circulated to all participants and to Working Party 3 of the O.E.C.D. The Governors of the central banks of the Group, when they meet at the bank, also exchange information at the earliest practicable stage on undertakings between members of the Group for new or enlarged credit facilities. Thus the basis has been created for multilateral surveillance of the various elements of liquidity creation. The year 1965 showed how useful the co-operation can be.

Finally, the B.I.S. has been associated in the work carried out by the Group of Ten, in particular its Study Group on the creation of reserve assets.

The development of co-operation between central banks has also strengthened the relation between the B.I.S. on the one hand, and the O.E.C.D. and the International Monetary Fund on the other, by extending their collaboration to new fields.

The bank's balance-sheet total on 31 March 1965 amounted to 7,850,380,538 gold francs (units of 0·29032258 grammes fine gold).

This table shows the development of the balance-sheet total at the end of each of the last eight accounting periods.

Annual balance-sheets
(In millions of gold francs)

Period ending 31 March	Balance-sheet total	Differences
1958	2,232	..
1959	3,528	+1,296
1960	3,430	− 98
1961	3,973	+ 543
1962	4,732	+ 759
1963	4,950	+ 218
1964	5,778	+ 828
1965	7,850	+2,072

The following items are not included in the balance-sheet: gold under earmark, bills and other securities held in custody for the account of central banks and other depositors; the assets (gold under earmark, bank balances, bills and other securities) held by the bank as Agent for the Organisation for Economic Co-operation and Development in connection with the European Monetary Agreement, as Depository under the Act of Pledge concluded with the High Authority of the European Coal and Steel Community and as Trustee or Fiscal Agent for international government loans.

Balance-sheet as at 31 March 1965
(In thousands of Swiss gold francs)

Liabilities		Assets	
Capital authorised and issued		Gold in bars and coins	3,397,866
200,000 shares, each of 2,500		Cash on hand and on sight	
gold francs, 500,000,000 of		account with banks	300,199
which 25% paid up	125,000	Rediscountable Treasury bills	270,275
Reserves	25,843	Bills and securities cashable on	
Provision for contingencies	214,500	demand	62,758
Deposits (gold)	4,132,916	Time deposits and advances	2,190,334
Deposits (currencies)	2,820,005	Other bills and securities	1,559,297
Notes	463,920	Miscellaneous assets	1,360
Miscellaneous	36,933	Buildings and equipment	1
Profit and Loss Account		Own funds employed in exe-	
Balance brought forward	8,745	cution of The Hague Agree-	
Profit for the financial year		ments of 1930 for invest-	
ended 31 March 1965	22,519	ment in Germany	68,291
TOTAL	7,850,381	TOTAL	7,850,381

The total volume of the bank's operations amounted to the equivalent of 72·2 milliard Swiss francs in 1964–5, compared with 58·9 milliard Swiss francs in 1963–4 and 38·6 milliard Swiss francs in 1962–3.

Funds, bills and other securities administered or held by the bank for account of third parties:

	Gold francs
Earmarked gold	1,382,422,831
Bank balances	38,886,250
Bills and other securities	780,407,060
TOTAL of items not included in the balance sheet . .	2,201,716,141

The B.I.S. acts as Trustee and Fiscal Agent for the following international government loans:

German External Loan 1924 (Dawes Loan),
German Government International Loan 1930 (Young Loan),
Austrian Government International Loan 1930,

and in conformity with an Act of Pledge concluded between the B.I.S. and the High Authority of the European Coal and Steel Community on 28 November 1954, the bank performs the functions of Depositary in respect of the international loans of the High Authority which are secured in accordance with the provisions of that Act.

At present the Board of Directors of this 'super central bank', which grows more and more powerful, consists of thirteen persons, representing the eight member-countries — Belgium, France, Germany, Holland, Italy, Sweden, Switzerland and United Kingdom:

> Dr. M. W. Holtrop, Amsterdam, *President*
> Maurice Frère, Brussels, *Vice-President*
> Hubert Ansiaux, Brussels
> The Earl of Cromer, London
> M. J. Babington Smith, London
> Karl Blessing, Frankfurt (Main)
> Dr. Rudolf Brinckmann, Hamburg
> Jacques Brunet, Paris
> Henri Deroy, Paris
> Dr. Guido Carli, Rome
> Dr. Donato Menichella, Rome
> Per Asbrink, Stockholm
> Dr. Walter Schwegler, Zürich
>
> Gabriel Ferras, *General Manager*

4. THE EUROPEAN INVESTMENT BANK

A protocol added to the Treaty of Rome (Article 129) provided for the creation of a European Investment Bank, whose object is to further the smooth and balanced development of the Common Market, using its own resources and mobilising those of the capital-markets.

The present head office of the bank is in Brussels. It is intended that the bank should finance the modernisation or conversion of industrial undertakings, or the creation of new enterprises which — either because of their scope or their nature — cannot justify national investment or which are beyond the resources of local finance. The bank is a non-profit-making institution and facilitates, by the means of loans or guarantees, the financing of projects in all sectors of the economy in the six states of the Common Market.

The bank is endowed with a milliard units of account (the value of the unit of account is 0·88867088 gramme of fine gold, that is to say, one American dollar). The capital was subscribed by the six member-states of the European Economic Community in the following amounts:

				Million units of account
France	.	.	.	300
Germany	.	.	.	300
Italy	.	.	.	240
Belgium	.	.	.	86·5
Holland	.	.	.	71·5
Luxembourg	.	.	.	2
TOTAL	.	.	.	$1,000

Up to 31 December 1965 only 250 million had been paid up, 25% in gold or dollars and 75% in national currencies, the latter being safeguarded by special clauses against any possible de-valuation.

It is not the intention of the bank to compete with private banks but to act as an official European credit institution, supplementing the banking system of each of the member-states of the Common Market.

The bank was planned on the same principles as the World Bank in Washington and with the benefit of its experience; within the framework of the Common Market it exercises similar functions. The articles of the European Investment Bank are analogous to those of a joint-stock company; with this difference, that no general meeting is provided for. The normal functions of a general meeting are undertaken by the Board of Governors, chosen by the member-states.

The articles lay down that the bank must work in close collaboration with the European Economic Commission and exclusively in the service of the Community; and in Article 130 of the Treaty of Rome even the type of project it may foster is defined.

The bank is run:

1. by a Board of Governors (six ministers appointed by each of the member-states) whose function is to work out the credit policy of the bank as a contributory factor in the development of the Common Market;

2. by a Board of Directors of twelve members (of which France appoints three), appointed for five years and having authority to grant credits and determine their conditions (rate of interest, guarantees, etc.);

3. by a Committee of Management, which deals with routine business, composed of a President and two Vice-Presidents, appointed for six years by the Board of Governors on the recommendation of the Board of Directors.

Table of approved loans from 1 January 1958 to 31 December 1964

Country	Number of enterprises	Amount of loan in units of account	Share of each country as percentage of whole
1. Ordinary Operations (member-states)			
Italy	59	310·7	67
France	11	71·0	15
Germany	3	32·4	7
Belgium	1	4·8	1
Luxembourg	1	4·0	1
	75	422·9	91
Greece (associate state)	8	36·8	8
2. Special Operations			
Turkey (associate state)	2	5·4	1
TOTAL	85	465·1	100

On 31 December 1964 the balance-sheet of the European Investment Bank showed assets of 584,968,287·59 units of account (1 unit of account = 1 U.S. dollar).

Since its establishment (1 January 1958) up to 31 December 1964 the bank has approved eighty-five loans, totalling 465·1 units of account, each loan averaging therefore about $5·5 million. The enterprises which the bank has supported represent a total investment of about $2 milliard: the bank's share in their financing has averaged about 23%, with considerable variations depending on the nature and importance of the enterprise. The geographical distribution of the loans granted up to 31 December 1964 is indicated in the table on p. 262.

Current loans total 394,536,399·63 units of account. As for the conditions on which loans are granted, current rates of interest for ordinary operations were fixed, taking into account the general trend of the money-market, at the following rates, operative from 8 October 1964:

Duration of loan: up to 7 years	.	.	.	.	5%
Duration of loan: from 7 to 12 years	.	.	.		6%
Duration of loan: from 12 to 20 years	.	.	.		$6\frac{1}{4}$%

On 27 May 1963 the Board of Governors established a special section; this is not an entity legally separate from the bank, but operations conducted by this section are financed by special resources and are administered separately from other operations. They are, in fact, conducted on the authority of a mandate given by the Community or by member-states, at the mandator's sole risk. The normal resources of the bank may not be used to finance special operations. The funds to be used are specified for each particular case and are either provided directly by the mandator or are assembled on his behalf. The duration of loans granted by the special section may be longer and the rate of interest lower than normal.

On 31 December 1964 the funded debt of the bank amounted to the equivalent value of 153,694,512·61 units of account, issued in the following states:

Germany	.	.	.	.	47,500,000
Holland	.	.	.	.	34,806,629·84
U.S.A. .	.	.	.	.	25,000,000
Italy	.	.	.	.	24,000,000
France .	.	.	.	.	12,152,981·73
Belgium	.	.	.	.	8,000,000
Switzerland .	.	.	.	.	1,234,901·04
Luxembourg .	.	.	.	.	1,000,000

TOTAL	.	.	.	.	153,694,512·61

The bank's own resources:

Capital	.	.	.	.	250,000,000
Reserves	.	.	.	.	26,615,682·50
Various provisions .	.	.	.	28,000,000

TOTAL	.	.	.	.	458,310,195·14

To turn to regional policies, the principal problem of the European Economic Community remains the raising of the standard of living in the south of Italy. In this region, where 19 million people live, that is, 37% of the Italian population (11% of the population of the Community) the product per head is only a third of the average product in the Community.

The economic integration of southern Italy with the developed regions of the Community, principally by investment in basic industrial and agricultural projects, remains one of the priority objectives not only of the Italian state, but also of the Community as a whole. For this reason the bank continues to devote particular attention to this region.

In the less-developed regions of the other countries of the Community, in which the product per head has already reached a high level, it is more a question of remedying structural deficiencies and giving a fresh direction to economic activity of solving an acute problem of unemployment or of chronic underemployment.

Greece was the first European country to enter into association with the European Economic Community. Under the terms of the agreement which came into force on 1 November 1962 the Community will aid Greece in her economic development by loans amounting over a period of five years to $125 million. Of this total, $50 million will be handed over by the bank during the first two years. In 1963 the bank decided to participate in financing five undertakings, to the extent of $25 million.

The agreement by which Turkey became associated with the European Economic Community was signed on 12 September 1963 in Ankara and came into force on 1 December 1964. This agreement provides for loans to a possible total of $175 million in five years, to further the economic development of Turkey. These loans will be made by the bank through its special section from funds provided by member-states or raised on their behalf.

The Convention of Association of 1 June 1964 between the European Economic Community and eighteen African states and Madagascar was signed on 20 July 1963, at Yaoundé (Cameroon). It provides for financial aid from the Community to the amount of $730 million. In addition, aid from the Community to the amount of $70 million is pledged to the French overseas possessions and the four French overseas departments. The bank contributes to this aid, either by granting loans from its own funds, or by co-operating with other Community institutions in handling loans on special conditions from the resources of the European Development Fund.

Within the framework of the European Economic Community, the role played by the European Investment Bank will be of the utmost importance. It will have to mobilise considerable amounts of capital and put them at the disposal of the various countries of the Community. The year 1964 was a period of intense activity for the bank. The number of its operations has increased, foreshadowing the important tasks which await it in the future.

5. THE FIFTY MOST IMPORTANT BANKS OF THE EUROPEAN ECONOMIC COMMUNITY

The figures for each bank are based on deposits, total as of 31 December 1964 (in thousands of U.S. dollars).

	Name	Founded	Head Office	Country	Deposits
1	Banca Nazionale del La- voro (excluding special sections)	1913	Rome	Italy	4,542,561
2	Crédit Lyonnais	1863	Paris	France	4,252,023
3	Société Générale	1864	Paris	France	3,544,147
4	Deutsche Bank	1870	Frankfurt	Germany	3,419,923
5	Banca Commerciale Itali- ana	1894	Milan	Italy	3,130,652
6	Banque Nationale pour le Commerce et l'Industrie[1]	1932	Paris	France	3,004,440
7	Credito Italiano	1870	Milan	Italy	2,673,115
8	Dresdner Bank	1872	Frankfurt	Germany	2,623,356
9	Banco di Roma	1880	Rome	Italy	2,317,644
10	Commerzbank	1870	Düsseldorf	Germany	2,259,839
11	Banco di Napoli	1539	Naples	Italy	1,934,298
12	Banque de la Société Générale de Belgique[2]	1934	Brussels	Belgium	1,721,697
13	Comptoir National d'Es- compte de Paris[1]	1848	Paris	France	1,621,677
14	Bayerische Hypotheken- und Wechsel-Bank	1835	Munich	Germany	1,615,917
15	Amsterdam–Rotterdam Bank	1863	Amsterdam	Netherlands	1,499,198
16	Algemene Bank Neder- land	1824	Amsterdam	Netherlands	1,441,644
17	Istituto Bancario San Paolo di Torino	1563	Turin	Italy	1,326,969
18	Banque de Bruxelles	1871	Brussels	Belgium	1,288,793
19	Banco di Sicilia	1843	Palermo	Italy	1,272,884
20	Monte dei Paschi di Siena	1624	Siena	Italy	1,265,293
21	Bayerische Vereinsbank	1869	Munich	Germany	1,211,624
22	Banca Popolare di Novara	1872	Novara	Italy	1,159,518

[1] As from 1 July 1966 the Banque Nationale pour le Commerce et l'Industrie and the Comptoir National d'Escompte de Paris have merged to form a new bank called Banque Nationale de Paris.

[2] As from 1 January 1965 the bank is called Société Générale de Banque.

Name	Founded	Head Office	Country	Deposits
23 Bank für Gemeinwirtschaft	1958	Frankfurt	Germany	1,033,582
24 Banca Nazionale dell' Agricoltura	1921	Rome	Italy	931,908
25 Kredietbank	1935	Brussels	Belgium	701,923
26 Bayerische Staatsbank	1870	Munich	Germany	701,269
27 Deutsche Genossenschafts- kasse	1895	Frankfurt	Germany	600,565
28 Crédit du Nord	1848	Lille	France	576,257
29 Banco di Santo Spirito	1605	Rome	Italy	538,207
30 Banque de Paris et des Pays-Bas	1872	Paris	France	519,200
31 Banca d'America e d'Italia	1918	Milan	Italy	490,303
32 Crédit Commercial de France	1894	Paris	France	474,685
33 Banca Popolare di Milano	1865	Milan	Italy	472,001
34 Nederlandsche Midden- standsbank	1927	Amsterdam	Netherlands	463,061
35 Crédit Industriel et Com- mercial	1859	Paris	France	461,597
36 Banco Ambrosiano	1896	Milan	Italy	450,585
37 Banque Française du Commerce Extérieur	1947	Paris	France	434,441
38 Credito Commerciale	1907	Milan	Italy	345,087
39 Compagnie Française de Crédit et de Banque	1877	Paris	France	340,743
40 Banca Toscana	1904	Florence	Italy	328,928
41 Berliner Bank	1950	Berlin (West)	Germany	312,307
42 Banque de l'Union Pari- sienne	1904	Paris	France	296,296
43 Hollandsche Bank-Unie	1914	Amsterdam	Netherlands	288,401
44 Banque Française et Italienne pour l'Améri- que du Sud S.A.	1910	Paris	France	287,741
45 Berliner Handels- Gesell- schaft	1856	Frankfurt	Germany	286,401
46 Société Marseillaise de Crédit	1865	Marseilles	France	275,278
47 Westfalenbank	1921	Bochum	Germany	268,922
48 Crédit Industriel d'Alsace et de Lorraine	1920	Strasbourg	France	265,432
49 Banca Cattolica del Veneto	1892	Vicenza	Italy	259,654
50 Caisse Centrale des Banques Populaires	1921	Paris	France	251,988

In Luxembourg, the sixth partner in the Common Market, the most important commercial banks are:

the Banque Internationale à Luxembourg, with deposits of about $100 million,
the Banque Générale du Luxembourg, with deposits of about $70 million.

The banks listed in the above table are institutions of an essentially commercial nature.

We have not listed on pp. 266–7 specialised public or semi-public credit institutions, such as the fourteen provincial banks of Federal Germany, listed below:

Deutsche Girozentrale-Deutsche Kommunalbank, Frankfurt;
Badische Kommunale Landesbank-Girozentrale, Mannheim;
Bayerische Gemeindebank (Girozentrale), Munich;
Braunschweigische Staatsbank, Brunswick;
Bremer Landesbank, Bremen;
Hamburgische Landesbank-Girozentrale, Hamburg;
Hessische Landesbank-Girozentrale, Frankfurt;
Landesbank für Westfalen-Girozentrale, Münster;
Landesbank und Girozentrale Rheinland-Pfalz, Mainz;
Landesbank und Girozentrale Saar, Saarbrücken;
Landesbank und Girozentrale Schleswig-Holstein, Kiel;
Niedersächsische Landesbank-Girozentrale, Hannover;
Rheinische Girozentrale und Provinzialbank, Düsseldorf;
Württembergische Girozentrale-Würtembergische Landeskommunalbank, Stuttgart.

These are the central institutions of the 863 German public savings banks and their 12,048 branch offices. On 31 December 1964 these fourteen institutions were administering approximately 50 billion Deutsche Marks equivalent to about $12·5 billion.

Also omitted from the list is the Société Nationale de Crédit a l'Industrie, Brussels, a state institution, which on 31 December 1964 was administering deposits totalling $1,181 million.

Within the framework of the European Economic Community, the national banking systems retain their own character. In France, Italy and Belgium there is a clear separation between commercial banks and deposit banks. In contrast, no such separation exists in Germany, Holland and Luxembourg. In these three countries the mixed type of bank remains normal and commercial banks are at liberty to invest as they like, even though their funds derive to a great extent from deposits on call.

5

THE 110 MOST IMPORTANT
COMMERCIAL BANKS IN
THE WORLD

SINCE 1957 the daily banking newspaper *American Banker* in New York has been publishing an annual tabulation of the 500 largest commercial banks of the free world.

This tabulation lists all institutions considered to be commercial banks, excluding banks of issue, banks making loans on the security of real estate, mutual savings banks and bank holding companies.

This publication is of great interest to the banking world; it permits one to study the gradual development of each institution, to make realistic comparisons and to judge the vitality of the nation's leading banks. These statistics paint a picture of growth and geographical diversity in the economy of the free world.

The figures for each bank, expressed in U.S. dollars, are based on total deposits on 31 December of each year. Total funds at the banks' disposal is indeed the best criterion of their power.

For several years the correct definition of the term 'deposits' has been under discussion. In the interests of uniformity, 'deposits' can be taken to mean funds subject to withdrawal by depositors on demand or at predetermined periods of maturity.

The phenomenal growth of the economy of all countries in the world makes it clear that the trends in international banking established in recent years continue unabated.

The number of banks with $1 milliard or more in deposits continues to increase, reaching a total of 110 up to 31 December 1964.

The list for 31 December 1964 is reproduced by courtesy of Mr. Upton E. Liptrott, President of the *American Banker* in New York.

1. List of 110 banks holding 1 milliard dollars or more in deposits (31 December 1964; amounts in thousands of U.S. dollars).

Name	Founded	Head Office	Country	Deposits
1 Bank of America N.T. and S.A.	1904	San Francisco	U.S.A.	14,000,123
2 The Chase Manhattan Bank	1799	New York	U.S.A.	11,357,072
3 First National City Bank	1812	New York	U.S.A.	10,806,051
4 Manufacturers Hanover Trust Co.	1831	New York	U.S.A.	6,039,651
5 Barclays Bank Ltd.	1694	London	England	6,022,501
6 Midland Bank Ltd.	1836	London	England	5,463,399
7 Chemical Bank New York Trust Co.	1824	New York	U.S.A.	5,296,634
8 The Royal Bank of Canada	1869	Montreal	Canada	4,859,217
9 Morgan Guaranty Trust Co.	1864	New York	U.S.A.	4,788,346
10 Canadian Imperial Bank of Commerce	1867	Toronto	Canada	4,776,277
11 Banca Nazionale del Lavoro	1913	Rome	Italy	4,542,561
12 Lloyds Bank Ltd.	1765	London	England	4,531,091
13 Continental Illinois National Bank & Trust Co. of Chicago	1857	Chicago	U.S.A.	4,300,102
14 Crédit Lyonnais	1863	Paris	France	4,252,023
15 Security-First National Bank	1875	Los Angeles	U.S.A.	4,236,414
16 Bank of Montreal	1817	Montreal	Canada	4,201,142
17 National Provincial Bank Ltd.	1833	London	England	4,123,694
18 Westminster Bank Ltd.	1834	London	England	4,017,938
19 Bankers Trust Co.	1903	New York	U.S.A.	3,900,370
20 Fuji Bank Ltd.	1880	Tokyo	Japan	3,895,305
21 Mitsubishi Bank Ltd.	1919	Tokyo	Japan	3,752,897
22 Sanwa Bank Ltd.	1933	Osaka	Japan	3,683,730
23 Sumitomo Bank Ltd.	1895	Osaka	Japan	3,639,720
24 First National Bank of Chicago	1863	Chicago	U.S.A.	3,612,996

Name	Founded	Head Office	Country	Deposits
25 Société Générale	1864	Paris	France	3,544,147
26 Deutsche Bank	1870	Frankfurt/M	Germany	3,419,923
27 Wells Fargo Bank	1852	San Francisco	U.S.A.	3,312,129
28 Banco do Brasil	1808	Brasilia	Brazil	3,287,801
29 Crocker-Citizens National Bank	1870	San Francisco	U.S.A.	3,216,457
30 Banca Commerciale Italiana	1894	Milan	Italy	3,130,652
31 Banque Nationale pour le Commerce et l'Industrie	1932	Paris	France	3,004,440
32 Industrial Bank of Japan Ltd.	1902	Tokyo	Japan	2,922,268
33 Tokai Bank Ltd.	1941	Nagoya	Japan	2,899,063
34 Irving Trust Co.	1851	New York	U.S.A.	2,781,315
35 United California Bank	1903	Los Angeles	U.S.A.	2,745,681
36 Mellon National Bank & Trust Co.	1902	Pittsburgh	U.S.A.	2,689,465
37 Credito Italiano	1870	Milan	Italy	2,673,114
38 Bank of Nova Scotia	1832	Halifax	Canada	2,656,881
39 Dresdner Bank	1872	Frankfurt/M	Germany	2,623,356
40 Barclays Bank D.C.O.	1925	London	England	2,611,944
41 Dai-Ichi Bank Ltd.	1873	Tokyo	Japan	2,545,184
42 National Bank of Detroit	1933	Detroit	U.S.A.	2,507,803
43 Mitsui Bank Ltd.	1876	Tokyo	Japan	2,467,585
44 Rheinische Girozentrale und Provinzialbank	1854	Düsseldorf	Germany	2,437,038
45 Nippon Kangyo Bank Ltd.	1897	Tokyo	Japan	2,333,191
46 Banco di Roma	1880	Rome	Italy	2,317,644
47 The Toronto-Dominion Bank	1855	Toronto	Canada	2,302,969
48 Commerzbank	1870	Düsseldorf	Germany	2,259,839
49 Hessische Landesbank-Girozentrale	1940	Frankfurt/M	Germany	2,252,164
50 Long Term Credit Bank of Japan Ltd.	1952	Tokyo	Japan	2,084,755
51 Banco di Napoli	1539	Naples	Italy	1,934,298
52 First National Bank of Boston	1784	Boston	U.S.A.	1,884,813
53 Swiss Bank Corporation	1872	Basle	Switzerland	1,872,987
54 Union Bank of Switzerland	1912	Zürich	Switzerland	1,861,837
55 Swiss Credit Bank	1856	Zürich	Switzerland	1,856,172
56 Svenska Handelsbanken	1871	Stockholm	Sweden	1,758,340

	Name	Founded	Head Office	Country	Deposits
57	Banque de la Société Générale de Belgique	1934	Brussels	Belgium	1,721,697
58	Kyowa Bank Ltd.	1945	Tokyo	Japan	1,650,097
59	The Cleveland Trust Co.	1894	Cleveland	U.S.A.	1,640,026
60	Comptoir National d'Escompte de Paris	1848	Paris	France	1,621,677
61	Bank of New South Wales	1817	Sydney	Australia	1,616,753
62	Bayerische Hypotheken- und Wechsel-Bank	1935	Munich	Germany	1,615,917
63	Mitsubishi Trust & Banking Co. Ltd.	1927	Tokyo	Japan	1,586,465
64	Sumitomo Trust & Banking Co. Ltd.	..	Osaka	Japan	1,560,051
65	Daiwa Bank Ltd.	1918	Osaka	Japan	1,557,484
66	The Bank of Tokyo Ltd.	1946	Tokyo	Japan	1,533,200
67	Landesbank für Westfalen-Girozentrale	1832	Münster	Germany	1,518,948
68	Amsterdam–Rotterdam Bank	1863	Amsterdam	Netherlands	1,499,198
69	Mitsui Trust & Banking Co. Ltd.	1925	Tokyo	Japan	1,491,899
70	Banco Español de Credito	1902	Madrid	Spain	1,482,866
71	Bayerische Gemeindebank (Girozentrale)	1914	Munich	Germany	1,446,097
72	Algemene Bank Nederland	1824	Amsterdam	Netherlands	1,441,644
73	Banco Hispano Americano	1900	Madrid	Spain	1,403,060
74	Skandinaviska Banken	1864	Stockholm	Sweden	1,377,361
75	State Bank of India	1955	Bombay	India	1,377,277
76	The Hongkong & Shanghai Banking Corporation	1865	Hong Kong	Hong Kong	1,360,165
77	Coöperatieve Centrale Raiffeisen-Bank	1898	Utrecht	Netherlands	1,354,006
78	First Pennsylvania Banking & Trust Co.	1812	Philadelphia	U.S.A.	1,351,778
79	The Chartered Bank	1853	London	England	1,338,523
80	Istituto Bancario San Paolo di Torino	1563	Turin	Italy	1,326,969
81	The Bank of Kobe Ltd.	1936	Kobe	Japan	1,322,619
82	The Standard Bank Ltd.	1852	London	England	1,304,586
83	Banque de Bruxelles	1871	Brussels	Belgium	1,288,793
84	Republic National Bank of Dallas	1920	Dallas	U.S.A.	1,284,355

Name	Founded	Head Office	Country	Deposits
85 Banco di Sicilia	1843	Palermo	Italy	1,272,884
86 The Franklin National Bank	1926	Mineola, N.Y.	U.S.A.	1,269,745
87 Monte dei Paschi di Siena	1624	Siena	Italy	1,265,293
88 Manufacturers National Bank of Detroit	1933	Detroit	U.S.A.	1,260,138
89 Harris Trust & Savings Bank	1882	Chicago	U.S.A.	1,258,391
90 Australia & New Zealand Bank Ltd.	1835	London	England	1,214,256
91 Detroit Bank & Trust Co.	1849	Detroit	U.S.A.	1,212,173
92 Bayerische Vereinsbank	1869	Munich	Germany	1,211,624
93 First National Bank in Dallas	1874	Dallas	U.S.A.	1,206,597
94 Seattle–First National Bank	1870	Seattle	U.S.A.	1,203,398
95 Martins Bank Ltd.	1831	Liverpool	England	1,182,345
96 Société Nationale de Crédit à l'Industrie	1919	Brussels	Belgium	1,180,581
97 Philadelphia National Bank	1803	Philadelphia	U.S.A.	1,173,482
98 Banca Popolare di Novara	1872	Novara	Italy	1,159,518
99 Bank of London & South America Ltd.	1862	London	England	1,141,608
100 Banque Cantonale de Zürich	1869	Zürich	Switzerland	1,136,002
101 First National Bank of Oregon	1865	Portland	U.S.A.	1,132,980
102 Saitama Bank Ltd.	1943	Urawa	Japan	1,122,649
103 Pittsburgh National Bank	1863	Pittsburgh	U.S.A.	1,121,960
104 Yasuda Trust & Banking Co. Ltd.	..	Tokyo	Japan	1,113,720
105 Union Bank	1914	Los Angeles	U.S.A.	1,113,585
106 United States National Bank	1891	Portland	U.S.A.	1,096,270
107 Bank of California N.A.	1864	San Francisco	U.S.A.	1,061,104
108 Bank für Gemeinwirt schaft	1958	Frankfurt/M	Germany	1,033,582
109 Marine Midland Trust Co. of Western New York	1850	Buffalo	U.S.A.	1,018,404
110 The Northern Trust Co.	1889	Chicago	U.S.A.	1,010,915

2. Geographical distribution of the 110 banks holding $1 milliard or more in deposits (31 December 1964; amounts in thousands of U.S. dollars).

Country	Number of banks	Deposits
1 United States of America	34	107,890,723
2 Japan	19	43,161,882
3 England . . .	11	32,951,885
4 Germany . . .	10	19,818,488
5 Italy	9	19,622,933
6 Canada . . .	5	18,796,486
7 France	4	12,422,287
8 Switzerland . . .	4	6,726,998
9 Netherlands . . .	3	4,294,848
10 Belgium . . .	3	4,191,071
11 Sweden . . .	2	3,135,701
12 Spain	2	2,885,926
13 Brazil	1	3,287,801
14 Australia . . .	1	1,616,753
15 India	1	1,377,277
16 Hong Kong . . .	1	1,360,165
TOTAL . . .	110	283,541,224

The study of these statistics leads to some extremely interesting facts, such as the banking gigantism of the Anglo-Saxon bloc (U.S.A., England, Australia, Canada and Hong Kong). In fact, of the 110 greatest commercial banks with deposits exceeding $283 milliard, 52 have English names and hold more than $162 milliard.

In the table, European banks (excluding Great Britain) total 37, with $73 milliard in deposits.

Japan alone can parade 19 banks with more than $43 milliard in deposits.

The great Anglo-Saxon banks, because of their long existence, their experience, their tradition, their organisation and their power, form the aristocracy of the international banking world. They do indeed operate on a world scale and handle an enormous amount of business, which itself increases their power. Their activity extends across oceans and continents, indeed over the whole world. The predominance of the great Anglo-American banking institutions, in relation to the rest of the world, makes them the real masters of international credit.

One can form an idea of the potential political and financial influence which the Anglo-Saxon banking empire exercises in the world, if one adds to the great private banks of the Anglo-Saxon bloc with their world-wide ramifications, the seven great international banking and financial institutions of Washington, which we describe in Chapter 3, that is:

> the International Bank for Reconstruction and Development (World Bank);
> the International Finance Corporation;
> the International Development Association;
> the International Monetary Fund;
> the Inter-American Development Bank;
> the Export–Import Bank of Washington;
> the Agency for International Development.

The Americans and the British are attached to the concept of leadership in world finance; they consider it legitimate and frankly expect to enjoy the profits of leadership. The chiefs of the super-banks are hardly known to the general public. Because of the enormous financial power which they represent, they enjoy exceptional prestige and reputation in political circles the world over.

6

THE 475 CENTURY-OLD BANKS
OF THE WORLD

IN the whole world there exist at present about 35,000 banks
and private banking-houses. Which are the oldest? Which are
those who have survived the vicissitudes of history, economic
débâcles, financial disasters, catastrophic devaluations, political
storms, military adventures, the collapse of once-powerful
empires, social upheavals; which swept away so many other
institutions, yet still exist today and are therefore to be considered
the doyens of the banking profession?

As far as we know, this is the first time that an attempt has
been made to enumerate the banks and private banking-houses
which are at least a hundred years old. I do not claim that the
list is complete; it may well be that I have committed involuntary
errors of omission in my investigations. Since errors are always
possible, I apologise in advance for any which have escaped my
notice and which the reader may detect. I should be grateful to be
informed of any such errors, so that they may be corrected in
future editions.

Among the banks listed there are some veritable giants of high
international finance; institutions of dazzling prestige, occupying
a dominant position on the international scene and whose name
sometimes appears in the financial history of the various countries
of the world. How much wealth, how much power are often
hidden behind a simple, prosaic company name!

The list also contains the names of modest banks and private
banking-houses with a national, a regional or a purely local
reputation, whose establishment may date back several centuries.

Among the throng of private banking-houses, the true banking aristocracy, are banks bearing famous names which have played an important role in world history. Their line of descent is often complicated, their fascinating history reaches back through the centuries. Their names are worth knowing.

Thanks to the ability of their leaders, certain banking dynasties have become, and remain today, the equals of the most important international financiers. Very often the founders of these dynasties were adventurers, setting out with nothing, or almost nothing, to conquer vast financial empires. Their success demanded much initiative, courage and a taste for risks, since in the world of banking success is never a matter of luck. Success in the business world is always based on sound knowledge and mature reflection.

It is not speaking too lyrically to admit of these great strategists — who loved and who still love the struggle — that all these names, indiscriminately, fill us with admiration for their wisdom, which, across the centuries, against wind and tide, has always held high the standards of their houses and preserved the inheritance of their ancestors.

The table (p. 279) showing the geographical distribution of the 475 century-old banks reveals some very interesting facts. The United States heads the list with a total of 111 banks, but they include only two private banking-houses. In the United States the concentration of capital in the form of limited companies has favoured the emergence of large banks, which have gradually absorbed almost all private banking-houses. A recent and startling example was the disappearance of the firm J. P. Morgan & Co. of New York (founded in 1861), considered the most powerful international banking house of the world. On 24 April 1959 it merged with the Guaranty Trust Company to form the Morgan Guaranty Trust Company of New York, which today ranks as sixth greatest among American banks and as the ninth most powerful commercial bank in the world.

On 31 December 1964, out of 14,281 banks established in the U.S.A., only 82 are private banking-houses, of which 56 are in the state of Georgia.

Great Britain comes in second place, with a total of 67 century-old banks, of which 38 are private banking-houses.

1. Geographical distribution of the 475 century-old banks

Country	Banks	Private banking-houses	Total
1 United States of America . .	109	2	111
2 Great Britain	29	38	67
3 Germany	20	39	59
4 France	22	22	44
5 Guiana (French)	1	..	1
6 Martinique (French) . . .	1	..	1
7 Guadeloupe (French) . . .	1	..	1
8 Réunion (French) . . .	1	..	1
9 Switzerland	18	21	39
10 Netherlands	7	16	23
11 Italy	14	1	15
12 Denmark	10	1	11
13 Belgium	3	6	9
14 Sweden	9	..	9
15 Spain	8	1	9
16 Austria	2	4	6
17 Australia	6	..	6
18 Portugal	3	2	5
19 Brazil	5	..	5
20 Canada	5	..	5
21 Ireland	4	..	4
22 Norway	4	..	4
23 Malta	2	1	3
24 Luxembourg	2	..	2
25 Finland	2	..	2
26 Turkey	2	..	2
27 Argentina	2	..	2
28 Indonesia	2	..	2
29 Dutch West Indies . . .	2	..	2
30 Bermuda (British) . . .	1	..	1
31 Ceylon	..	1	1
32 Chile	1	..	1
33 Costa Rica	1	..	1
34 Gibraltar	..	1	1
35 Greece	1	..	1
36 Hong Kong (British) . . .	1	..	1
37 Madeira (Portuguese) . . .	..	1	1
38 Mauritius (British) . . .	1	..	1
39 India	1	..	1
40 Liechtenstein	1	..	1
41 Mexico	1	..	1
42 New Zealand	1	..	1
43 Philippines	1	..	1
44 Uruguay	1	..	1
TOTALS	307	157	464
Banks of issue . . .	..	..	11
TOTAL	..	..	475

Germany comes in third place with a total of 59 century-old institutions, of which 20 are banks and 39 private banking-houses.

France, including the four overseas departments, comes in fourth place, with a total of 48 century-old banks, of which 22 are private banking-houses.

Fifth place is held by Switzerland, with a total of 39 century-old institutions, of which 18 are banks and 21 private banking-houses.

There is a total of 23 Dutch banks in the table, of which 16 are private banking-houses.

Italy can display only 15 century-old banks, but among them there are 4 which are considered to be the oldest in the world.

2. *The eleven century-old banks of issue*

Name	Founded	Head Office	Country
1 Sveriges Riksbank . . .	1668	Stockholm	Sweden
2 Bank of England . . .	1694	London	England
3 Banque de France . . .	1800	Paris	France
4 Suomen Pankki (Bank of Finland)	1811	Helsinki	Finland
5 Nederlandsche Bank . .	1814	Amsterdam	Holland
6 Norges Bank	1816	Oslo	Norway
7 Danmarks Nationalbank . .	1818	Copenhagen	Denmark
8 Bank Indonesia . . .	1828	Djakarta	Indonesia
9 Banco de España . . .	1829	Madrid	Spain
10 Banco de Portugal . . .	1846	Lisbon	Portugal
11 Banque Nationale de Belgique .	1850	Brussels	Belgium

3. The 307 century-old commercial banks

Name	Founded	Head Office	Country
1 Banco di Napoli . . .	1539	Naples	Italy
2 Istituto Bancario San Paolo di Torino	1563	Turin	Italy
3 Banco di Santo Spirito . .	1605	Rome	Italy
4 Monte dei Paschi di Siena .	1624	Siena	Italy
5 Barclays Bank Ltd. . .	1694	London	Great Britain
6 Bank of Scotland . . .	1695	Edinburgh	Great Britain
7 Royal Bank of Scotland. .	1727	Edinburgh	Great Britain
8 Banca Jover S.A. . . .	1737	Barcelona	Spain
9 British Linen Bank . .	1746	Edinburgh	Great Britain
10 Banque Leu & Cie S.A.. .	1755	Zürich	Switzerland
11 Banque Courtois S.A. . .	1760	Toulouse	France
12 Lloyds Bank Ltd. . .	1765	London	Great Britain
13 Braunschweigische Staatsbank	1765	Brunswick	Germany
14 Williams Deacon's Bank Ltd..	1771	Manchester	Great Britain
15 Banco Pastor S.A.. . .	1776	Corunna	Spain
16 Banque Dubois S.A. . .	1778	Liège	Belgium
17 Banca Rossi & Cie S.A.. .	1780	Genoa	Italy
18 Bayerische Staatsbank . .	1780	Munich	Germany
19 First Pennsylvania Banking & Trust Company . .	1782	Philadelphia	U.S.A.
20 Bank of Ireland . .	1783	Dublin	Eire
21 Bank of New York . .	1784	New York	U.S.A.
22 First National Bank of Boston	1784	Boston	U.S.A.
23 Industrial National Bank of Providence . . .	1791	Providence	U.S.A.
24 Hartford National Bank & Trust Co.	1792	Hartford	U.S.A.
25 First New Haven National Bank	1792	New Haven	U.S.A.
26 Banque Chalus S.A. . .	1797	Clermont-Ferrand	France
27 Philadelphia National Bank .	1803	Philadelphia	U.S.A.
28 State Bank of Albany . .	1803	Albany	U.S.A.
29 Trenton Banking Company .	1804	Trenton	U.S.A.
30 Worcester County National Bank	1804	Worcester	U.S.A.
31 National Newark & Essex Banking Company . .	1804	Newark	U.S.A.
32 Farmers National Bank of Annapolis. . . .	1805	Annapolis	U.S.A.
33 First National Bank of Baltimore	1806	Baltimore	U.S.A.
34 Kas-Associatie . . .	1806	Amsterdam	Netherlands
35 Connecticut National Bank .	1806	Bridgeport	U.S.A.
36 Banco do Brasil S.A. . .	1808	Brasilia	Brazil
37 National Bank of Washington, D.C.	1809	Washington, D.C.	U.S.A.
38 Banque Tarneaud Frères & Co. S.A.	1809	Limoges	France
39 National Bank of Malta. .	1809	Valetta	Malta
40 National Commercial Bank of Scotland . . .	1810	Edinburgh	Great Britain
41 Alexanders Discount Company Ltd..	1810	London	Great Britain

Name	Founded	Head Office	Country
42 National State Bank . .	1812	Newark	U.S.A.
43 First National City Bank .	1812	New York	U.S.A.
44 Marine Midland Trust Company of the Mohawk Valley	1812	Utica	U.S.A.
45 First Camden National Bank & Trust Company . .	1812	Camden	U.S.A.
46 Connecticut Bank & Trust Company	1814	Hartford	U.S.A.
47 National Bank of Geneva .	1817	Geneva	U.S.A.
48 National Bank of West Virginia	1817	Wheeling	U.S.A.
49 Bank of Montreal . . .	1817	Montreal	Canada
50 Bank of New South Wales .	1817	Sydney	Australia
51 Banca Vonwiller S.A. . .	1819	Milan	Italy
52 Banque Dupont S.A. . .	1819	Valenciennes	France
53 Deutsche Effecten- und Wechsel-Bank	1821	Frankfurt	Germany
54 Banco de la Provincia de Buenos Aires . . .	1822	Buenos Aires	Argentina
55 Northern Bank Ltd. . .	1824	Belfast	Great Britain
56 Chemical Bank New York Trust Co. .	1824	New York	U.S.A.
57 Algemene Bank Nederland .	1824	Amsterdam	Netherlands
58 Provincial Bank of Ireland Ltd.	1825	Dublin	Eire
59 Hibernian Bank Ltd. . .	1825	Dublin	Eire
60 National Commercial Bank & Trust Co.	1825	Albany	U.S.A.
61 Merchants National Bank of New Bedford . . .	1825	New Bedford	U.S.A.
62 Fall River National Bank .	1825	Fall River	U.S.A.
63 Banque J. Joire S.A. .	1826	Tourcoing	France
64 Belfast Banking Company .	1827	Belfast	Great Britain
65 Banque d'Anvers . . .	1827	Antwerp	Belgium
66 Curaçaosche Bank N.V. .	1828	Fort Amsterdam	Dutch West Indies
67 Banque Bastide–Société de Banque de l'Ariège . .	1828	Lavelanet	France
68 Central-Penn National Bank of Philadelphia . . .	1828	Philadelphia	U.S.A.
69 District Bank Ltd. . . .	1829	Manchester	Great Britain
70 Sciclunas Bank . . .	1830	Valetta	Malta
71 Banque Hervet S.A. . .	1830	Bourges	France
72 Banco Tornquist S.A. . .	1830	Buenos Aires	Argentina
73 Manufacturers Hanover Trust Co.	1831	New York	U.S.A.
74 Martins Bank Ltd. . .	1831	Liverpool	Great Britain
75 New England Merchants National Bank of Boston .	1831	Boston	U.S.A.
76 Landesbank für Westfalen-Girozentrale . . .	1832	Münster	Germany
77 Bank of Nova Scotia . .	1832	Halifax	Canada
78 Wermlands Enskilda Bank .	1832	Karlstad	Sweden
79 National Provincial Bank Ltd.	1833	London	Great Britain
80 Chemung Canal Trust Company	1833	Elmira	U.S.A.
81 National Bank & Trust Company of Fairfield County .	1834	Stamford	U.S.A.

Name	Founded	Head Office	Country
82 Commercial Banking Co. of Sydney	1834	Sydney	Australia
83 Hohenzollerische Landesbank	1834	Sigmaringen	Germany
84 Indiana National Bank of Indianapolis . . .	1834	Indianapolis	U.S.A.
85 South Carolina National Bank	1834	Charleston	U.S.A.
86 Banco Economico de Bahia .	1834	Salvador (Bahia)	Brazil
87 Banque Cantonale de Berne .	1834	Berne	Switzerland
88 Westminster Bank Ltd. .	1834	London	Great Britain
89 National Bank Ltd. . .	1835	London	Great Britain
90 Australia & New Zealand Bank Ltd. . . .	1835	London	Great Britain
91 Western National Bank of Baltimore . . .	1835	Baltimore	U.S.A.
92 Bayerische Hypotheken- und Wechsel-Bank . . .	1835	Munich	Germany
93 Midland Bank Ltd. . .	1836	London	Great Britain
94 Clydesdale Bank Ltd. . .	1836	Glasgow	Great Britain
95 Ulster Bank Ltd. . .	1836	Belfast	Great Britain
96 Royal Bank of Ireland Ltd. .	1836	Dublin	Eire
97 National Shawmut Bank of Boston	1836	Boston	U.S.A.
98 Oneida National Bank & Trust Co. of Central New York . . .	1836	Utica	U.S.A.
99 Girard Trust Bank .	1836	Philadelphia	U.S.A.
100 Riggs National Bank of Washington . . .	1836	Washington, D.C.	U.S.A.
101 Östergötlands Enskilda Bank	1837	Lindköping	Sweden
102 Smålands Bank . .	1837	Jönköping	Sweden
103 Mauritius Commercial Bank Ltd.	1838	Port Louis	Mauritius
104 Banque Scalbert S.A. . .	1838	Lille	France
105 Hambros Bank Ltd. . .	1839	London	Great Britain
106 Ionian Bank Ltd.. .	1839	London	Great Britain
107 Northern New York Trust Co.	1839	Watertown	U.S.A.
108 Marine National Exchange Bank of Milwaukee . .	1839	Milwaukee	U.S.A.
109 National Bank of Greece .	1841	Athens	Greece
110 Mittelrheinische Kreditbank-Dr. Horbach & Co. K.G. .	1841	Mainz	Germany
111 State Savings Bank of Victoria	1841	Melbourne	Australia
112 Banco José Enriques Totta S.A.	1843	Jerez de la Frontera	Spain
113 Banco di Sicilia . .	1843	Palermo	Italy
114 Banco de Andalucia . .	1844	Jerez de la Frontera	Spain
115 Banque Cantonale Vaudoise .	1845	Lausanne	Switzerland
116 National City Bank of Cleveland . . .	1845	Cleveland	U.S.A.
117 Banco de A. Edwards y Cia. Ltd. . . .	1846	Valparaiso	Chile
118 Fyens Diskonto Kasse . .	1846	Odensee	Denmark
119 Montreal City & District Savings Bank . .	1846	Montreal	Canada
120 Solothurner Handelsbank .	1847	Soleure	Switzerland

Name	Founded	Head Office	Country
121 Bay State–Merchants National Bank . . .	1847	Lawrence	U.S.A.
122 Boatmen's National Bank .	1847	St. Louis	U.S.A.
123 Marshall & Ilsley Bank .	1847	Milwaukee	U.S.A.
124 Provident Tradesmens Bank and Trust Co.. . .	1847	Philadelphia	U.S.A.
125 Comptoir National d'Escompte de Paris ★ .	1848	Paris	France
126 Banca Belinzaghi S.A. . .	1848	Milan	Italy
127 Union du Crédit de Bruxelles	1848	Brussels	Belgium
128 Christiana Bank og Kreditkasse	1848	Oslo	Norway
129 Crédit du Nord . . .	1848	Lille	France
130 Göteborgs Bank . . .	1848	Göteborg	Sweden
131 Society National Bank of Cleveland . . .	1849	Cleveland	U.S.A.
132 Detroit Bank & Trust Company	1849	Detroit	U.S.A.
133 Banque de la Martinique .	1849	Fort-de-France	Martinique
134 Banque de la Réunion . .	1849	Saint-Denis	Réunion
135 Banque Hypothécaire Argovienne	1849	Brugg	Switzerland
136 Banque Régionale de l'Ain .	1849	Bourg-en-Bresse	France
137 Banque Cantonale Lucernoise	1850	Lucerne	Switzerland
138 Mesdag & Groeneveld's Bank	1850	Groningen	Netherlands
139 Merchants National Bank & Trust Co. . . .	1850	Syracuse	U.S.A.
140 Marine Trust Co. of Western New York . . .	1850	Buffalo	U.S.A.
141 Bank of the Philippine Islands	1851	Manila	Philippines
142 Irving Trust Company .	1851	New York	U.S.A.
143 Wells Fargo Bank . .	1852	San Francisco	U.S.A.
144 Manufacturers National Bank of Troy	1852	Troy	U.S.A.
145 Fulton County National Bank & Trust Co of Gloversville	1852	Gloversville	U.S.A.
146 First National Bank in Oshkosh	1852	Oshkosh	U.S.A.
147 English, Scottish & Australian Bank, Ltd. . . .	1852	London	Great Britain
148 Banco Moreira Gomes S.A. .	1852	Belem	Brazil
149 Bank in Menziken . .	1852	Menziken	Switzerland
150 Sofibanque Hoskier S.A. .	1852	Paris	France
151 Chartered Bank . . .	1853	London	Great Britain
152 Old Kent Bank & Trust Co.	1853	Grand Rapids	U.S.A.
153 Banque de la Guadeloupe .	1853	Pointe-à-Pitre	Guadeloupe
154 Österreichische Industriekredit A.G. . . .	1853	Vienna	Austria
155 Banque Populaire de la Gruyère	1853	Bulle	Switzerland
156 First National Bank of St. Paul	1853	St. Paul	U.S.A.
157 First Wisconsin National Bank	1853	Milwaukee	U.S.A.

★ From 1 July 1966 merged with the Banque Nationale de Paris.

Name	Founded	Head Office	Country
158 Genesse Valley Union Trust Co.	1853	Rochester	U.S.A.
159 Merchants National Bank .	1853	Manchester	U.S.A.
160 United States Trust Co. of New York . . .	1853	New York	U.S.A.
161 First Hutchings–Sealy National Bank . . .	1854	Galveston	U.S.A.
162 Banca Mas-Sardá S.A. . .	1854	Barcelona	Spain
163 Banque Brière & Co. S.A.	1854	Noyon (Oise)	France
164 First National Bank . .	1854	Madison	U.S.A.
165 Home National Bank & Trust Co.	1854	Meriden	U.S.A.
166 Frankfurter Bank . .	1854	Frankfurt	Germany
167 Rheinische Girozentrale und Provinzialbank . .	1854	Düsseldorf	Germany
168 Aargauische Kantonalbank .	1854	Aarau	Switzerland
169 St. Gallische Creditanstalt .	1854	St. Gall	Switzerland
170 Veile Bank . . .	1854	Veile	Denmark
171 Middelfart Bank . .	1854	Middelfart	Denmark
172 Randers Disconto-og Laanebank	1854	Randers	Denmark
173 Aalborg Diskontobank .	1854	Aalborg	Denmark
174 Bergens Privatbank . .	1854	Bergen	Norway
175 City Trust Company . .	1854	Bridgeport	U.S.A.
176 Mercantile Trust Company .	1855	St. Louis	U.S.A.
177 Banque Lenoir & Bernard S.A.	1855	Amiens (Somme)	France
178 First National Bank of Fond du Lac . . .	1855	Fond du Lac	U.S.A.
179 First National Bank of Winona	1855	Winona	U.S.A.
180 Keene National Bank . .	1855	Keene	U.S.A.
181 Second National Bank of New Haven . . .	1855	New Haven	U.S.A.
182 Banque de la Guyane . .	1855	Cayenne	Guiana
183 Creditanstalt-Bankverein .	1855	Vienna	Austia
184 Hjørring Discontobank .	1855	Hjørring	Denmark
185 Ribe Discontobank .	1855	Ribe	Denmark
186 Banque Internationale à Luxembourg . . .	1856	Luxembourg	Luxembourg
187 Caisse d'Épargne de l'État, Luxembourg . . .	1856	Luxembourg	Luxembourg
188 Crédit Suisse . . .	1856	Zürich	Switzerland
189 National Discount Co. Ltd. .	1856	London	Great Britain
190 Toronto–Dominion Bank .	1856	Toronto	Canada
191 Berliner Handels-Gesellschaft	1856	Frankfurt	Germany
192 Stockholms Enskilda Bank .	1856	Stockholm	Sweden
193 Bank Edward Henriquez & Cie, N.V.	1856	Curaçao	Dutch West Indies
194 Kolding Laane-og Diskontokasse Bank . . .	1856	Kolding	Denmark
195 Vereinsbank in Hamburg .	1856	Hamburg	Germany
196 Handelsbank in Lübeck .	1856	Lübeck	Germany
197 Banca Rasini di C. Rasini & C., S.a.S. . . .	1856	Milan	Italy

Name	Founded	Head Office	Country
198 Manufacturers & Traders Trust Co. . . .	1856	Buffalo	U.S.A.
199 United States National Bank	1856	Omaha	U.S.A.
200 First National Bank of Minneapolis	1857	Minneapolis	U.S.A.
201 Union National Bank of Pittsburgh . . .	1857	Pittsburgh	U.S.A.
202 Banken for Slagelse og Omegn	1857	Slagelse	Denmark
203 Continental Illinois National Bank & Trust Co. of Chicago	1857	Chicago	U.S.A.
204 Privatbanken i Kjøbenhavn .	1857	Copenhagen	Denmark
205 Banco de Bilbao . .	1857	Bilbao	Spain
206 Banco de Santander . .	1857	Santander	Spain
207 Bergens Skillingsbank . .	1857	Bergen	Norway
208 Den Norske Creditbank . .	1857	Oslo	Norway
209 Banco Comercial . .	1857	Montevideo	Uruguay
210 Escomptobank . . .	1857	Djakarta	Indonesia
211 Bank of N. T. Butterfield & Son Ltd. .	1858	Hamilton	Bermuda
212 Yorkshire Bank Ltd. . .	1858	London	Great Britain
213 National Bank of Australasia.	1858	Melbourne	Australia
214 Banco da Provincia do Rio Grande do Sul . . .	1858	Porto Alegre	Brazil
215 Banco de Bahia . . .	1858	Salvador (Bahia)	Brazil
216 Fifth Third Union Trust Co.	1858	Cincinnati	U.S.A.
217 Walker Bank & Trust Co. .	1859	Salt Lake City	U.S.A.
218 Banque Graveneau & Co. S.A.	1859	Paris	France
219 Crédit Industriel & Commercial . . .	1859	Paris	France
220 Harvard Trust Co. . .	1860	Cambridge	U.S.A.
221 Millikin National Bank of Decatur	1860	Decatur	U.S.A.
222 New Britain National Bank .	1860	New Britain	U.S.A.
223 First National Bank of Denver	1860	Denver	U.S.A.
224 Finlands Hypotekarförening .	1960	Helsinki	Finland
225 Wiesbadener Bank . .	1860	Wiesbaden	Germany
226 Handwerkerbank, Basel .	1860	Basle	Switzerland
227 Société de Banque et de Participations . . .	1860	Paris	France
228 Banque Journel & Cie S.A.*	1860	Saint-Quentin	France
229 Kreditbank Hameln . .	1861	Hamelin	Germany
230 Banco Fonsecas, Santos & Vianna	1861	Lisbon	Portugal
231 The Provincial Bank of Canada	1861	Montreal	Canada
232 Bank of New Zealand . .	1861	Wellington	New Zealand
233 Central Trust Company .	1862	Cincinnati	U.S.A.
234 Colorado National Bank .	1862	Denver	U.S.A.
235 Nordiska Föreningsbanken .	1862	Helsinki	Finland

* From 1 January 1966 merged with the Banque Dupont (see No. 52).

Name	Founded	Head Office	Country
236 Liechtensteinische Landes-bank . . .	1862	Vaduz	Liechtenstein
237 Frankfurter Volksbank . .	1862	Frankfurt	Germany
238 Frankfurter Hypothekenbank	1862	Frankfurt	Germany
239 Bank of London & South America Ltd. . . .	1862	London	Great Britain
240 Standard Bank Ltd. . .	1862	London	Great Britain
241 Ulmer Volksbank . .	1863	Ulm	Germany
242 Bank Wädenswil . .	1863	Wädenswill	Switzerland
243 Banco Aliança . .	1863	Oporto	Portugal
244 Banco Anglo-Costarricense .	1863	San José	Costa Rica
245 Crédit Lyonnais . . .	1863	Lyons	France
246 Ottoman Bank . .	1863	Istanbul	Turkey
247 Nationale Handelsbank .	1863	Amsterdam	Netherlands
248 Amsterdam–Rotterdam Bank	1863	Amsterdam	Netherlands
249 Internationale Crediet- en Handels-Vereeniging 'Rot-terdam' . . .	1863	Rotterdam	Netherlands
250 Türkiye Cumhuriyeti Ziraat Bankasi (Agricultural Bank of the Turkish Republic) .	1863	Ankara	Turkey
251 National & Grindlays Bank Ltd. . . .	1863	London	Great Britain
252 Credito Navarro . . .	1863	Pamplona	Spain
253 Northeastern Pennsylvania National Bank & Trust Co.	1863	Scranton	U.S.A.
254 Pittsburgh National Bank .	1863	Pittsburgh	U.S.A.
255 First National Bank of Chicago . . .	1863	Chicago	U.S.A.
256 First National Bank of Cincinnati . . .	1863	Cincinnati	U.S.A.
257 First National Lincoln Bank of Louisville . . .	1863	Louisville	U.S.A.
258 First National Bank of Omaha . . .	1863	Omaha	U.S.A.
259 First National Bank of Richmond . . .	1863	Richmond	U.S.A.
260 First National Bank of Peoria . . .	1863	Peoria	U.S.A.
261 First National Bank of Memphis . . .	1864	Memphis	U.S.A.
262 First National Bank of Passaic County . .	1864	Paterson	U.S.A.
263 First National Bank of Rochester . . .	1864	Rochester	U.S.A.
264 First National Bank of York .	1864	York	U.S.A.
265 Bank of California . .	1864	San Francisco	U.S.A.
266 Concord National Bank .	1864	Concord	U.S.A.
267 Morgan Guaranty Trust Co.	1864	New York	U.S.A.
268 Third National Bank of Hampden County . .	1864	Springfield	U.S.A.
269 Société Générale . .	1864	Paris	France
270 Volksbank Tuttlingen . .	1864	Tuttlingen	Germany
271 Banco de Londres y Mexico .	1864	Mexico City	Mexico
272 Banco Nacional Ultramarino	1864	Lisbon	Portugal
273 Union Vaudoise du Crédit .	1864	Lausanne	Switzerland

Name	Founded	Head Office	Country
274 Bank in Burgdorf . .	1864	Burgdorf	Switzerland
275 Banque Populaire de la Broye	1864	Payerne	Switzerland
276 Banque Cantonale de Bâle-Campagne . . .	1864	Basle	Switzerland
277 Gewerbekasse Baden . .	1864	Baden	Switzerland
278 Skandinaviska Banken . .	1864	Stockholm	Sweden
279 Sundsvalls Banken . .	1864	Sundsvall	Sweden
280 Uplands Enskilda Bank .	1865	Uppsala	Sweden
281 Skaraborgs Enskilda Bank .	1865	Skövde	Sweden
282 Banca Popolare di Bologna e Ferrara	1865	Bologna	Italy
283 First National Bank of Atlanta	1865	Atlanta	U.S.A.
284 Hongkong & Shanghai Banking Corporation . .	1865	Hong Kong	Hong Kong
285 Bank of Adelaide . .	1865	Adelaide	Australia
286 Allahabad Bank Ltd. . .	1865	Calcutta	India
287 Surinaamsche Bank (De) .	1865	Paramaribo	Indonesia
288 Banca Popolare di Milano .	1865	Milan	Italy
289 Banca Popolare di Cremona .	1865	Cremona	Italy
290 Heidenheimer Volksbank .	1865	Heidenheim–Brenz	Germany
291 Feuerbacher Volksbank .	1865	Stuttgart–Feuerbach	Germany
292 Commerce Trust Co. . .	1865	Kansas City	U.S.A.
293 Merchants National Bank & Trust Co. of Indianapolis .	1865	Indianapolis	U.S.A.
294 First & Merchants National Bank	1865	Richmond	U.S.A.
295 First Security National Bank & Trust Company . .	1865	Lexington	U.S.A.
296 First National Bank of Mobile	1865	Mobile	U.S.A.
297 First National Bank of Oregon	1865	Oregon	U.S.A.
298 Société Marseillaise de Crédit	1865	Marseilles	France
299 Société Lyonnaise de Dépôts et de Crédit Industriel .	1865	Lyons	France
300 Union Discount Company of London Ltd. . . .	1866	London	Great Britain
301 Banca Popolare di Padova e Treviso	1866	Padua	Italy
302 Banca Popolare di Vicenza .	1866	Vicenza	Italy
303 Commercial Bank of Australia	1866	Melbourne	Australia
304 First National Bank of San Antonio	1866	San Antonio	U.S.A.
305 Fidelity–Philadelphia Trust Co.	1866	Philadelphia	U.S.A.
306 Omaha National Bank. .	1866	Omaha	U.S.A.
307 Huntington National Bank .	1866	Columbus	U.S.A.

4. The 157 century-old private banking-houses

Name	Founded	Head Office	Country
1 Koch, Lauteren & Co.. . .	1586	Frankfurt	Germany
2 Berenberg (Joh.), Gossler & Co. .	1590	Hamburg	Germany
3 Hoare (C.) & Co. . . .	1673	London	Great Britain
4 B. Metzler seel. Sohn & Co. .	1674	Frankfurt	Germany
5 Mocatta & Goldsmid Ltd. . .	1684	London	Great Britain
6 Vlaer & Kol	1691	Utrecht	Netherlands
7 Coutts & Co.	1692	London	Great Britain
8 Mallet Frères & Cie ★ .	1713	Paris	France
9 R. Mees & Zoonen . . .	1720	Rotterdam	Netherlands
10 J. A. Krebs	1721	Freibourg (Breisgau)	Germany
11 A. C. Fraser & Co. . . .	1736	Rotterdam	Netherlands
12 F. van Lanschot . . .	1737	'sHertogenbosch	Netherlands
13 Wegelin & Co.	1741	Saint-Gall	Switzerland
14 Nagelmackers Fils & Cie . .	1747	Liège	Belgium
15 Gebrüder Bethmann . . .	1748	Frankfurt	Germany
16 Orelli im Thalhof . . .	1749	Zürich	Switzerland
17 Rahn & Bodmer . . .	1750	Zürich	Switzerland
18 James Finlay & Co. Ltd. . .	1750	Glasgow	Great Britain
19 Glyn, Mills & Co. . . .	1753	London	Great Britain
20 von der Heydt-Kersten & Sohn .	1754	Wuppertal	Germany
21 Johannes Schuback & Söhne .	1757	Hamburg	Germany
22 Gebrüder Löbbecke & Co. . .	1761	Brunswick	Germany
23 Hope & Co.	1762	Amsterdam	Netherlands
24 Baring Brothers & Co. Ltd. . .	1763	London	Great Britain
25 A. van Hoboken & Co. . .	1774	Rotterdam	Netherlands
26 Hesse, Newman & Co. . .	1777	Hamburg	Germany
27 C. G. Trinkhaus	1785	Düsseldorf	Germany
28 La Roche & Cie . . .	1787	Basle	Switzerland
29 Hottinguer & Cie . . .	1787	Paris	France
30 R. Raphael & Sons . . .	1787	London	Great Britain
31 Sal. Oppenheim Jr. & Cie .	1789	Cologne	Germany
32 J. H. Stein	1790	Cologne	Germany
33 Wichelhaus (J.) P. Sohn . .	1790	Wuppertal	Germany
34 Heine & Cie	1790	Paris	France
35 Joseph J. Le Grelle . .	1792	Antwerp	Belgium
36 Ferrier, Lullin & Cie . .	1795	Geneva	Switzerland
37 C. L. Seeliger	1795	Wolfenbüttel	Germany
38 Hentsch & Co. . . .	1796	Geneva	Switzerland
39 H. Oyens & Zonen . .	1797	Amsterdam	Netherlands
40 Conrad Hinrich Donner .	1798	Hamburg	Germany
41 Brinckmann, Wirtz & Co. . .	1798	Hamburg	Germany
42 Lombard, Odier & Co. . .	1798	Geneva	Switzerland
43 H. J. Merck & Co. . . .	1799	Hamburg	Germany
44 de Neuflize, Schlumberger & Cie ★	1800	Paris	France
45 Demachy & Cie . . .	1800	Paris	France
46 R. Henriquez Jr.	1801	Copenhagen	Denmark
47 Bugnion & Cie	1803	Lausanne	Switzerland
48 J. Henry Schroder, Wagg & Co. Ltd.	1804	London	Great Britain
49 N. M. Rothschild & Sons .	1804	London	Great Britain
50 J. Ph. Kessler	1804	Frankfurt	Germany
51 Wm. Brandt's Sons & Co. Ltd. .	1805	London	Great Britain
52 Martin Friedburg & Co. . .	1805	Hamburg	Germany
53 Vve. Morin-Pons, Morin & Cie .	1805	Lyons	France

★ From 1 January 1966 merged with de Neuflize, Schlumberger & Cie. New name: de Neuflize, Schlumberger, Mallet & Cie.

Name	Founded	Head Office	Country
54 Pictet & Cie	1805	Geneva	Switzerland
55 Bankierskantoor van Lissa & Kann	1806	The Hague	Netherlands
56 van der Hoop, Offers & Zoon .	1807	Rotterdam	Netherlands
57 Antony Gibbs & Sons Ltd. . .	1808	London	Great Britain
58 Saint Olive & Cie . . .	1809	Lyons	France
59 Brown, Shipley & Co. Ltd. .	1810	London	Great Britain
60 Blyth, Greene, Jourdain & Co. Ltd.	1810	London	Great Britain
61 Armand von Ernst & Cie . .	1812	Berne	Switzerland
62 M. Varin-Bernier & Cie .	1812	Bar-le-Duc	France
63 B. Tagliaferro & Sons . .	1812	Valetta	Malta
64 Les Fils Dreyfus & Cie . .	1813	Basle	Switzerland
65 Magnus (J.) & Co. . . .	1813	Hamburg	Germany
66 Heinrich Gontard & Co. . .	1815	Frankfurt	Germany
67 Bonhôte & Co.	1815	Neuchâtel	Switzerland
68 Almeida, Basto & Piombimo & Co.	1815	Lisbon	Portugal
69 Blandy Brothers (Banquieros) .	1815	Funchal	Madeira
70 de Rothschild Frères . . .	1817	Paris	France
71 G. Vermeer Johz . . .	1817	Deventer	Netherlands
72 Brown Brothers, Harriman & Co.	1818	New York	U.S.A.
73 Patijn, van Notten & Co. . .	1819	Amsterdam	Netherlands
74 Mirabaud & Cie . . .	1819	Geneva	Switzerland
75 Ralli Brothers (Bankers) Ltd. .	1820	London	Great Britain
76 Vernes & Cie	1821	Paris	France
77 Nottebohm & Co. . . .	1822	Hamburg	Germany
78 Grunelius & Co. . . .	1824	Frankfurt	Germany
79 Ogilvy, Gillanders & Co. Ltd. .	1825	London	Great Britain
80 Martin Frères	1825	Marseilles	France
81 Banque Jules Joire . . .	1826	Brussels	Belgium
82 Carl F. Plump & Co. Bankhaus .	1828	Bremen	Germany
83 Karl Schmidt Bankgeschäft. .	1828	Hof-am-Saal	Germany
84 Knowles & Foster★ . . .	1828	London	Great Britain
85 Bankhaus Carl Spängler & Co. .	1828	Salzburg	Austria
86 Kleinwort, Benson Ltd.† .	1830	London	Great Britain
87 John Stuart & Co. Ltd. .	1830	London	Great Britain
88 Arm. Theod. Sölling & Co. .	1830	Rotterdam	Netherlands
89 Schneider & Münzing . .	1830	Munich	Germany
90 Hill, Samuel & Co. Ltd. . .	1831	London	Great Britain
91 Banque Frederic Jacobs & Cie .	1832	Antwerp	Belgium
92 Bankhaus Hengst (Friedrich) & Co.	1832	Offenbach (Main)	Germany
93 Bankhaus Schelhammer & Schat-tera	1832	Vienna	Austria
94 Stern Brothers . . .	1833	London	Great Britain
95 Teissonnière & Cie . . .	1833	Alès	France
96 Schöller & Co. . . .	1833	Vienna	Austria
97 L. J. Carregosa & Co. .	1833	Oporto	Portugal
98 Arbuthnot Latham & Co. Ltd. .	1833	London	Great Britain
99 Fratelli Ceriana . . .	1835	Turin	Italy
100 George Steuart & Co. . .	1835	Colombo	Ceylon
101 Guinness Mahon & Co. Ltd. .	1836	London	Great Britain
102 Darier & Co.	1837	Geneva	Switzerland
103 De Baecque, Beau & Cie .	1837	Paris	France
104 Morgan Grenfell & Co. Ltd. .	1838	London	Great Britain
105 Vermeer & Co. . . .	1839	Amsterdam	Netherlands
106 Burkhardt & Co. . . .	1841	Essen	Germany

★ Suspended payment in 1964.
† First established in Cuba in 1792, moved to London in 1830.

Name	Founded	Head Office	Country
107 Bechetoille & Cie . . .	1841	Annonay	France
108 A. Sarasin & Cie . . .	1841	Basle	Switzerland
109 Gonet & Cie	1842	Nyon	Switzerland
110 Laidlaw & Co.	1842	New York	U.S.A.
111 Bordier & Cie	1844	Geneva	Switzerland
112 Banque Dupuy, de Parseval & Cie	1845	Sète	France
113 Banque Arnaud Pallier & Cie .	1845	Nîmes	France
114 Schröder Gebrüder & Co. . .	1846	Hamburg	Germany
115 Münchmeyer & Co. . . .	1846	Hamburg	Germany
116 Hijos de Olimpio Perez . .	1847	Santiago	Spain
117 Worms & Cie	1848	Paris	France
118 Inschauspé & Cie . . .	1848	Bayonne	France
119 Bates (Edward) & Sons Ltd. .	1848	Liverpool	Great Britain
120 Matheson & Co. Ltd.. . .	1848	London	Great Britain
121 T. Goedewaagen & Zoonen .	1849	Gouda	Netherlands
122 Balfour, Williamson & Co. Ltd. .	1851	London	Great Britain
123 Jean Degroof & Cie . .	1851	Brussels	Belgium
124 Teixeira de Mattos Bros. . .	1852	Amsterdam	Netherlands
125 J. & P. Hirigoyen . . .	1852	Saint-Vincent-de-Tyrosse	France
126 Wilhelm Ahlmann . . .	1852	Kiel	Germany
127 Bankhaus Hermann Lampe . .	1853	Bielefeld	Germany
128 Samuel Montagu & Co. Ltd. .	1853	London	Great Britain
129 De Clermont & Donner Ltd. .	1853	London	Great Britain
130 Lazard Frères & Cie . . .	1854	Paris	France
131 von Wangenheim & Co. . .	1854	Kassel	Germany
132 Heusser & Cie	1855	Basle	Switzerland
133 A. L. Galliano	1855	Gibraltar	Gibraltar
134 Louis Hirsch & Cie . . .	1855	Paris	France
135 Kirchholtes & Co. . . .	1856	Frankfurt	Germany
136 Gebrüder Röchling Bank . .	1856	Saarbrücken	Germany
137 C. A. Steinhäusser . . .	1856	Vienna	Austria
138 Delbrück, Schickler & Co. . .	1856	Hamburg	Germany
139 B. W. Blydenstein & Co. . .	1858	London	Great Britain
140 Eug. de Buren & Cie . . .	1858	Berne	Switzerland
141 Sedy & Co. Ltd. . . .	1858	London	Great Britain
142 Werner & Frese . . .	1858	Hamburg	Germany
143 Lippmann, Rosenthal & Co. .	1859	Amsterdam	Netherlands
144 P. P. Rodocanachi & Co. Ltd. .	1860	London	Great Britain
145 Piguet & Cie	1860	Yverdon	Switzerland
146 David Sassoon & Co. Ltd. . .	1860	London	Great Britain
147 Hauck (Georg) & Sohn . .	1861	Frankfurt	Germany
148 Bass & Herz	1862	Frankfurt	Germany
149 Gellatly, Hankey & Co. Ltd. .	1862	London	Great Britain
150 De L'Harpe & Cie . . .	1863	Geneva	Switzerland
151 Thomas Barlow & Bro. . .	1863	London	Great Britain
152 Wallace Brothers & Co. (Holdings) Ltd.	1863	London	Great Britain
153 Page & Gwyther . . .	1863	London	Great Britain
154 Banque Dreze	1863	Dison	Belgium
155 Raphael & Cie	1865	Paris	France
156 Gray, Dawes & Co. Ltd. . .	1865	London	Great Britain
157 Gerald Quin, Cope & Co. . .	1866	London	Great Britain

INDEX

NOTE

Principal page references are set in bold type.

Banks which occur only in lists of major banks have not been indexed. Such lists will be found under each country with a major entry, and also on pages 149, 266–7, 271–4, 280–91.